A HISTORY OF SPIRITUALITY IN SANTA FE

The City of Holy Faith

Ana Pacheco

THE History PRESS

Published by The History Press
Charleston, SC
www.historypress.net

Front cover, top, left to right: A 1948 photo of Archbishop Edwin V. Byrne, clergy members and La Conquistadora in front of the Cathedral Basilica of St. Francis of Assisi. *Photo by Robert H. Martin*; Two member musicians of the Pecos Valley Cowboy Church. *Courtesy Glen Strock*; *Prayer Song* sculpture (1994) by Allan C. Houser. *Courtesy Allan Houser Gallery*. *Middle*: Amma in 2015 at an outdoor meditation gathering at the Buffalo Thunder Resort. *Courtesy M.A. Center, San Ramon, California*; A 1934 photo of the Santa Fe Christian Brothers. *Courtesy New Orleans–Santa Fe Christian Brothers District Archives*. *Bottom*: Spruce Tree House looking north, Mesa Verde National Park, Colorado, 1907. *Photo by Jesse Nussbaum. Courtesy Palace of the Governors [NMHM/DCA]. No. 060587*; A painting of Temple Beth Shalom by Tommy Macaione. *Courtesy Raphael Shapiro.*
Back cover, top: The mural by Ed O'Brien on the wall of the Gurdwara at the Hacienda de Guru Ram Das (ashram) at the Sikh Dharma community in Española. *Courtesy Sunstone Press*; *bottom*: Yogi Bhajan teaching Kundalini yoga in 1969 at the Hog Farm and Friends Summer Solstice celebration in Aspen Meadows, Tesuque, New Mexico. *Photo by Lisa Law.*

First published 2016

Manufactured in the United States

ISBN 978.1.46711.819.4

Library of Congress Control Number: 2015956823

Contents

Foreword

And sometimes it's the very otherness of a stranger, someone who doesn't belong to our ethnic or ideological or religious group, an otherness that can repel us initially, but which can jerk us out of our habitual selfishness, and give us intonations of that sacred otherness, which is God.
—Karen Armstrong, author of A History of God

From an early age, Ana Pacheco understood Armstrong's "sacred otherness, which is God." Deeply rooted in the Hispanic Catholicism of her family, Pacheco grew up interacting with Santa Feans of diverse backgrounds and spiritual traditions—Native Americans, Jews, Protestants, New Age hippies, Sikhs and the Hare Krishnas who chanted and "paraded around downtown" during her teen years.

As Pacheco notes, such diversity is a hallmark of large urban areas like New York City or Los Angeles. But Santa Fe was, and still is, a small city—thirty-five thousand in the 1960s, seventy thousand in 2014. Yet the community's size actually enhanced Pacheco's experience of that diversity In the Santa Fe of her childhood and teen years, you couldn't go downtown or hang out on the Plaza without rubbing shoulders with people who were different from you.

Despite its growth, Santa Fe still offers opportunities to engage people who don't look, speak, think or believe like you do. In and of itself, living in a diverse community doesn't foster understanding. One has to be intentional and willing to engage the "other." Pacheco has done that all her life, and her book reflects that commitment. It also demonstrates a unique blend of her insatiable curiosity about the diverse spiritual communities of Santa Fe and her deep respect for each tradition.

Her book is impressive if only because of its scope, from geology to theology. She begins with an exploration of the landscape that has shaped northern New Mexico spiritually and every other way through the centuries. In the chapters that follow, her descriptions of various Santa Fe spiritual communities dig into their historical roots and help the reader appreciate the depth of our diversity in the present day. I have been a pastor for a local Santa Fe Protestant church for almost thirty years and active in interfaith work the entire time. Yet I learned something new on almost every page of Pacheco's book.

While celebrating Santa Fe's many spiritual paths and communities, Pacheco also tells the truth about the challenges and inevitable conflicts that come with such diversity. Sometimes the conflicts have been between people of different faiths, as when either Spanish Catholics or Anglo Protestants encountered native spiritual traditions. But often they are "all in the family," such as the conflict in the late 1800s between local Hispanic priests and their Rome-appointed French bishops or the demonizing of Roman Catholicism by the nineteenth-century Protestant missionaries.

Such disputes aren't limited to Christianity in Santa Fe or anyplace else. As Pacheco outlines, the city is home to multiple and diverse Jewish congregations, different Buddhist communities with varying practices and a whole variety of New Age groups. One could argue (no pun intended) that our celebrated diversity is the direct result of the fact that we *don't* agree on what to believe or how to practice a particular faith.

Yet, as Pacheco points out, time and again most of Santa Fe's history has been one of "harmonious spirituality." Why is that true? What has made such diversity possible? Perhaps it is the vortices or the spiritual energy of the landscape. But as a spiritual leader in Santa Fe, I think there are other reasons. As the former rector of St. Francis Cathedral monsignor Jerome Martínez Alire affirms, one reason is that in northern New Mexico, "every group is a minority." The fourteenth-generation Santa Fean observes, "We've learned how to get along because we've had to. No one group dominated the last two centuries. To survive, you had to cooperate. We still do."

"Besides," the monsignor often adds, "whether we see ourselves as Hispanic, native or Anglo, we're all a mixture of all kinds of backgrounds and ethnicities. Basically, we're all mutts." Pacheco's discovery of her Hispanic Catholic family's Sephardic Jewish roots (that led to her writing this book) demonstrates that truth.

Another reason for the cooperation and understanding among diverse spiritual groups has been a shared commitment to the wider community. Looking back to the 1800s, Pacheco writes of the hospitals, schools, clinics, sanatoriums, orphanages and prison ministries started by a variety of Santa Fe faith communities. That "cooperation for the common good" continues to this day. Following the horrific riot at the State Penitentiary in 1980, Santa Fe faith communities came together to start the Prison Family Center to care for the children of the prisoners' families so the parents can visit. In 1987, Protestant, Catholic and Jewish congregations started Santa Fe's chapter of Habitat for Humanity to build homes and hope for lower-income families.

St. Elizabeth (Santa Fe's first shelter for the homeless), Esperanza Shelter for Battered Families and the Interfaith Shelter were initiated by Santa Fe faith groups. At all three, Jews, Christians, Muslims and Buddhists can be found working side by side to care for Santa Fe's poorest of the poor. Partnerships with Santa Fe public schools, now part of Communities in Schools, were also started by local congregations committed to living out their faith by caring for others.

A similar spirit of care and cooperation is manifested when individual faith communities have come under siege. When Temple Beth Shalom was graffitied with anti-Semitic slogans or St. Bede's Episcopal Church was vandalized because of its support for LGBT rights or a state political candidate made slurs against Muslims, Santa Fe faith communities of all traditions came together to offer support and show solidarity across religious lines.

As Pacheco's book illustrates, the diverse spiritual communities of Santa Fe may call God by different names. We may worship in different ways. We may not agree on the "basics" of faith. But as she also affirms, whatever our differences, we do agree on our commitment to the wider community, and we do, in all our diverse ways, give thanks for one another and for the One who draws us together into this community called Santa Fe.

I thank Ana Pacheco for the depth and breadth of her work. With this comprehensive overview of Santa Fe's spiritual legacy and current communities, she reminds us of one of Santa Fe's most valuable gifts—the opportunity to experience that "sacred otherness, which is God."

REVEREND TALITHA ARNOLD
Senior Minister, the United Church of Santa Fe

Acknowledgements

My sincere gratitude goes to all the individuals and institutions that gave so generously of their time and knowledge, as well as to the following individuals who know far more than I ever will and did their best to make me look good:

Jacqueline Dunnington
DeeDee Downs
Lisa Law
Nancy Zimmerman
Felicia Lujan
Jonathan Crews
Talitha Arnold
Robert Harcourt
Stanley M. Hordes
Olinda Hodges
Emily Brock
Hannah Abelbeck
Theresa Strottman
Barb Lamont
Lance Bell

Also, in memory of my dearly departed friends whose work shines through with their spirit in this book:

Robert H. Martin
Cary Herz
Gunther Aaron
Andrea "Drew" Bacigalupa

Introduction

In 1610, the capital city of New Mexico was christened La Villa Real de la Santa Fe de San Francisco de Asís. Santa Fe is the fourth of thirteen official commemorative cities named Santa Fe, which means "holy faith" in Spanish. It's also the first city in the world outside Spain to bear the name. I'm sure our founding fathers had no inkling of the ramifications that name would conjure four centuries later. Catholicism was the first religion introduced to the area, but Native American spirituality had been entrenched in the land for thousands of years. The presence of ancient religions of the East, old European faiths, American-made religions, mysticism and New Age are all found in Santa Fe. Just as the earliest settlers began their own type of worship in small groups in private homes, people continue to gather in a similar fashion as they home in on a spiritual foundation to fit their needs and lifestyles. Reminiscent of those early days, these new missionaries reach out in the Spanish language to the state's burgeoning immigrant community from Mexico and Central America.

Since the mid-twentieth century, Santa Fe has been referred to as "the City Different" because of our "anything goes" attitude. This mindset includes the diversity of its spirituality. In a city with a population of some seventy thousand, it's a place of refuge not just for spiritual seekers but also for His Holiness the Dalai Lama. Having lived in exile from his beloved Tibet for more than half a century, he has been instrumental in establishing a strong Mahayana Buddhist presence in Santa Fe, including all four major lineages: Nyingma, Kagyu, Sakya and Gelug traditions. The presence of such a strong Buddhist community might not be uncommon in large metropolitan cities like New York or Los Angeles, but for a small town like Santa Fe, it's unprecedented.

Spirituality was never far from my mind while growing up in a devout Catholic family in Santa Fe. My cousin Ralph Herrera was a Diocesan priest, my cousin Charles Ortiz was a Trappist monk and my cousin Stella Córdova was a member of the Sisters of Loretto for sixty years. Another cousin on my paternal side, Steve Armenta, was a La Sallian Christian Brother who spent part of his life as a missionary in Central America, returning to Santa Fe in the 1990s to teach at St. Michael's High School. My mother's eldest brother, Daniel Ortiz, was also a Christian Brother. He lived abroad for fifty years, spreading the word of St. John-Baptist de La Salle, who devoted his life to education—first in Monterrey, Mexico, where he helped to start a school for boys, and then in the Philippines, where he was the founding president of La Salle University in Manila.

On my mother's side of the family, five generations of women received both their primary and secondary education from the Sisters of Loretto. Alas, I broke my mother's heart when I became the first one in my family to attend public school. I transitioned away from Catholic school after committing an infraction at St. Francis Parochial School that resulted in my expulsion. Even back then, I subconsciously questioned the notion of a singular God.

Fortunately, growing up in a small town meant it wasn't hard to absorb the inner workings of the community. As a child, I was familiar with the Jewish merchants on the Plaza, where my family shopped. I knew they didn't attend my church and always wondered if they were members of the other churches in town, the ones that had crosses but weren't the same kind of church I went to. Back in the late 1960s, Santa Fe, Boulder and Taos were known as the three sister cities of cosmic consciousness. I'm not sure why, but I think it had to do with the surrounding mountain vortex and the remnants of volcanic activity from millions of years ago. Whatever the reason, there were plenty of hippies with their crystals and all their New Age stuff around. As a teenager, I loved eating the ice cream made by the Sikhs at the Golden Temple restaurant while watching the Hare Krishna parade around town, banging on tambourines and chanting. And I remember listening to Marianne, my mother's beautician, while she excitedly talked about her I AM religion. So by the time I had learned to drive a car, I had been introduced to spirituality from different parts of the world, as well as an American-born sect.

When I returned to Santa Fe in 1991 after living in New York for sixteen years, I wasn't surprised by the proliferation of spiritual groups that I encountered because so many changes had taken place in my absence. But what caught me off guard was the revelation that I was a Sephardic Jew. Toward the latter part of the twentieth century, a lot of information began to surface on the *conversos*, the Spanish Jews who had converted to Catholicism to avoid persecution, all the while practicing their Jewish faith in secrecy.

This newfound spiritual identity hasn't changed my life; if anything, it's made me more cognizant of the need to nurture the inner core of existence through something greater than oneself. While writing this book, I learned so much from all the people who so graciously gave of their time and knowledge. This book is not meant to be a scholarly or theological work but, rather, a history of the harmonious spirituality that abounds in Santa Fe, the City of Holy Faith.

God is not what you imagine or think you understand.
—St. Augustine

Chapter 1

A Sacred Land

And ye came near and stood under the mountain; and the mountain burned with fire unto the midst of heaven, with darkness, clouds, and thick darkness.
—Deuteronomy 4:11

Descending from the crest of La Bajada Hill into Santa Fe, one's first glimpse is of the surrounding Sangre de Cristo, Jemez and Ortiz Mountains. These ranges are part of a broader landscape created from widespread volcanic activity that occurred seventy million years ago. New Mexico is known as the Volcano State, having the most diverse and largest number of volcanoes in North America. In addition, it contains one of the world's five continental rifts.

The greatest concentration of craters created by volcanic stream explosions occurred in New Mexico. The Valles Caldera (*caldera* is Spanish for "cauldron"), located fifty-eight miles from Santa Fe, is one of the largest super volcanoes in the world and one of three in the United States. (The other two are Yellowstone in Wyoming and Long Valley in California.) The Valles Caldera spans almost fourteen miles and was formed from the collapse of molten rocks, creating a magma chamber. Two of the largest basaltic lava flows in the world are in Carrizozo, in the southern part of the state, and McCartys Village to the west. It was in New Mexico, not Hawaii, that lava flows were first studied by geologists.

The Sangre de Cristo Mountains, whose name, given by the early Spanish explorers, means "blood of Christ," are part of the Rocky

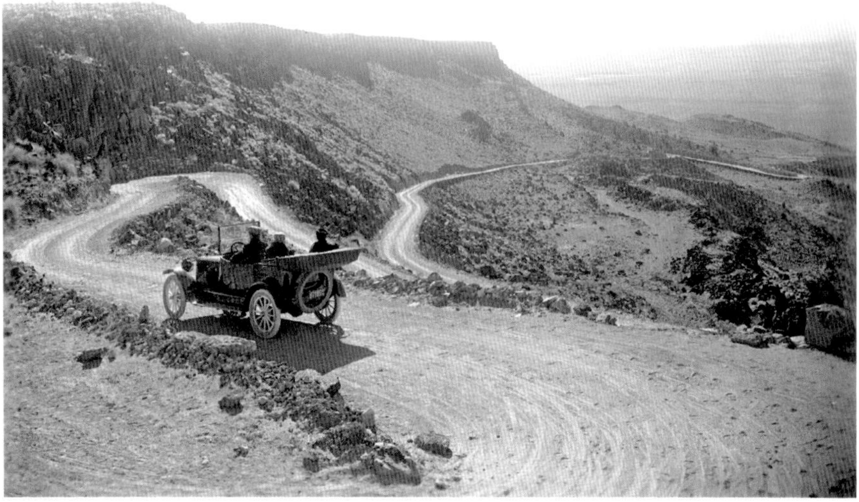

La Bajada Hill, New Mexico. *Courtesy Palace of the Governors [NMHM/DCA]. No. 008231.*

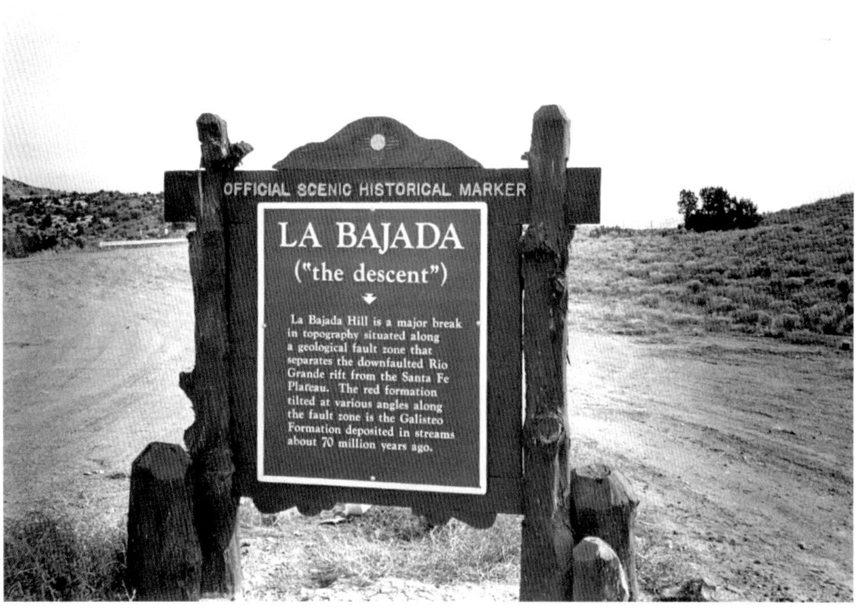

La Bajada (the descent) road sign south of Santa Fe. *Courtesy Palace of the Governors [NMHM/DCA]. No. HP.2014.14.*

Mountains, one of the longest mountain chains on earth. They were formed from volcanic activity. Major fault lines run along both the east and west sides of the Sangres, with the Rio Grande fault line at the range overlooking Santa Fe.

In addition to New Mexico's volcanic terrain, the spiritual landscape can be further explained by the Four Corners region of the United States. It's the only location in the United States where four states—New Mexico, Colorado, Utah and Arizona—connect. The Four Corners are part of the larger region known as the Colorado Plateau, which sprawls across Utah, northern Arizona, northwestern New Mexico and western Colorado and covers 130,000 square miles. For geographers, the Colorado Plateau has always been an enigma. While the Rocky Mountains to the east and the basin and land to the west were being thrust, stretched and fractured into existence during volcanic eruptions, the Colorado Plateau remained structurally intact. Geologists and geographers remain puzzled by this phenomenon, which many have described as mystical.

Within the Four Corners, Chaco Canyon in northwest New Mexico is the largest, best preserved and architecturally most advanced of all the early villages of the Anasazi, often referred to as Ancestral Puebloans. First

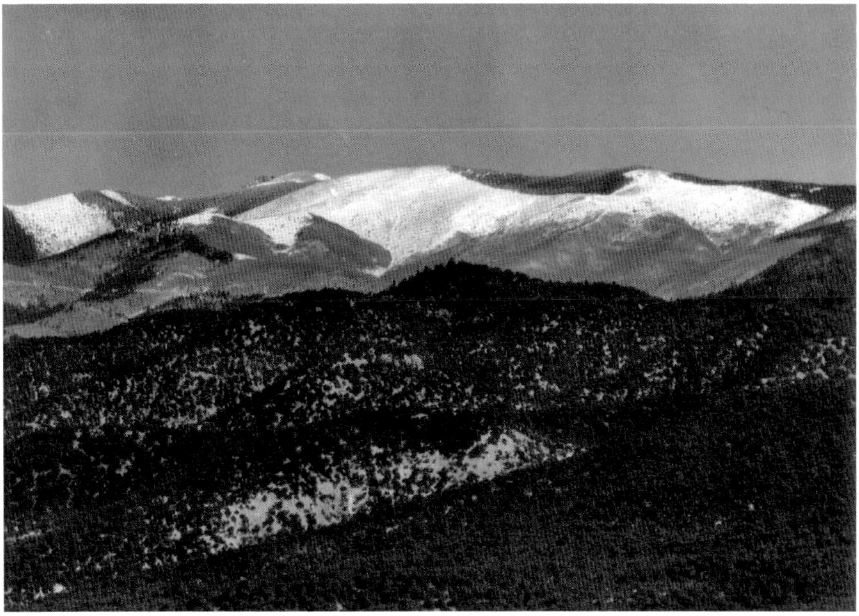

The image of a horse's head on the Sangre de Cristo Mountains northeast of Santa Fe in 1948. *Photo by Robert H. Martin.*

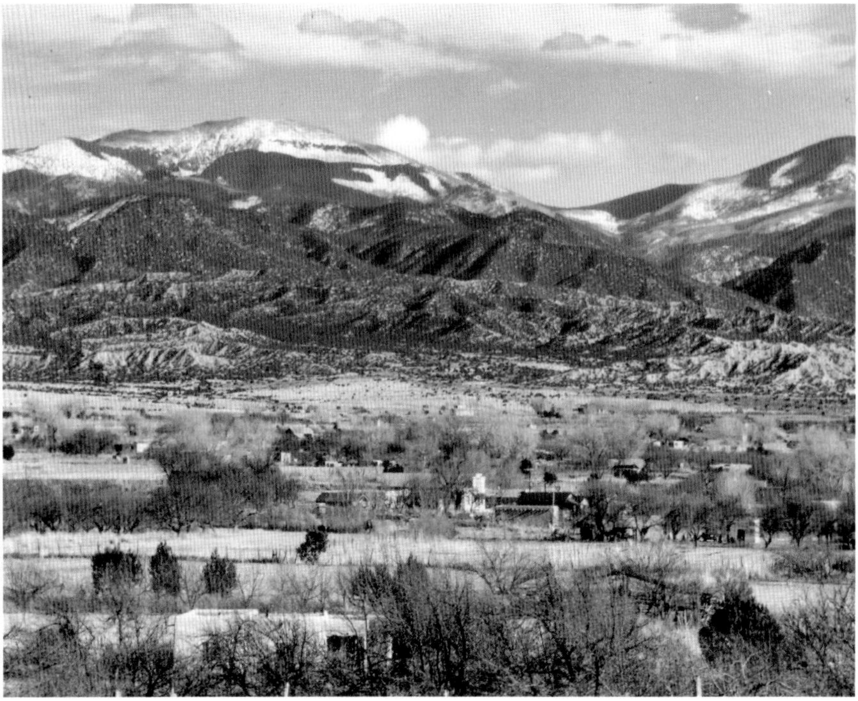

The image of a thunderbird on the Sangre de Cristo Mountains northeast of Santa Fe in 1948. *Photo by Robert H. Martin.*

Opposite, top: Tenth-century apartment house, Chaco Canyon, New Mexico, 1959. *Courtesy Palace of the Governors [NMHM/DCA]. No. 058339.*

inhabited in the ninth century AD, it was designated a national monument in 1907 and a UNESCO World Heritage site in 1987.

In 1978, Mesa Verde National Park in southwestern Colorado also became a UNESCO World Heritage Site. The inhabitants built their first pueblos after 650 BC and by the end of the twelfth century had begun to construct massive dwellings in the earth that are thought to be the largest cliff dwellings in North America.

Over millions of years, wind and water have sculpted the unique sandstone formation at Monument Valley in Utah. In 1884, the area surrounding Monument Valley was designated a Navajo reservation by President Chester A. Arthur, and it became a tribal park under the direction of the Navajo Tribal Council in 1958.

Canyon de Chelly National Monument, located within the boundaries of the Navajo Nation in Arizona, spans 131 square miles and encompasses

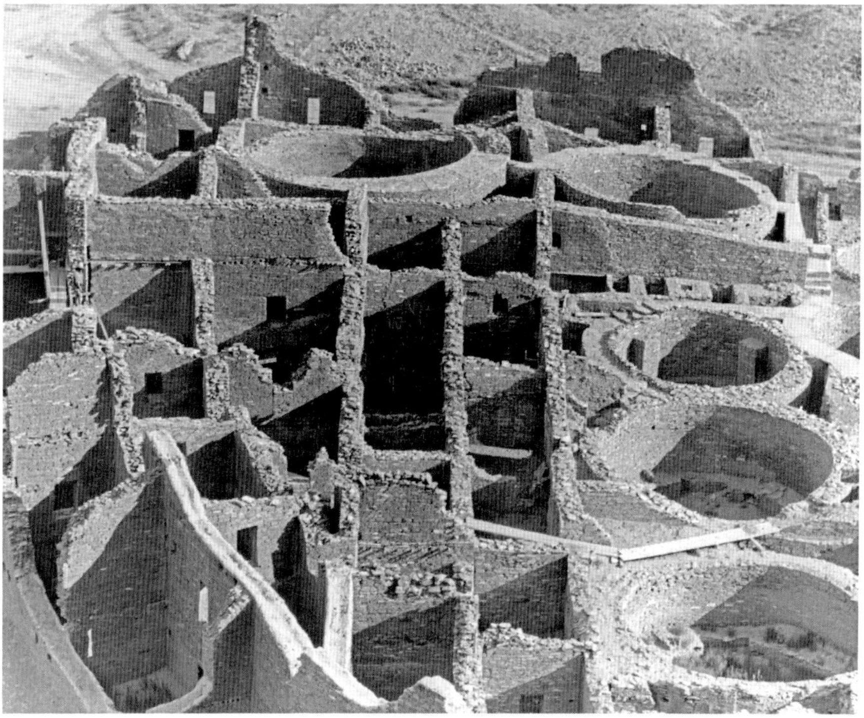

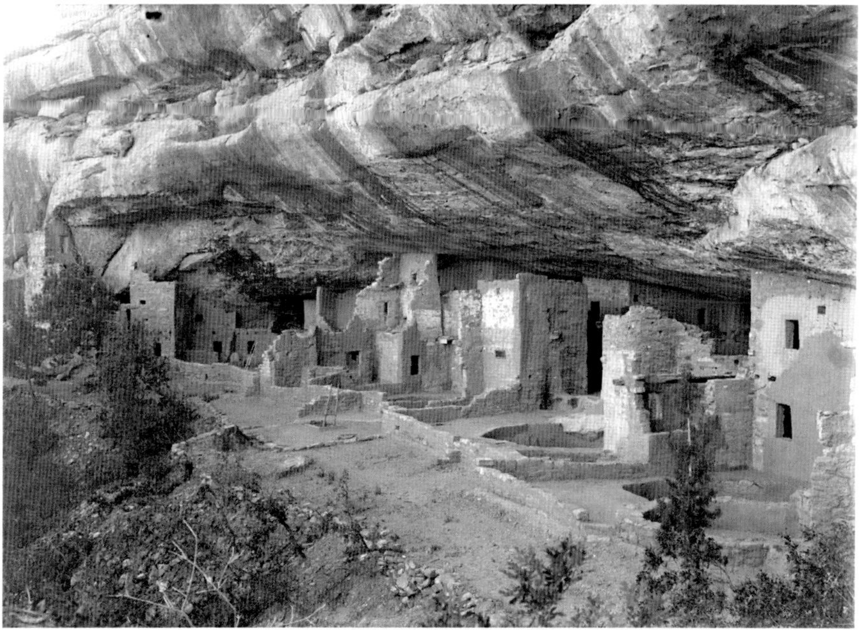

Spruce Tree House looking north, Mesa Verde National Park, Colorado, 1907. *Photo by Jesse Nussbaum. Courtesy Palace of the Governors [NMHM/DCA]. No. 060587.*

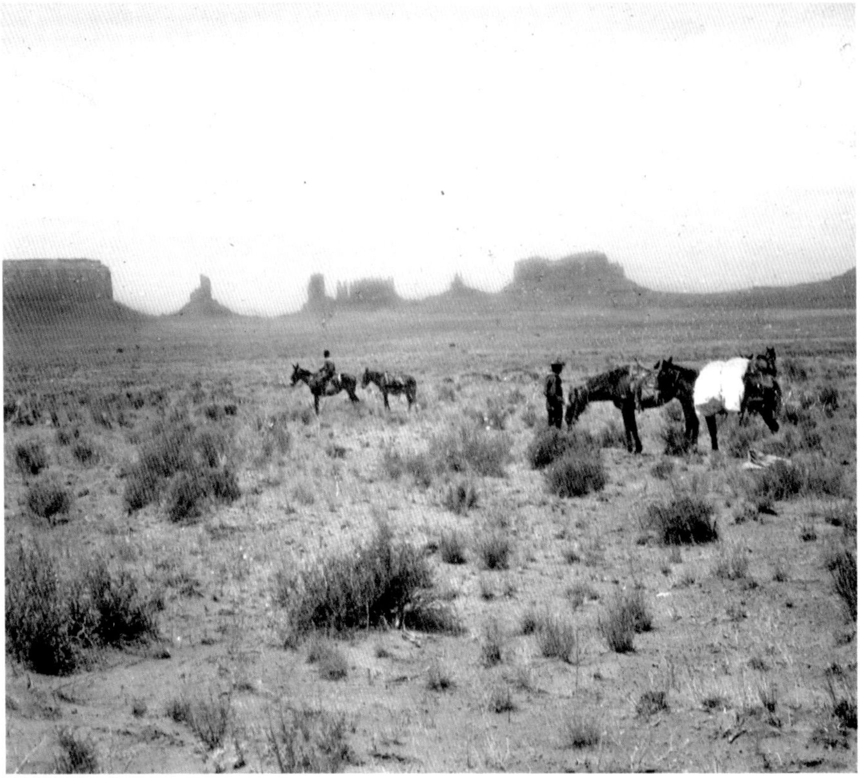

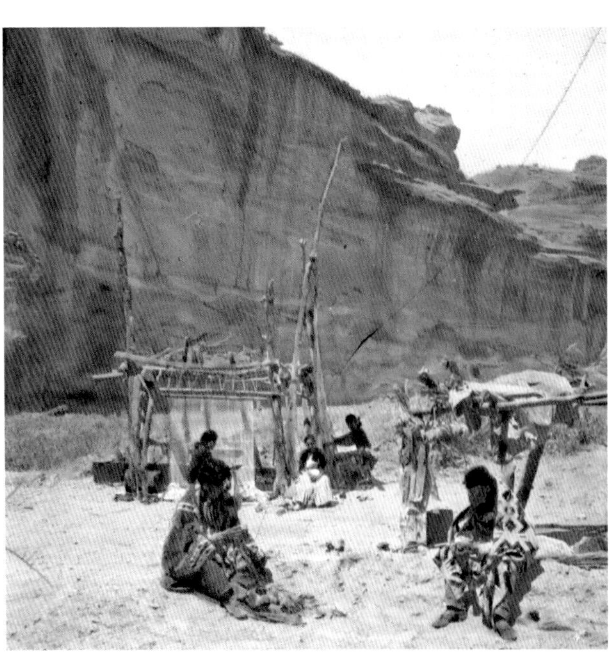

Above: Riders in Monument Valley, Arizona, 1915. *Courtesy Palace of the Governors [NMHM/DCA]. No. LS.1499.*

Left: Navajo camp in Canyon de Chelly, Arizona, circa. 1925. *Photo by Edward Kemp. Courtesy Palace of the Governors [NMHM/DCA]. No. LS.1482.*

three major canyons: Canyon de Chelly, Canyon del Muerto and Monument Canyon. It became a national park in 1931.

In the summer of 1987, thousands of people traveled to Chaco Canyon to observe the Harmonic Convergence, a worldwide meditation event that coincided with the end of one of the cycles of the Mayan calendar. The alignment of the moon, sun, earth and other planets during this time is believed to have marked the beginning of a new age. Like the Native Americans who settled in the Four Corners, the Spanish explorers who founded Santa Fe and the geologists and archaeologists who study this area, droves of spiritual seekers continue to be drawn to this sacred landscape.

Chapter 2

Honoring Spirit

Native American isn't blood; it is what is in the heart. The love for the land. The respect for it, those who inhabit it; and the respect and acknowledgement of the spirits and elders. That is what it is to be Indian.
—White Feather, Navajo medicine man

Over the past two centuries, geologists have learned through New Mexico's volcanic activity that it's a special place, something the native people knew long before. To them, the volcanic boulders that surround the area are a sacred landscape where they have carved petroglyphs and communicated with their ancestral spirits since the beginning of time. There's evidence of human presence in this area as early as 2900 BC. Until AD 200, the Anasazi were largely nomadic, but they settled in this region and began to farm and build small pit houses.

Around AD 850, some unknown event occurred that caused them to radically change the way they built their dwellings. The living quarters and communal spaces began to soar four and five stories high, connecting hundreds of rooms and kivas (round ceremonial chambers). These multistory caves were structured in a way that made them difficult to access, providing protection from enemy intruders. In addition to these structures, archaeologists have identified characteristic types of basketry, art, tools and architecture that go along with settlement patterns and agriculture. Between AD 1200 and 1300, the building style changed again, and the Anasazi built their homes in shallow caves, today known as cliff dwellings. These

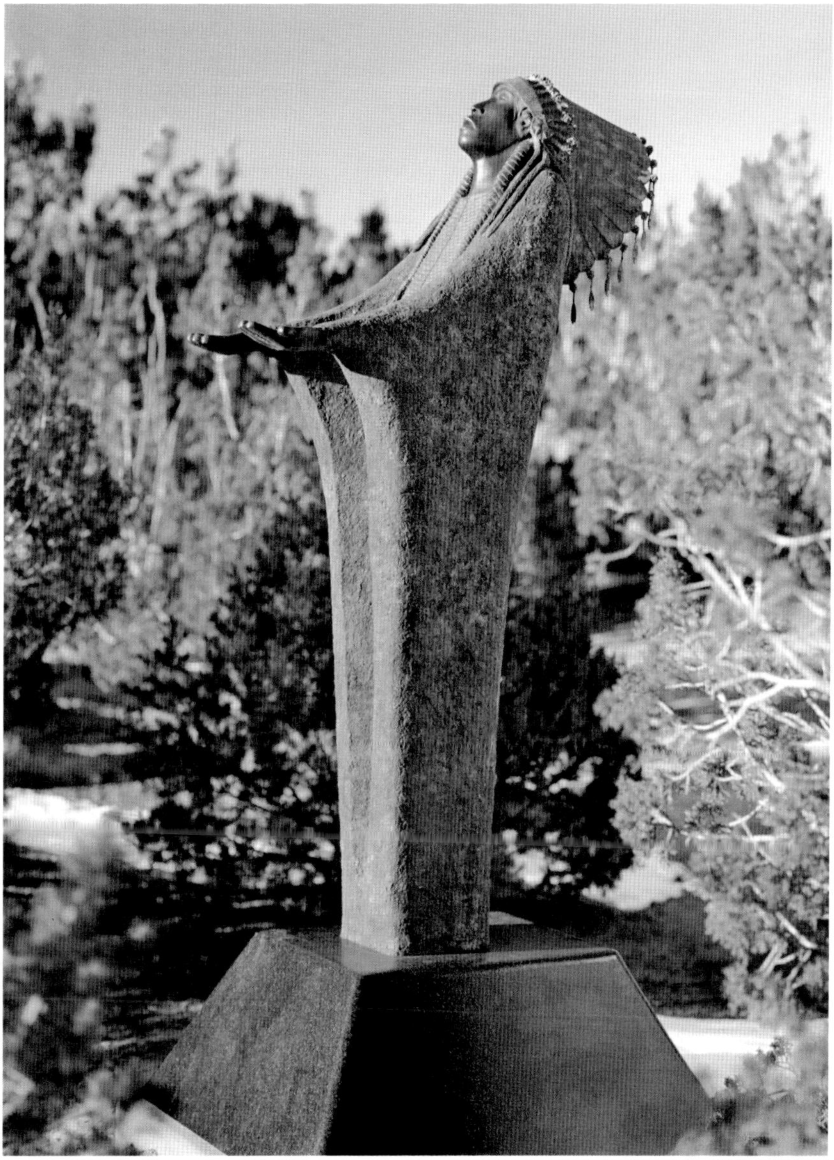

The 1994 sculpture *Prayer*, by Allan C. Houser. *Courtesy Allan Houser Gallery.*

were built in a manner that provided shelter, with shade in the summer and exposure to sun in the winter.

New Mexico's Pueblo Indians are believed to be descendants of the Anasazi, who populated the Four Corners region of the Colorado Plateau.

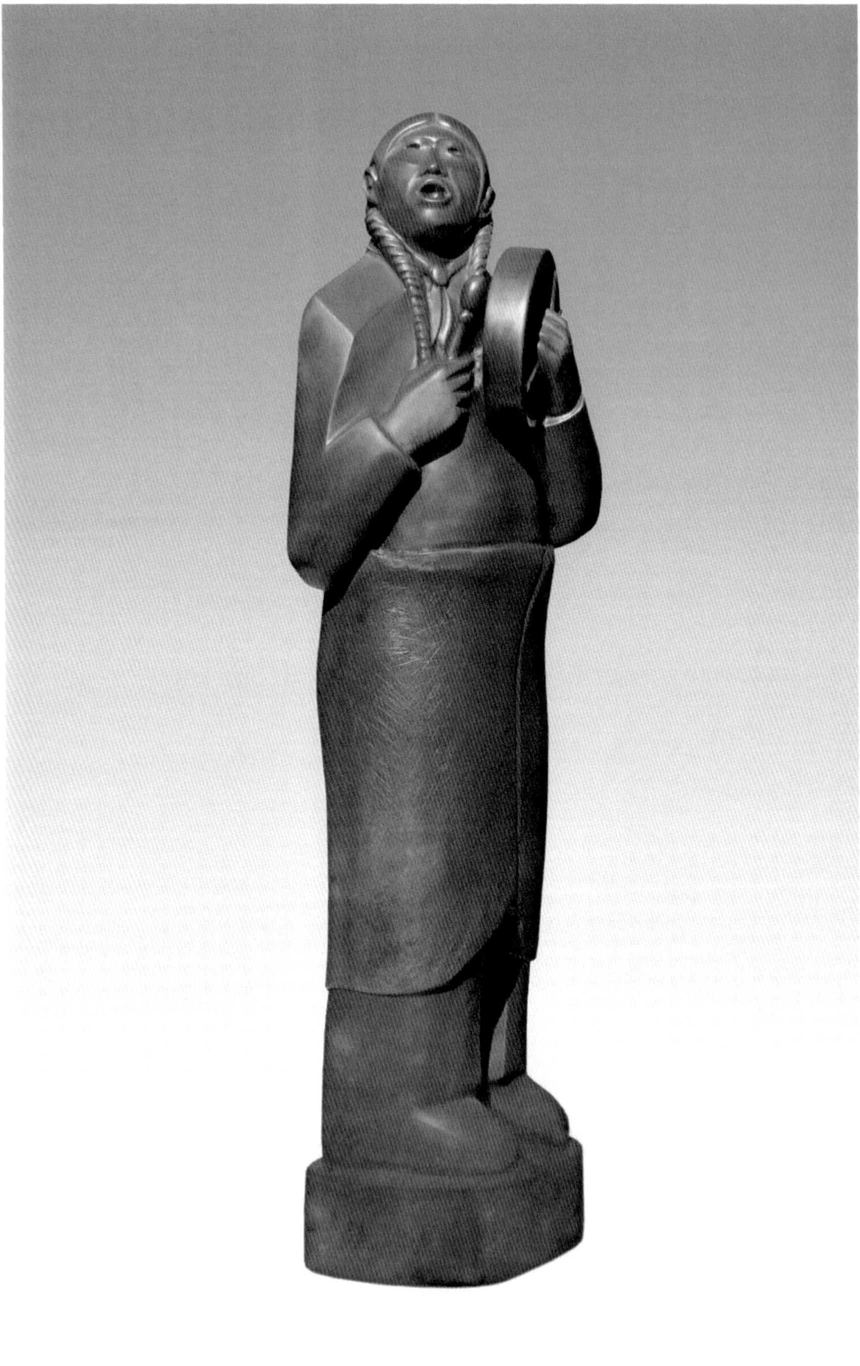

The 1990 sculpture *Inspiration* by Allan C. Houser. *Courtesy Allan Houser Gallery.*

In these areas of Utah, Arizona, New Mexico and Colorado, the Anasazi practiced rituals linked to the lunar and solar cycles. The dwellings they built were feats of engineering, often constructed in accordance with the celestial alignments. Evidence suggests that these people were expert sky watchers, with clear knowledge of the cyclical and seasonal patterns of the sun, moon and stars. This knowledge is reflected throughout the architectural ruins of the great houses and observational and ceremonial sites. The most famous among these is the Sun Dagger, a petroglyph crafted to mark the cycles of the sun at Chaco Canyon in northwest New Mexico.

Chaco Canyon was first inhabited in the middle of the ninth century, and it grew and prospered for two hundred years. At its peak, the population reached four thousand, with satellite villages spread across the northern part of what is now New Mexico. By AD 1300, the population centers of the Anasazi villages in the Four Corners had migrated to the Rio Grande Valley of New Mexico and the Mogollon Rim in Arizona, probably because of drought conditions.

In *God Is Red* by Vine Deloria Jr., the seminal book on Native American cosmology, the author underscores the importance to their belief system of space, time and the chronology of events. As he states, "Christianity puts a great deal of focus on creation and what it means to the religion. Indian tribal religions prefer to think of creation as the environment as it presents itself in a specific place."

Unlike Christianity and its use of the Bible as a spiritual guide, Native American spiritual practices relied on oral traditions. They didn't adhere to a single form of religion with a universal set of beliefs but, rather, to an array of religious practices that varied from location to location. These early beliefs continue today in a syncretic form at New Mexico's nineteen pueblos: Acoma, Cochití, Isleta, Jemez, Laguna, Nambé, Picurís, Pojoaque, San Ildefonso, San Juan (Ohkay Owingeh), Sandia, San Felipe, Santa Ana, Santa Clara, Santo Domingo, Taos, Tesuque, Zia and Zuni.

Just as their ancestors had to adapt to a harsh and changing environment, in the seventeenth century the Pueblo Indians were forced to adapt to the Christian doctrine introduced by the Spanish settlers in order to survive. Fortunately, many of their cultural rituals were woven into this new doctrine. Today, most of the native traditional dances are aligned with the changing seasons and coincide with Catholic feast days. Six of the nineteen pueblos are named in honor of saints, and all of them have a patron saint as their protector.

One curiosity, possibly the earliest evidence of the convergence of spiritual practices in this country, arrived from the Arab world via Spain. The dance

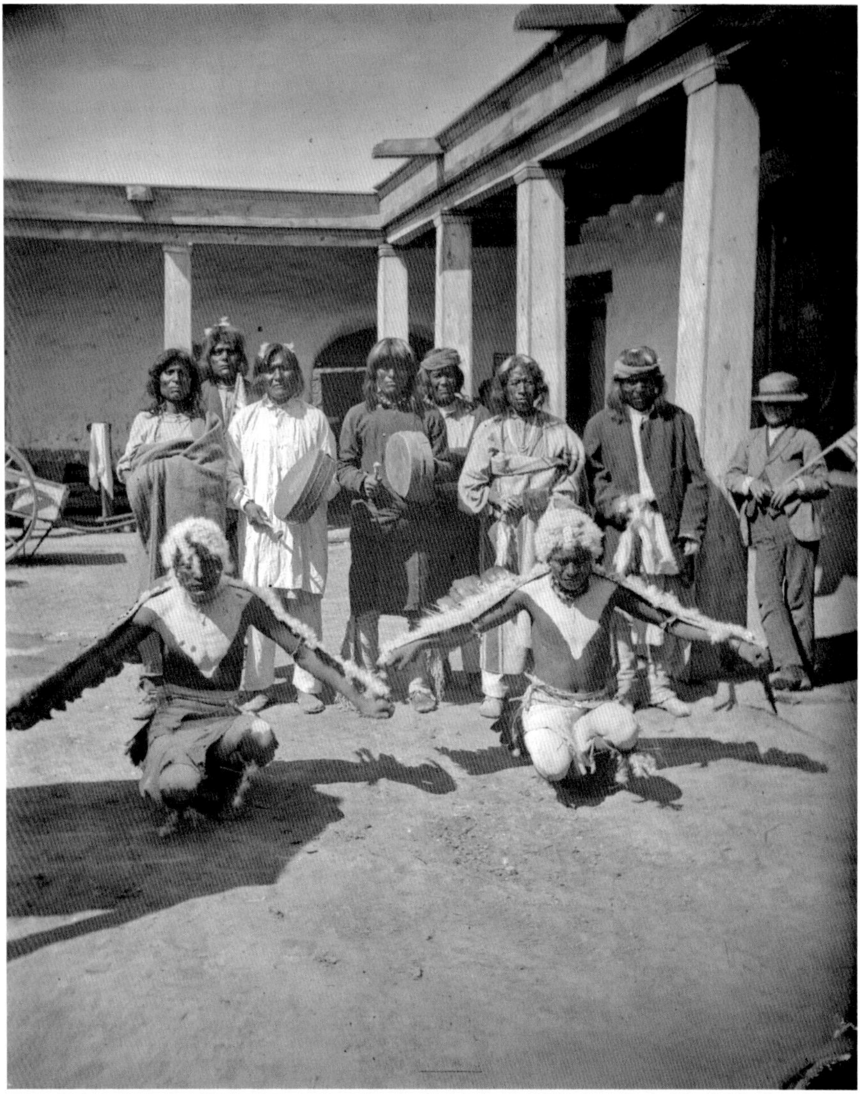

Tesuque Pueblo feather dancers, New Mexico, circa 1880. *Photo by Ben Wittick. Courtesy Palace of the Governors [NMHM/DCA]. No. 015580.*

known as Los Matachines is a performance ritual believed to be of Arabic origin that was used by the Franciscan missionaries as a proselytizing instrument to teach Catholicism to the Indians. The Matachín dancers most probably entered Spain from Morocco. In the *Diccionario de la lengua española*, *matachín* is translated from the Arabic word meaning "masked." The

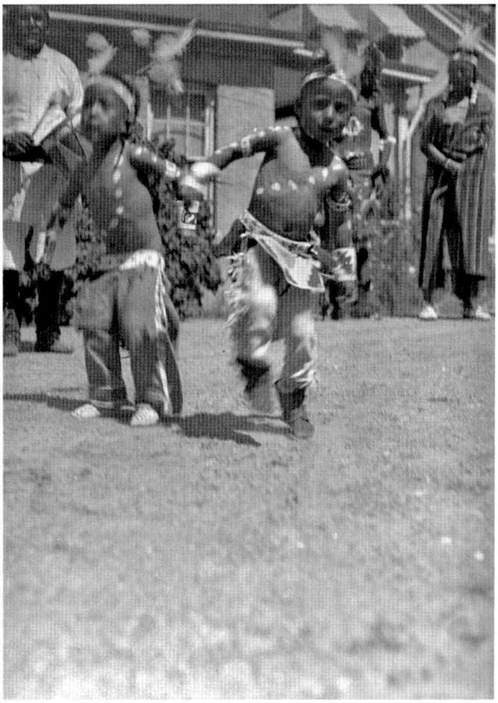

Right: Dancers at the Santa Fe Indian School, Santa Fe, New Mexico, circa 1925. *Photo by T. Harmon Parkhurst. Courtesy Palace of the Governors [NMHM/DCA]. No. 001417.*

Below: Catholic baptism, Jemez Pueblo, New Mexico, circa 1945. *Photo by Ferenz Fedor. Courtesy Palace of the Governors [NMHM/DCA]. No. 100371.*

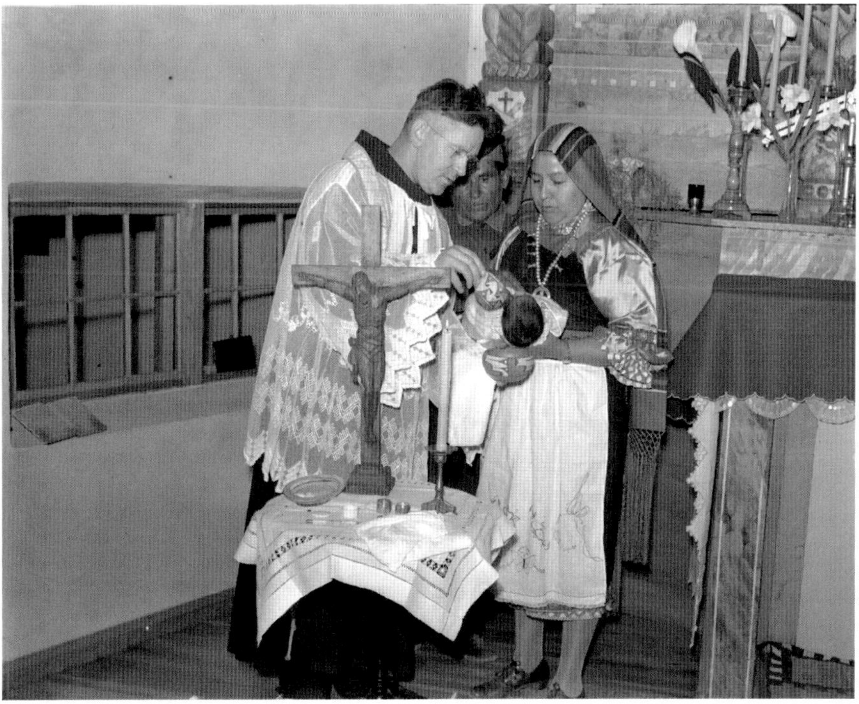

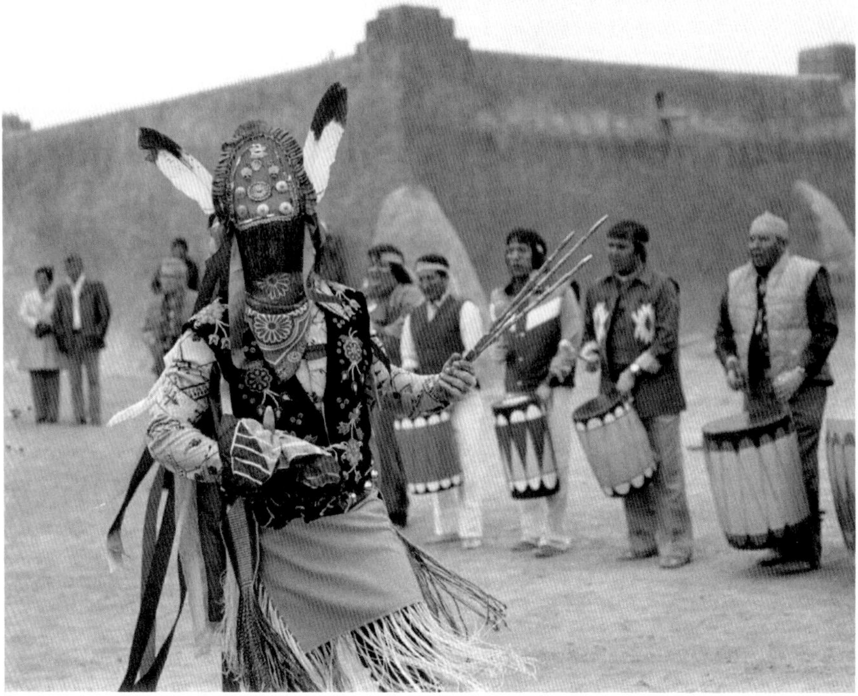

Matachines dance, Santa Clara Pueblo, New Mexico, 1981. *Photo by Nancy Hunter Warren. Courtesy Palace of the Governors [NMHM/DCA]. No. HP.2003.29.15.*

twelve masked dancers are said to be representative of the twelve apostles. But because the dance is performed as a form of entertainment, the Matachines are more akin to sacred clowns, like the amusing trickster genre found in Native American myths. The Abuelo, or grandfather, is a central figure in the dance, and it is to Grandfather, the Great Spirit, that Native Americans pray.

Chapter 3

Evangelizing the West

Santa Fe wouldn't exist as the City of Holy Faith if it weren't for the longest war in recorded history. From AD 718 through 1492, the Spanish and the Moors battled over territory and religious dominance. In 1491, following the last Ten Year War with the Moors, Queen Isabel and King Ferdinand reconquered an area located twelve kilometers south of Granada in Andalucía. Since it had been a crusade of the cross against the Moors, Isabel refused to have the newly constructed town named in her honor, preferring to call it Santa Fe de la Vega. It was there that Christopher Columbus signed the famous *capitulaciones* with the Catholic kings a few months after the end of the war, which granted him license and financial incentives to search for the newfound land. Two more cities in Spain were also given that name: Santa Fe del Penedés in the region of Barcelona and Santa Fe de Mondújar in the province of Almería. In 1610, the capital city of New Mexico was christened La Villa Real de la Santa Fe de San Francisco de Asís, the fourth of thirteen official cities around the world named Santa Fe.

With the end of the Moorish occupation, Isabel la Católica, as the queen became known, began the largest evangelization of Christianity since the apostles when she sponsored the 1492 expedition to America. Queen Isabel's determination to promote Christianity throughout the New World was rooted in the early history of Spain's patron saint, Santiago de Compostela, or St. James. When St. Peter became the first pope, it was his duty to spread the word of God to a non-Christian world with the help of the other eleven apostles. St. James the Greater was sent to Roman Hispania, where he was

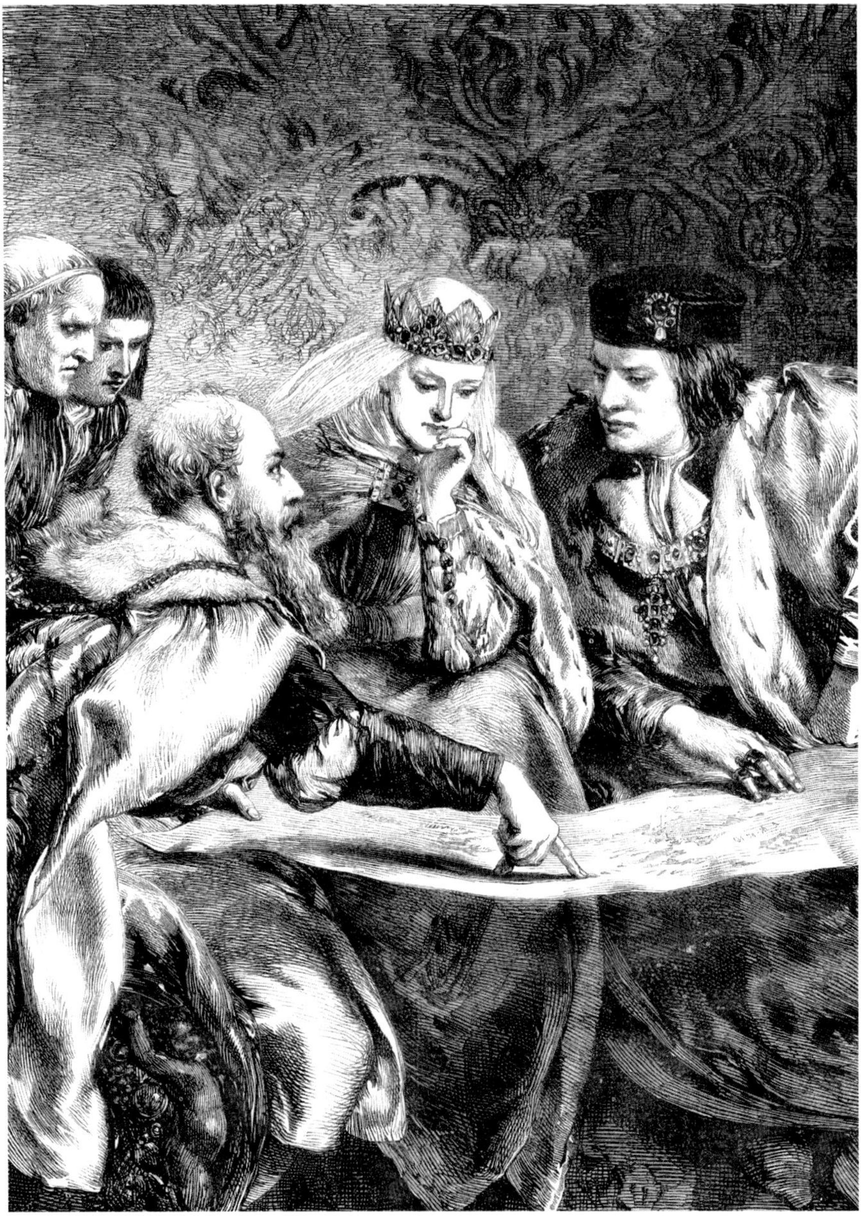

Queen Isabel and King Ferdinand meet Christopher Columbus. *Courtesy Getty Images.*

rebuked by the Roman Spaniards, who didn't want to convert to an observant religion, preferring the eclecticism of pagan Rome. Santiago converted just a few hundred Romans at most. Upon his return to Jerusalem, he had the misfortune of tangling with King Herod, one of the most merciless tyrants of his time, who in a rage ordered him beheaded. His body was brought to Spain and is entombed at Compostela, the Celtic region of Galicia in the northwestern part of the country. Today, Santiago de Compostela is a famous shrine rivaling those in Jerusalem and Rome. Millions of people make the annual pilgrimage to visit the tomb of St. James on foot, on horseback and by car on his July 25 feast day and throughout the year.

There's a movement underway in Spain to have Isabel canonized as a saint, but it may be a harder task than the canonization of St. James. Through the chronicles of history, it's been documented that the Spaniards from the peninsula did not go to America to work but to live off the exploitation of the native labor in a system that became known as the *encomienda*. Through this system, trusted Spanish noblemen exacted food and supplies from the Indians in a form of slavery. They believed, like their queen, that as Castilians they were superior, and they insisted that order be imposed through their language. They knew that language meant domination, leaving the task of communicating with the indigenous people to the missionaries.

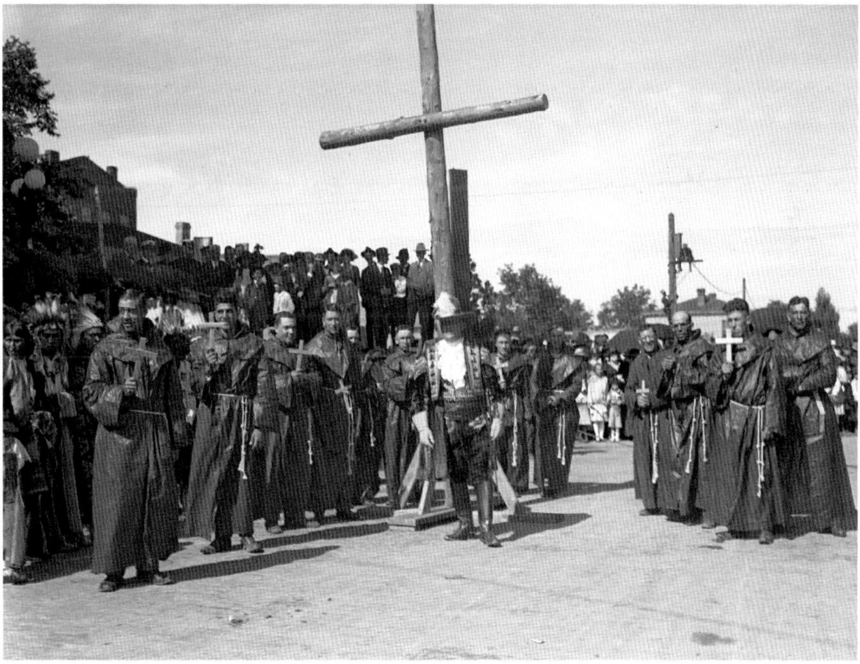

Reenactment at the 1919 Fiesta de Santa Fe pageant with the Franciscan friars and Diego de Vargas. *Photo by Wesley Bradfield. Courtesy Palace of the Governors [NMHM/DCA]. No. 052360.*

No one did a better job of executing these principles in New Mexico than Don Juan Pérez de Narriahonda y Salazar de Oñate, a Basque from a wealthy mining family in Zacatecas, Mexico. It was customary for both civil and religious leaders to want to immediately be identified by their *patria chica* (small country). The town of Oñate was in Las Vascongadas in the

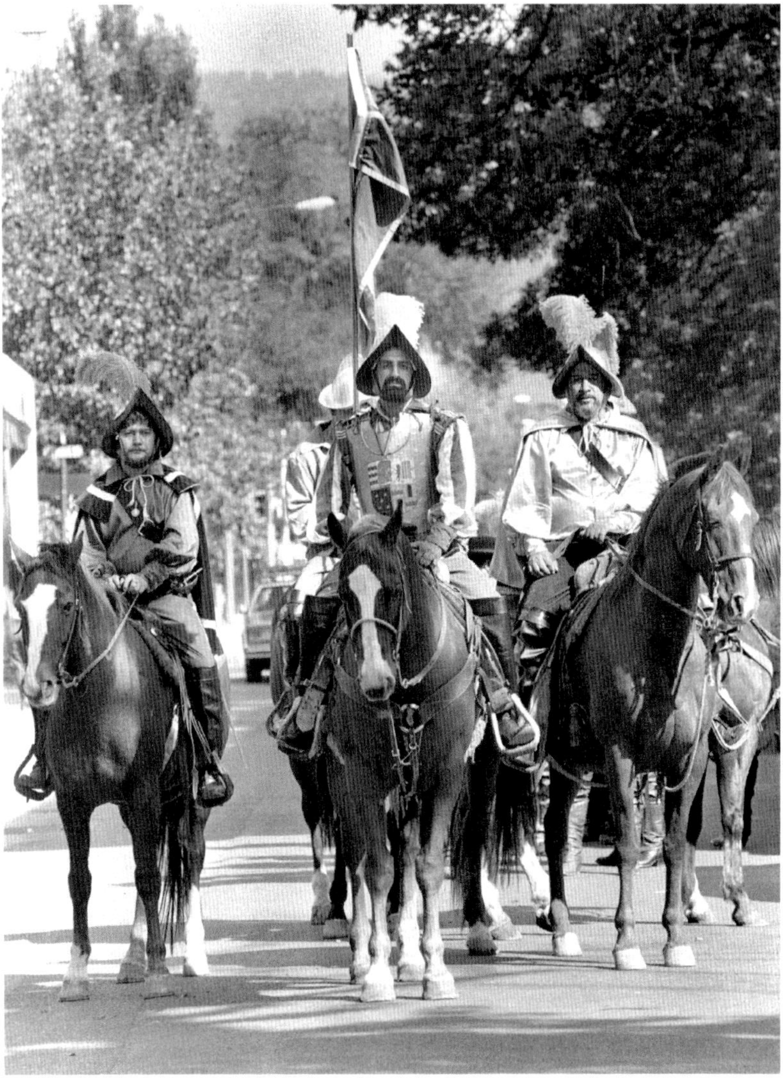

De Vargas mounted caballeros in Fiesta parade, 1988, Santa Fe, New Mexico. *Photo by Mark Nohl. Courtesy Palace of the Governors [NMHM/DCA]. No. HP.2014.14.319.*

Pyrenees Mountains of Spain. They were proud to be *vascos*, of Basque descent, with their own special language, customs and laws. Soon after the death of his wife, Isabel de Tolosa Cortés de Moctezuma, the granddaughter of Hernán Cortés, Oñate set out to find adventure and riches in the land that his ancestors had found in México-Tenochtitlán. He invited his son, Cristobalito, and two of his nephews from the Zaldívar family to serve as officers in his army. He also recruited more than 150 hearty soldiers and families. The caravan included 7 Franciscan friars whose main task was to Christianize the natives. On the second leg of the journey, a group of Tlaxcalan Indians from Mexico joined Oñate's colonizing expedition.

A captain in the Spanish military who traveled with the 1598 Oñate expedition was Gaspar Pérez de Villagra, who wrote *La Historia de la Nueva México* in 1610. In this epic poem, the soldier-scribe documented the establishment of the first European foothold in North America. The ancient narrative chronicles the arduous journey, including passage through a treacherous desert where both people and horses suffered from all-consuming thirst. It also provides a succinct depiction of the cruelty toward the native people by the Spanish explorers. Upon their arrival, there were close to one hundred Native American settlements; by the seventeenth century, that number had been reduced to the present number of nineteen Indian pueblos.

Early documents indicate that the first church built by the Franciscan missionaries around 1605 to 1608 in Santa Fe was the San Miguel Mission. The church was built on the south side of the Santa Fe River in the Barrio de Analco, the Aztec word meaning "the other side." It became the primary place of worship for missionaries, their Indian converts and the entire Hispanic population throughout the seventeenth century. Reputed to be the oldest church in the United States, it was burned during the 1680 Pueblo Revolt but was not completely destroyed. The thick adobe walls were not affected by the fire, which destroyed only the wooden roof and framework. When Diego de Vargas restored Spanish control of New Mexico in 1692, he ordered that the church be repaired. In 1859, the church was used as a chapel for the newly arrived Christian Brothers. Over its long history, the church has served as a mission, a barrio church, a military chapel, an oratory for the Christian Brothers and, most recently, a revered shrine to St. Michael, the patron saint of the dying.

The legend of the first church bell goes back to Spain and its eight-century-long battle with the Moors. The constant warring between the two groups created a state of fear among the Spanish population. In the

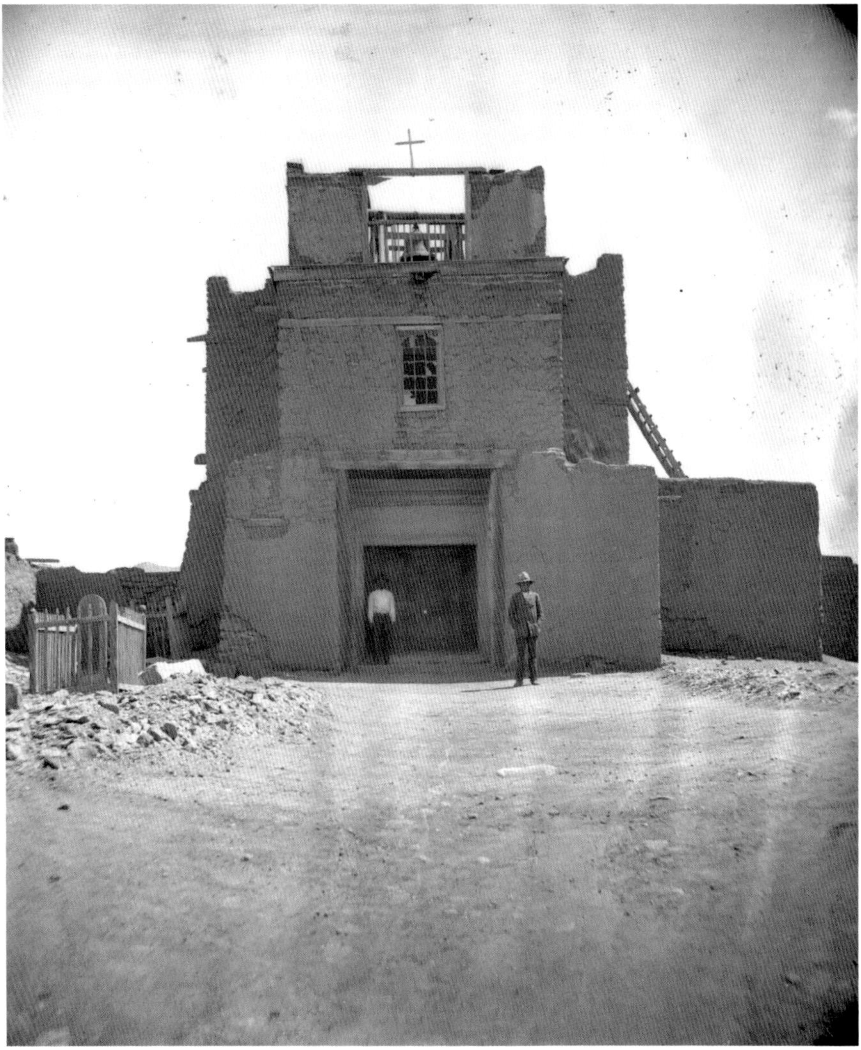

Ancient Chapel of San Miguel, Santa Fe, built between 1605 and 1608, photo circa 1880. *Photo by Ben Wittick. Courtesy Palace of the Governors [NMHM/DCA]. No. 015850.*

small hamlet of San José in Andalucía, the villagers prayed to St. Joseph for protection; they promised that if they were saved from the Moors, they would honor him. With their prayers answered, a bell was cast as a tribute of appreciation. Through their unrelenting faith and prayers, they believed that each time the bell rang, the power of the Moors declined. The bell rang triumphantly every time the Christians gained victory until their enemy was finally expelled from Spain. It is believed that the bell traveled from Spain to Mexico with Nicolás Ortiz Niño Ladrón de Guevara, a wealthy Spanish hidalgo. He brought it to Santa Fe, where it was placed in a *capilla* (small chapel) he built for his family. After the Pueblo Revolt, it was placed at San Miguel Chapel. In 1872, the bell was damaged by a storm and removed to the interior of the church for protection and preservation.

La Conquistadora, the oldest Madonna in the United States, arrived in Santa Fe in 1625. She was carried in the arms of Fray Alonzo de Benavides, a Franciscan priest who came across the twenty-eight-inch-tall statue depicting a Marian figure carved in willow wood with the liturgical title "One Assumption of Mary into Heaven." Padre Benavides, who was preparing to become the new superior for the Franciscan missionaries, believed that Mary Immaculate would provide the inspiration to the settlers of the barren northern frontier in the high desert. When he arrived with eleven Franciscans in his caravan, they received a warm welcome, and the legacy of this revered icon took root. The statue resided in the Santa Fe *parroquia* (parish), where it became the most important religious symbol for the Spanish pioneers. Sometime between 1625 and 1655, a rosary confraternity was founded around the statue's presence, and she was given the name La Conquistadora. For the next seventy-five years, she remained a symbol of religious devotion. During the Pueblo Revolt that drove the Spaniards from Santa Fe to El Paso del Norte (present-day El Paso, Texas), La Conquistadora was rescued from the burning chapel and carried by Josefa López Sambrano de Grijalva, wife of Francisco Lucero de Godoy, to safety. Lucero de Godoy was the eldest grandson of Francisco Gómez and Ana Robledo, who were two of Santa Fe's founding families.

La Conquistadora returned thirteen years later when she accompanied Diego de Vargas in the Spanish reconquest of New Mexico. The religious devotion of De Vargas was displayed by the banners representing the Marian figure in his *entrada* (parade entrance) to the capital city. De Vargas had petitioned La Conquistadora to assist him in his efforts, and he had vowed to establish a throne in her honor. She was enshrined at a chapel in the Casas Reales until 1714, ten years after the death of De Vargas, when the new chapel was completed.

The two central figures listed in the 1712 proclamation of the reconquest are Don Diego de Vargas and La Conquistadora. The proclamation is read each year at the Fiesta de Santa Fe, the oldest continual community celebration in the United States. In 1956, writer and historian Pedro Ribera Ortega and a group of devout men began La Cofradía de La Conquistadora.

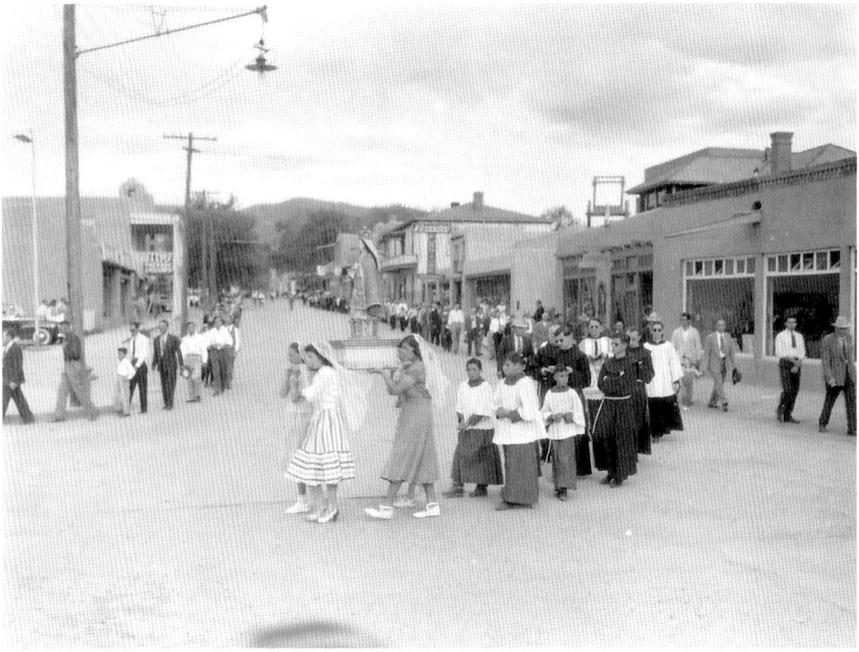

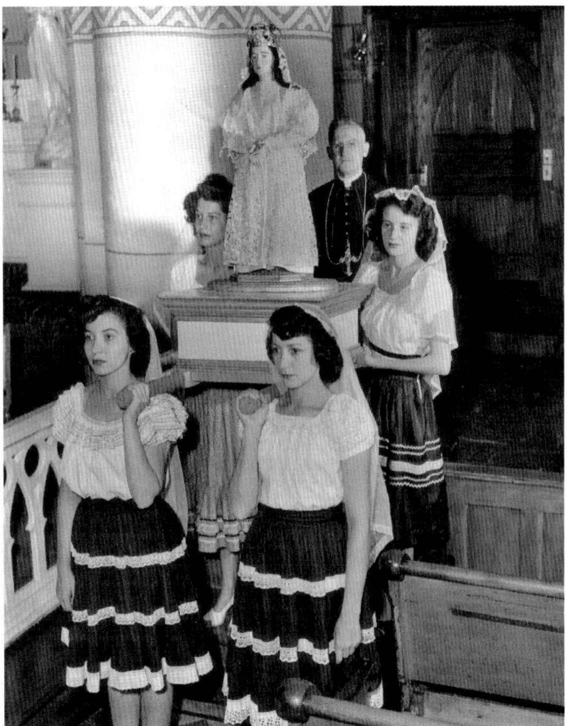

Above: A 1948 procession of La Conquistadora on Grant and Palace Avenues. *Photo by Robert H. Martin.*

Left: La Conquistadora inside the Cathedral Basilica of St. Francis of Assisi in 1948. *From left to right, front row*: Carmen Anchondo and Socorro Anchondo; *back row*: Pauline Padilla, Archbishop Edwin V. Byrne and Socorro López. *Photo by Robert H. Martin.*

Today, this group continues as the caretakers of New Mexico's most historical icon. Throughout Santa Fe's history, she has also been known as Our Lady of the Assumption, the Immaculate Conception, Our Lady of the Rosary, the Queen of New Mexico and, more recently, Our Lady of Peace. In the 1970s, she was given that name by the late archbishop Robert F. Sánchez, who rightly sensed a need to modify the name to better promote a deeper unity among the different cultural groups, especially within the Native

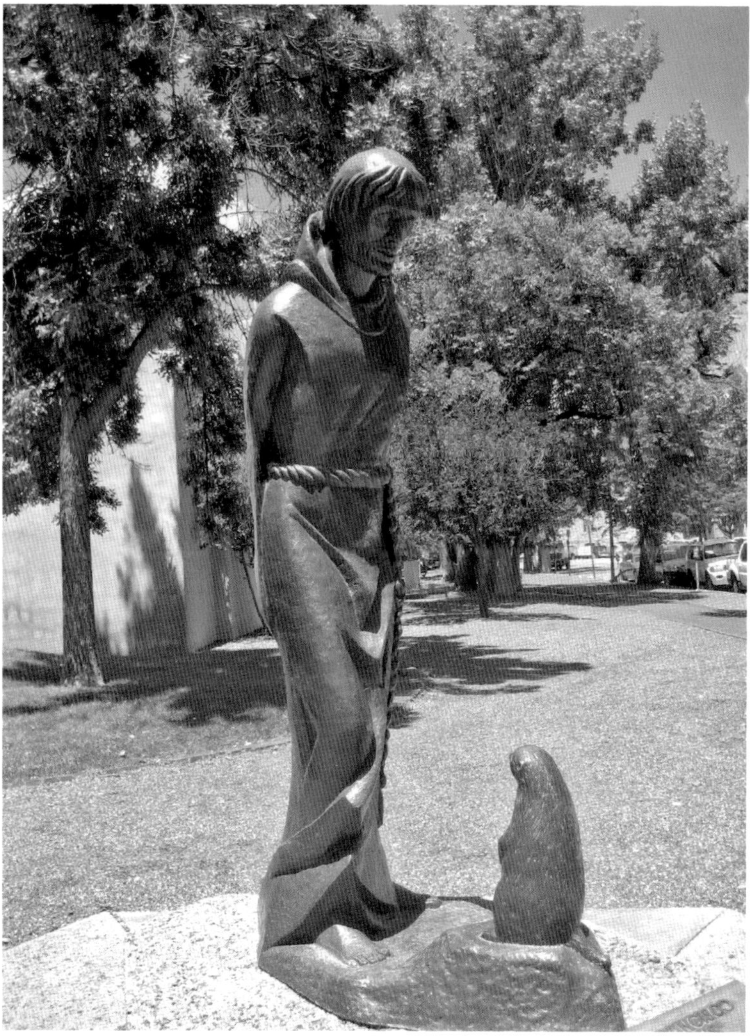

Sculpture of Santa Fe's patron saint, St. Francis of Assisi, by Andrea "Drew" Bacigalupa. *Photo by Ana Pacheco.*

American community. La Conquistadora has been in Santa Fe for 391 years and currently resides in the Cathedral Basilica of St. Francis of Assisi.

Santa Fe's second-most revered saint is St. Francis. Around 1717, San Francisco de Asís was named the patron saint of Santa Fe and the archdiocese. The First Order of St. Francis played an integral role in the history of Santa Fe and the surrounding region from the early 1600s through 2000. In addition to Oñate's explorations, members of the Franciscan order traveled on expeditions with Columbus, Cabeza de Vaca, Cortés and Narváez. They were instrumental in establishing Catholic missions throughout South America, Mexico and the southwestern United States.

Perhaps the best-known Franciscan priest to have an impact on New Mexico history was Fray Angélico Chávez. Considered the preeminent Hispanic writer and historian of New Mexico, he was born on April 10, 1910, in Wagon Mound, New Mexico. He was the first of ten children born to Fabián Chávez and Nicolasa Roybal. Chávez excelled in spiritual leadership, historical research, politics, the arts and church and military service. He served as a military chaplain at Fort Bliss, Texas, prior to World War II. He served with the Fighting 200th Division in the Philippines and was fluent in English, Spanish, French, German and Italian. He wrote twenty-two books, including five books of poetry, five *belles-lettres*, a novel titled *Our Lady of Toledo*, nine histories and two biographies. His book *Origins of New Mexico Families* is considered the Bible for genealogists researching the early Spanish settlements. The Fray Angélico Chávez Library at the Palace of the Governors in Santa Fe was named in his honor. He died in 1996.

In 1851, French-born Bishop Jean-Baptiste Lamy came from Baltimore, ending the reign of the Spanish clergy. Earlier he had been warned by the clergy in the East that the people of New Mexico were an immoral and dissolute lot. As he traveled throughout the diocese, he became disillusioned with the Spanish priests. In December 1852, Lamy sent a pastoral letter to all the priests, chastising their lack of moral standards as he witnessed dances, gambling and other community activities. The letter was also published in the local newspaper, *Gazeta de Santa Fe*, which caused a public uproar. Several local priests were suspended or left on their own volition after the publication of the historic letter. This was the beginning of a love-hate relationship with the new bishop that was made famous in the fictionalized Pulitzer Prize–winning book *Death Comes for the Archbishop*, written by Willa Cather in 1927.

In need of support, Lamy traveled to Mexico and Rome to obtain permission to recruit priests from France. After the arrival of the new French priests, Lamy invited the Sisters of Loretto, who arrived in covered wagons

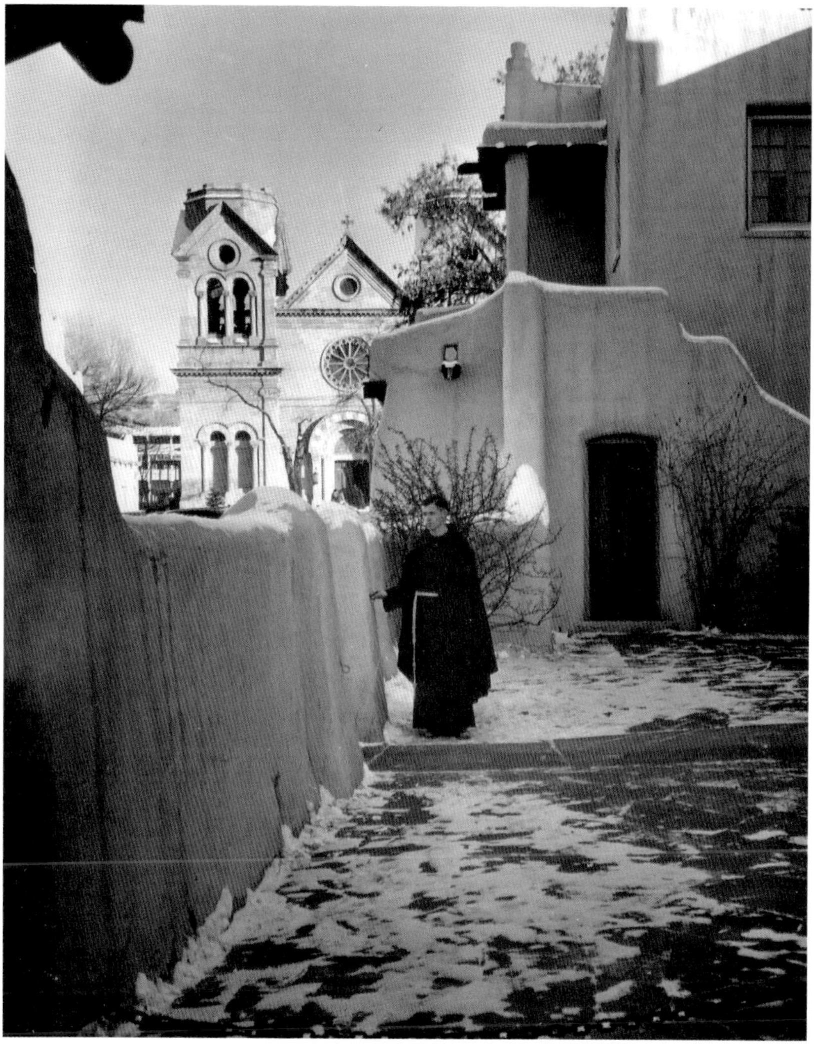

Fray Angélico Chávez in 1948 with the Cathedral Basilica of St. Francis of Assisi in the background. *Photo by Robert H. Martin.*

in 1852, to open a school for girls. The nuns founded an academy in Santa Fe the following year. During the next century, they founded schools throughout New Mexico. For 115 years, Loretto Academy provided thousands of young women with a rigorous, high-quality education and spiritual guidance.

In 1859, Lamy also brought the De La Salle Christian Brothers to Santa Fe, where they founded St. Michael's High School. St. John-Baptist de La Salle, the founder of the order, was born in the seventeenth century in France. De

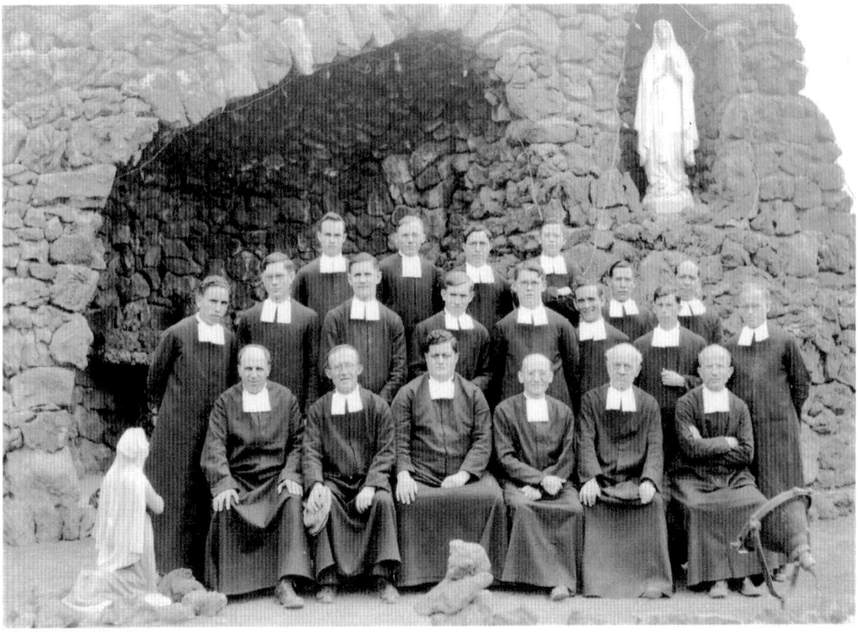

A 1934 photo of the Santa Fe Christian Brothers. *Courtesy New Orleans–Santa Fe Christian Brothers District Archives.*

La Salle worked tirelessly to ensure that poor children received an education during a time when only the wealthy were educated. He founded a training college for teachers and schools for languages, art and science. Today, there are De La Salle schools in eighty countries. In 1969, Loretto Academy and St. Michael's High School merged, becoming Santa Fe's only Catholic high school.

In 1881, Lamy brought Father De Fauri from Denver to raise funds to restore the church of Our Lady of Guadalupe. Originally built in 1777 on the banks of the Santa Fe River, the church had remained closed since 1826 after falling into disrepair. The following history of Santa Fe's Santuario of Our Lady of Guadalupe was documented by the Marian scholar Jacqueline Dunnington:

> *When it reopened, a 575-pound bell was added to complement the altar screen replica of Our Lady of Guadalupe that had been brought to Santa Fe by ox train in 1783. The Santuario de Guadalupe is the oldest continuously standing shrine to Our Lady of Guadalupe in the United States.*
>
> *The Santuario de Guadalupe honors the Mexican Mary of Guadalupe. The legend surrounding the Guadalupe of the Americas says that she*

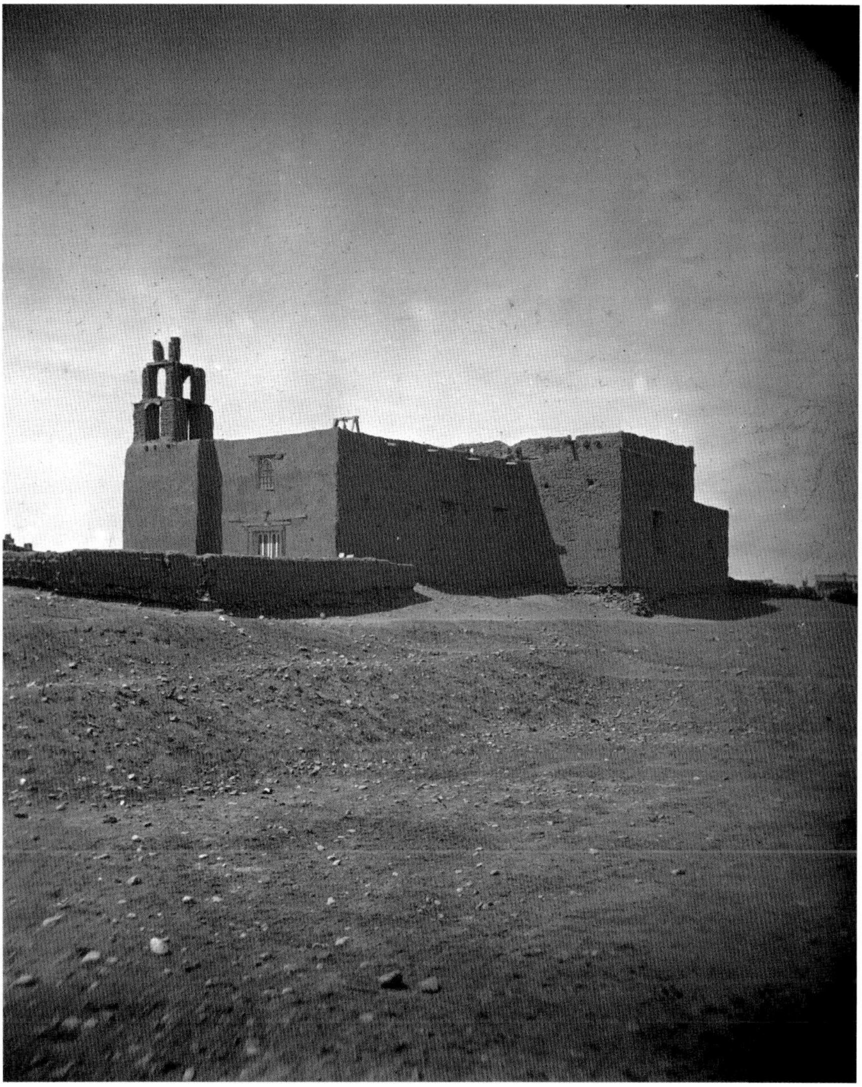

Church of Our Lady of Guadalupe from the northeast in Santa Fe, 1880. *Photo by Ben Wittick. Courtesy Palace of the Governors [NMHM/DCA]. No. 015847.*

appeared four times to Juan Diego, a Christianized Aztec Indian, in December of 1531. His age at the time of the Virgin's manifestations is still uncertain, but many scholars claim he was in his late 50s, and was not the young boy depicted in most of the artwork surrounding the legend.

The story unfolds through four different events that took place on Tepeyac Hill at the northeast rim of present-day Mexico City. One account of the 1531 apparitions records that the Virgin Mary of Guadalupe called herself the "Ever Virgin." Miguel Sánchez published the first Spanish-language imprint of the story in 1648, which was followed in 1649 by the Nahautal version written by Lasso (Lazo) de la Vega. The Virgin rapidly became the most popular Madonna of the masses, the one to whom they turned in time of need.

The original Santuario de Guadalupe in Santa Fe, built on a Latin cross plan, had three-foot-thick adobe walls and a bell tower at the southeast corner. It was an active mission church serving the immediate area populated by farmers and their families. The chapel was once surrounded by a camposanto *(cemetery); however, during the 1800s, many parishioners buried their dead under the Santuario floor. This was a common practice at the time to ward off grave robbers in search of jewelry and other memorabilia that were buried with the dead.*

Excavations in 1989, undertaken to locate the stress points created by the bell tower and heavy walls, produced unexpected results. Diggers unearthed the remains of 63 people who had been buried underneath the Santuario between 1820 and 1890. The dig did not turn up any religious articles pertaining to Guadalupe.

About a century after the original structure was completed, the old mission-style building was radically altered to resemble a typical east-coast church, with a steeple painted bright orange. The spire was centered above the entry instead of at the southeast corner where the bell tower once stood. Gothic-style windows were built into the walls and a white picket fence was erected to enclose the churchyard. One reason given for these drastic changes was the arrival of many English-speaking Catholics from the east, who brought their building style with them.

The eastern edge of the Santuario grounds has also withstood many changes. In 1889, the Denver and Rio Grande Railroad, later the Denver and Rio Grande Western, offered narrow-gauge rail service between Santa Fe and Denver out of a nearby depot. The line closed its service in 1941, and the rails and ties were torn from the Santuario's property line along Guadalupe Street.

In June of 1922, a disastrous fire engulfed the Santuario de Guadalupe: the roof was destroyed, the steeple was left a hollow shell, the new interior wall paintings were ruined, and fire-fighting efforts left the nave flooded. The altar and outer walls remained mostly unharmed. Repairs were made in the popular California Mission style. Cement was smoothed over the adobe bricks, a bell tower replaced the charred steeple, a massive stone wall

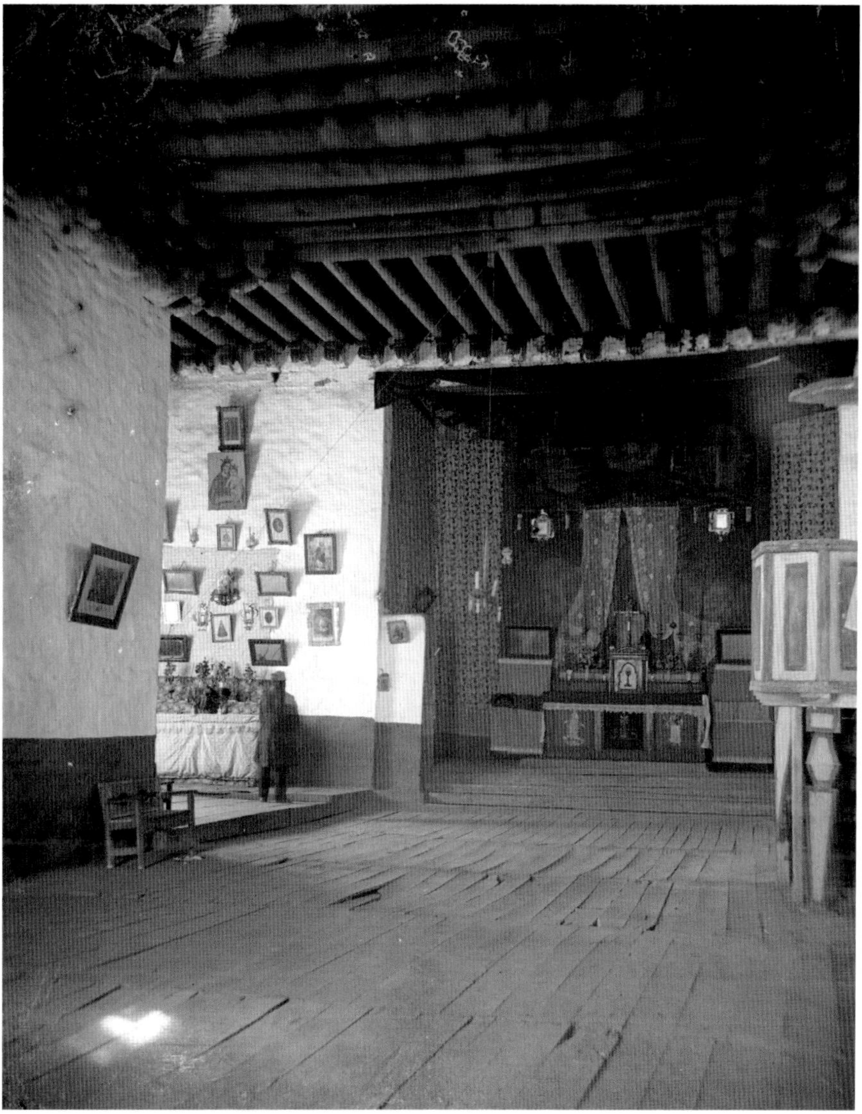

Interior of the Church of Our Lady of Guadalupe, Santa Fe, New Mexico, 1881. *Photo by Ben Wittick. Courtesy Palace of the Governors [NMHM/DCA]. No. 015848.*

supplanted the picket fence, and stained-glass windows featuring Marian themes decorated the interior walls.

The great fire spared a portrait of Our Lady of Guadalupe, which now hangs behind the area where the altar once stood. José de Alcíbar (Alzíbar), a Mexican baroque master, signed and dated this monumental work in

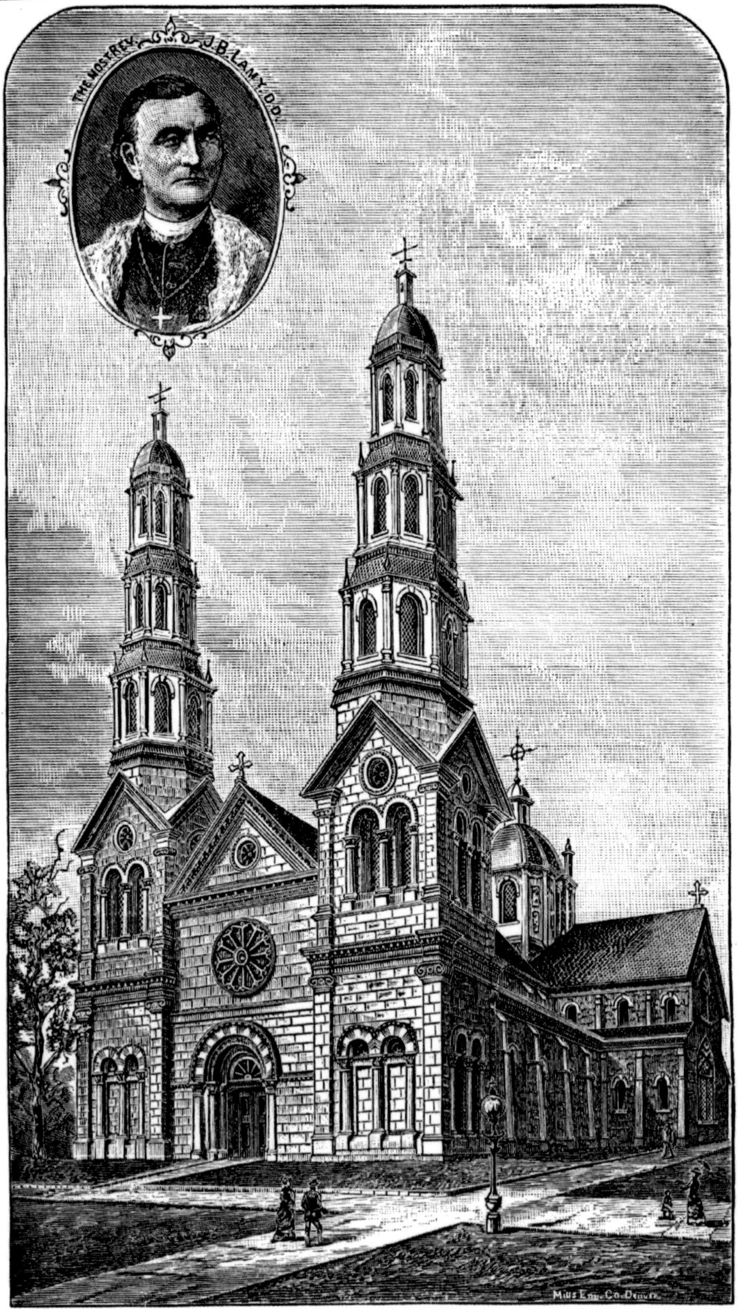

Archbishop Jean-Baptiste Lamy and the original rendering of St. Francis Cathedral. *Illustration from* Aztlan *by William Ritch, 1885. Courtesy Palace of the Governors [NMHM/DCA]. No. 010005.*

1783. It is the largest painting of Our Lady of Guadalupe in the United States and presents a central, full-body image of the Virgin surrounded by four illustrations of the main events of the 1531 apparition story. The painting made the journey north by cart and in sections, up the Camino Real from Mexico City to Santa Fe where the pieces were rejoined. It has found safety inside Guadalupe's Santuario in spite of the epic journey and near-fatal fire.

The most significant change brought by Lamy was his plan to build a Romanesque-style cathedral similar to those in his native France. The

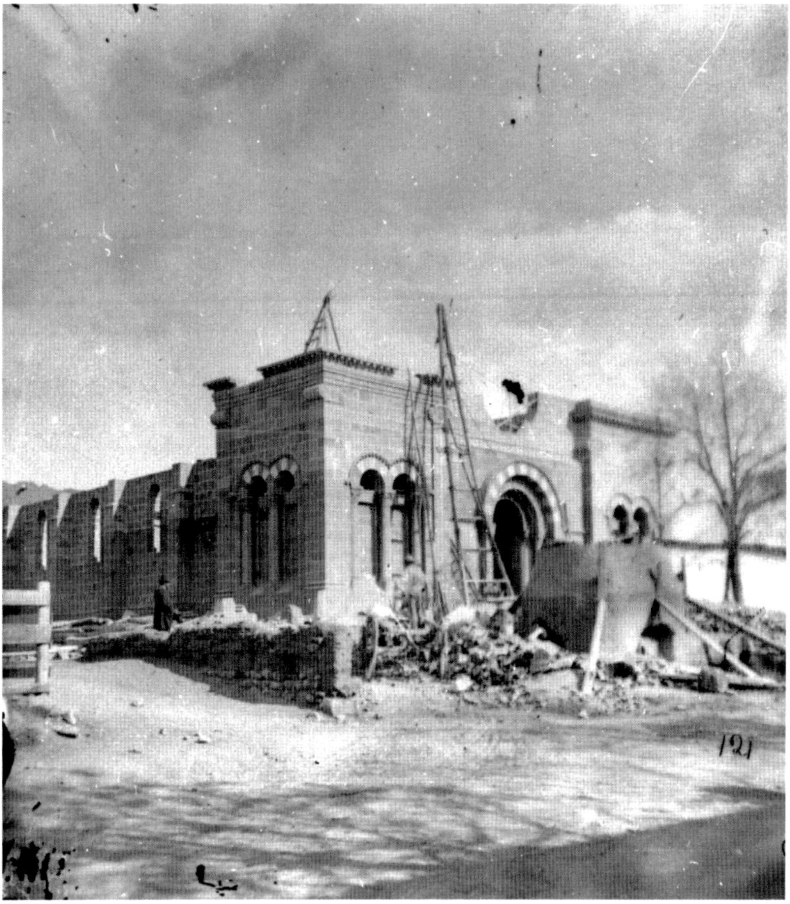

Cathedral Basilica of St. Francis of Assisi under construction, Santa Fe, New Mexico, circa 1880. *Photo by Ben Wittick. Courtesy Palace of the Governors [NMHM/DCA]. No. 058399.*

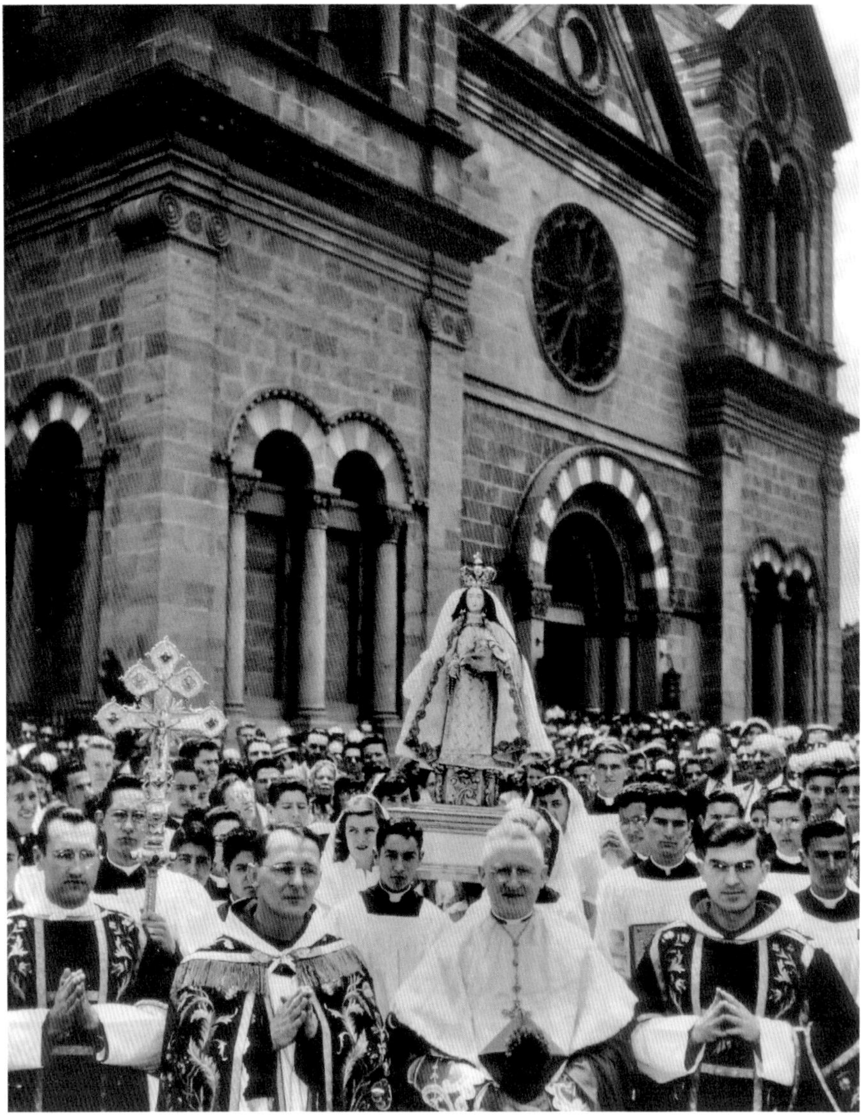

A 1948 photo of Archbishop Edwin V. Byrne, clergy members and La Conquistadora in front of the Cathedral Basilica of St. Francis of Assisi. *Photo by Robert H. Martin.*

cathedral, which opened in 1888, provided a stark contrast to Santa Fe's adobe structures.

The contempt and suspicion held by the Spanish settlers of Native American cultural practices was similar to those of Bishop Lamy, who had no respect for the confraternity La Fraternidad Piadosa de Nuestro Padre

Jesús Nazareno. From the seventeenth century until the mid-nineteenth century, the Spanish people of New Mexico were isolated both from the rest of the world and from the guiding hand of the church. Groups of men in the villages formed a religious brotherhood whose roots can be traced to the medieval *cofradías* of Spain.

What drew the ire of Bishop Lamy, and the curiosity of Anglo newcomers, was the practice of self-flagellation. During Holy Week, these men formed processions, carrying large wooden crosses and stopping periodically to whip themselves to express empathy for Christ's suffering. The first account of flagellation was recorded by Gaspar Pérez de Villagra during Holy Week at the camp of Oñate in 1598, where their leader and Franciscan priests honored the tradition, which was a practice followed by the Third Order of St. Francis.

The beliefs of these *penitentes*, or penitents, are rooted in Spanish and Roman Catholic tradition. During Holy Week in Spain, penitents disguised in robes and pointed hoods carry litters on which huge statues portray Gospel events, particularly Christ's passion and death. Today, the carrying of these heavy statues has replaced flagellation as a form of penance.

In New Mexico, the *penitentes* continue to play an important role in their communities. Their *moradas* (meeting places) come to life during Holy Week. Throughout the year, they contribute to the community's well-being, helping

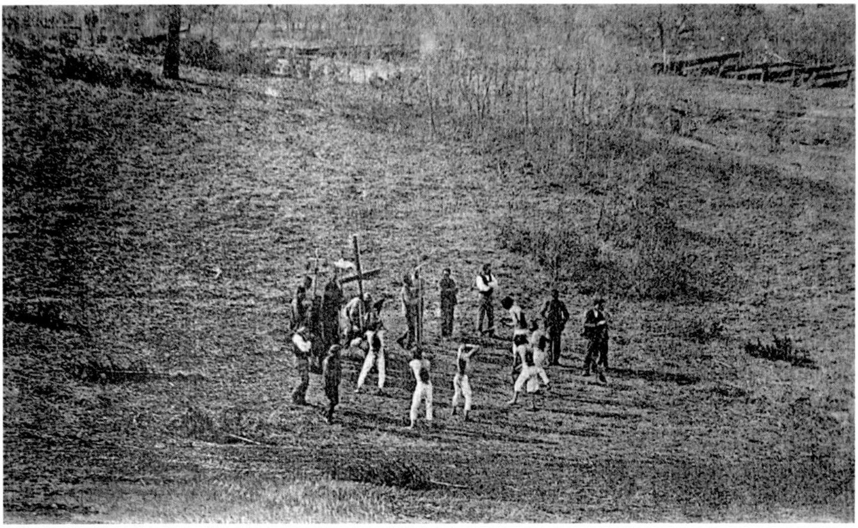

Los penitentes, penitent flagellants, northern New Mexico, circa 1896. *Courtesy Palace of the Governors [NMHM/DCA]. No. 013667.*

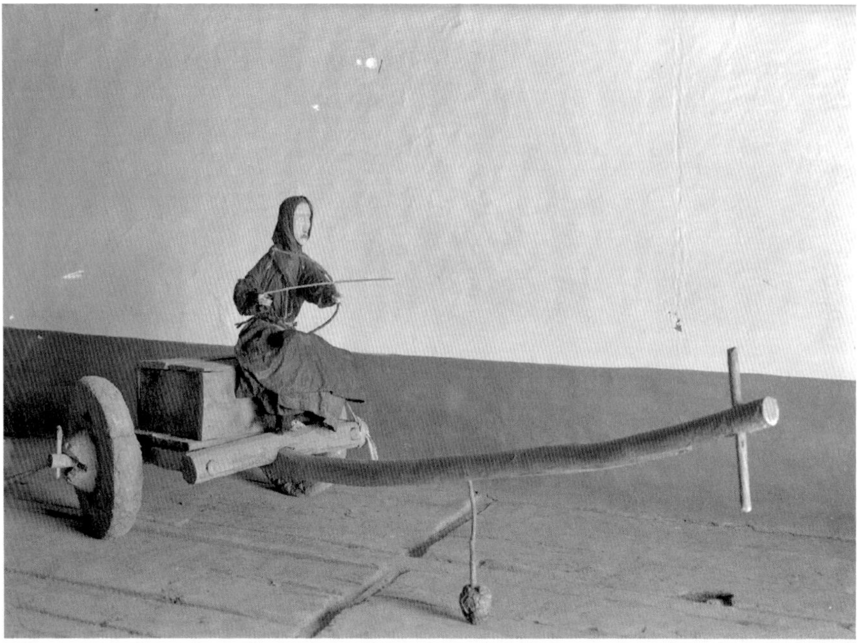

Doña Sebastiana in a wooden death cart of the *penitentes*, Las Trampas Church, New Mexico, circa 1912. Doña Sebastiana, or La Muerte, is an allegorical icon for death in the Penitente Brotherhood of New Mexico. *Photo by Jesse Nusbaum. Courtesy Palace of the Governors [NMHM/DCA]. No. 013671.*

the disadvantaged, the sick and the elderly. The roadside memorials found all over New Mexico known as *descansos* are attributed to the *penitentes*. A *descanso* is a remembrance to the *ánima* (soul) of the deceased. The practice of placing crosses or laying stones to mark a place of rest began with the Spaniards who died along the Camino Real, the royal highway that connected Mexico City with the northern reaches of New Spain. The *penitentes* were known to mark the ground with stones or crosses during Holy Week as they visited the various *moradas*. While carrying large crosses and flagellating themselves, they would stop periodically to pray. These stops were a form of the *descanso*, or rest.

Despite earlier misconceptions of the brotherhood promoted by the media during the twentieth century, the *penitentes* continue to practice their beliefs. In 1946, under the direction of Archbishop Edward Vincent Byrne, the Catholic Church of New Mexico approved the *penitente* official book of rules. The official state recognition of the Brothers of Nazareth was signed on January 28, 1947. The historian and writer Fray Angélico Chávez helped draft the document.

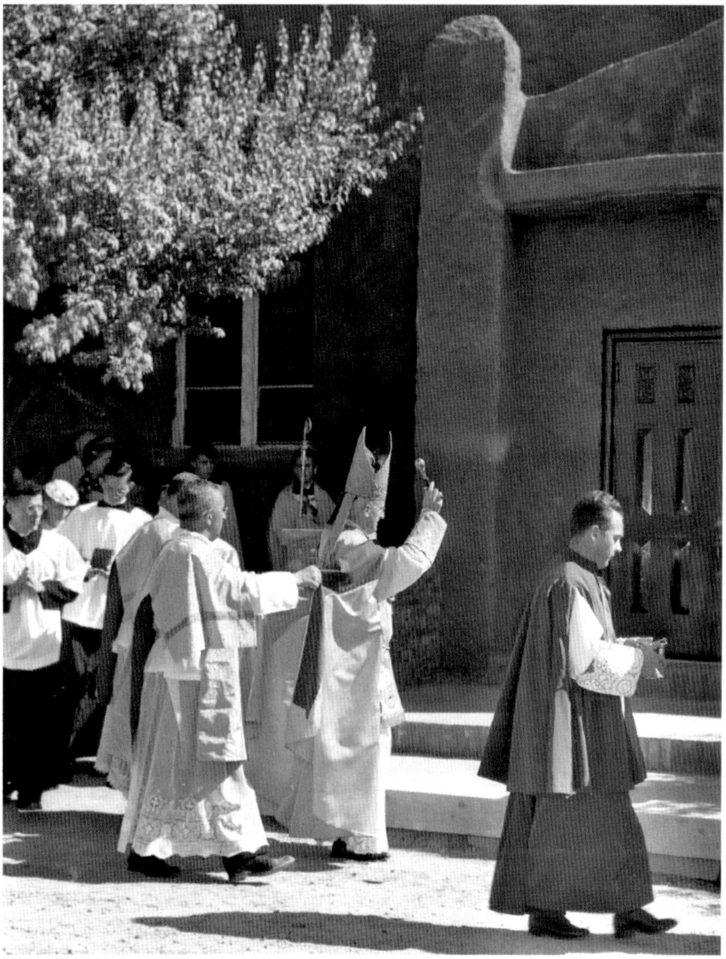

Archbishop Edwin V. Byrne christens the Carmelite Monastery in 1948.
Photo by Robert H. Martin.

On March 28, 2015, the 500th anniversary of the birth of St. Teresa de Ávila was celebrated throughout the world. The Carmelites of Santa Fe follow the Spanish tradition of order that was established during the sixteenth century by St. Teresa de Ávila, who entered the convent in 1535. She was born Teresa de Cepeda y Ahumada in 1515 in Gotarrendura in the province of Ávila, Spain. Her paternal grandfather, Juan de Toledo, was a *marrano*, a Jewish convert to Christianity, who was condemned by the Spanish Inquisition for allegedly returning to the Jewish faith. A writer and mystic, St. Teresa was a reformer of the Carmelite Order. In 1568, with the assistance of St. John of the Cross, they

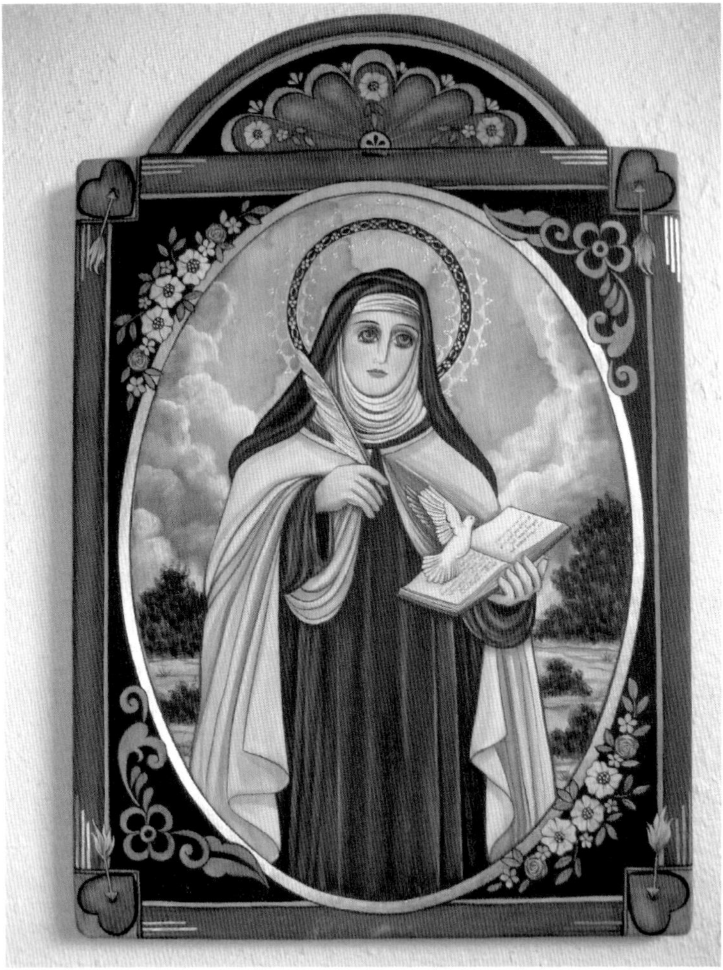

A painting of St. Teresa de Ávila of the Carmelite Order by artist Arlene Cisneros Sena.

restored the practice of the Ancient Order of the Carmelites. St. Teresa was canonized as a saint by Pope Gregory XV in 1622. In 1970, she was named the first female doctor of the church by Pope Paul VI. Diego de Vargas, who led the reconquest of Santa Fe in 1692, was St. Teresa of Ávila's second cousin through the family of his grandmother.

The Carmelites came to Santa Fe in 1945 and continue to honor the Spanish tradition of their founder. Although Santiago de Compostela is the patron saint of Spain, many Spaniards feel an equal if not greater affinity for St. Teresa de Ávila.

Chapter 4

Roots of Resilience

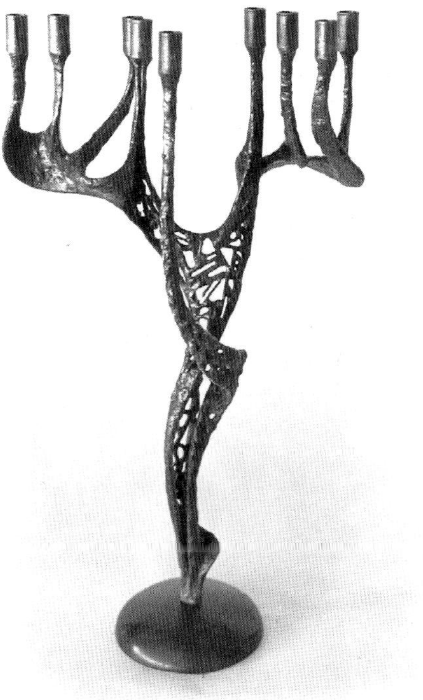

Menorah sculpture by Gunther Aaron. *Courtesy Geri Aaron.*

Like the Native Americans, who were forced to convert to Christianity while secretly honoring their own spirituality, many of New Mexico's early Spanish settlers also practiced a hidden faith. They were the Sephardic Jews who had eluded the Inquisition under the guise of being *conversos*, Jews who had converted to Catholicism. They became known as crypto-Jews because they practiced their Jewish faith secretly while presenting a different persona to the public. It wasn't until the mid-twentieth century that revelations of their existence came to light.

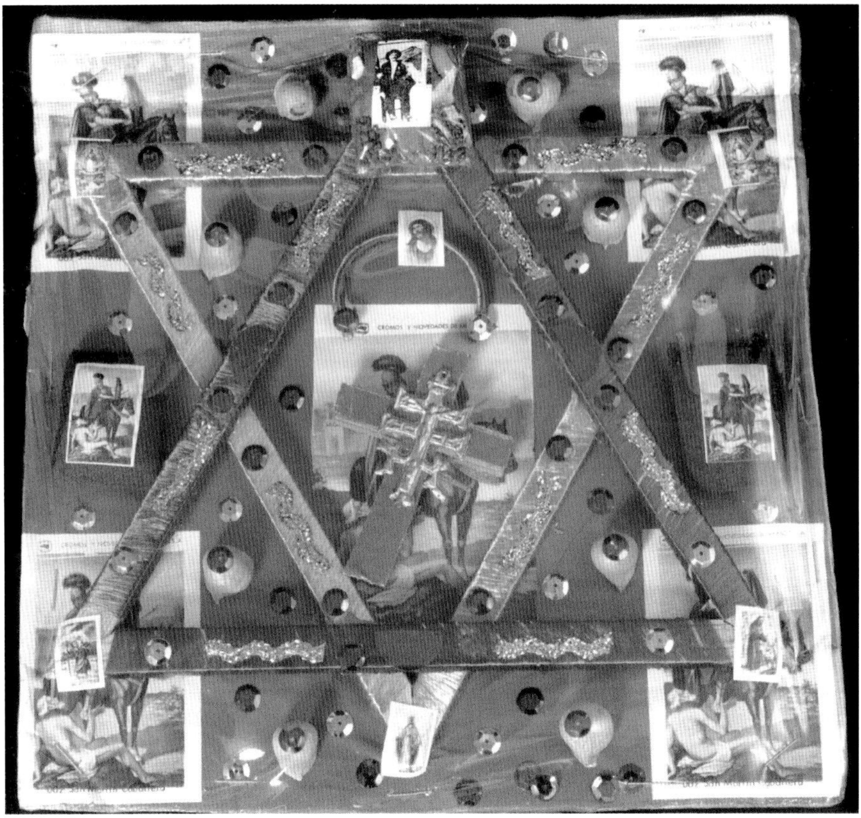

Star of David collage with Santiago de Compostela and other Catholic saints and imagery. *Photo by Cary Herz, circa 1990s. Courtesy Palace of the Governors Photo Archives [NMHM/DCA]. No. HP.2008.22.81.*

Since then, many books have been written on the subject, including the groundbreaking work of Henry J. Tobias in 1992, *A History of the Jews in New Mexico* (University of New Mexico Press). Tobias documented Judaism in New Mexico from the colonial period through the twentieth century. Another book, *To the End of the Earth: A History of the Crypto-Jews of New Mexico* by Stanley M. Hordes, was published by Columbia University Press in 2005. Hordes also provided a detailed account of the Sephardic Jews in New Mexico and this newfound identity for Hispanic New Mexicans in the twenty-first century.

In 2010, I had the opportunity to publish the official publication commemorating the 400th anniversary of Santa Fe. In that issue, the author and genealogist José A. Esquibel chronicled the history of the founders.

Of the nineteen first families, eleven were Jewish. In fact, it was a Jewish woman who rescued La Conquistadora from a burning chapel during the Pueblo Revolt of 1680. The Madonna was carried to safety by Josefa López Sambrano de Grijalva, wife of Francisco Lucero de Godoy. Lucero de Godoy was the eldest grandson of Francisco Gómez and Ana Robledo; both families were Jewish.

My first introduction to New Mexico's hidden Jews occurred when I was the publisher of *La Herencia*, a quarterly magazine covering New Mexico's Hispanic history. In the Winter 1996 issue, we ran a cover story on the subject by Emma Moya, a writer in her seventies who practiced both Catholicism and Judaism, just like her grandparents. The article listed some of the surnames of the people who were martyred because of their Jewish identity. It also included a list of Sephardic surnames. That issue opened up the floodgates, with inquiries coming in from all over the world, and I began to hear from New Mexicans with their own family remembrances of traditions that echoed those of Moya's childhood. Due to the overwhelming response, a quarterly column titled "Sephardim" was added to the magazine, which included references to archaic traditions with Jewish undertones. It also highlighted the use of Ladino, spoken by Sephardic Jews, which is sprinkled throughout New Mexico's Spanish vernacular.

In 2003, I was contacted by the late Cary Herz about a photo book she wanted to publish on New Mexico's crypto-Jews. In the winter of that year, I published aspects of her work on old gravestones that she found in Catholic and Protestant cemeteries in northern New Mexico and the region. Her gravestone photos included both Jewish and Catholic symbols. That essay brought to light the sometimes complex coexistence of dual religions. Cary died on September 1, 2008, at the age of forty-seven. Earlier that year, her book *New Mexico Crypto-Jews: Images and Memory* was published by the University of New Mexico Press.

In the 1996 article, the fact that my last name and that of Ortiz, my mother's surname, had been listed as being Sephardic piqued my curiosity. As the decade passed, information became available on do-it-yourself DNA kits. Every major media outlet was running features on the subject. The CBS program *60 Minutes* ran a segment documenting people's African lineage, while the *New York Times* reported that people in Spain, Portugal, Italy and France were all clamoring to give cheek swabs in the hope of finding out they were descendants of Christopher Columbus.

My mother died in 1992 and my father was in failing health, so at the urging of my friend Archie Perea, I ordered three DNA kits from the

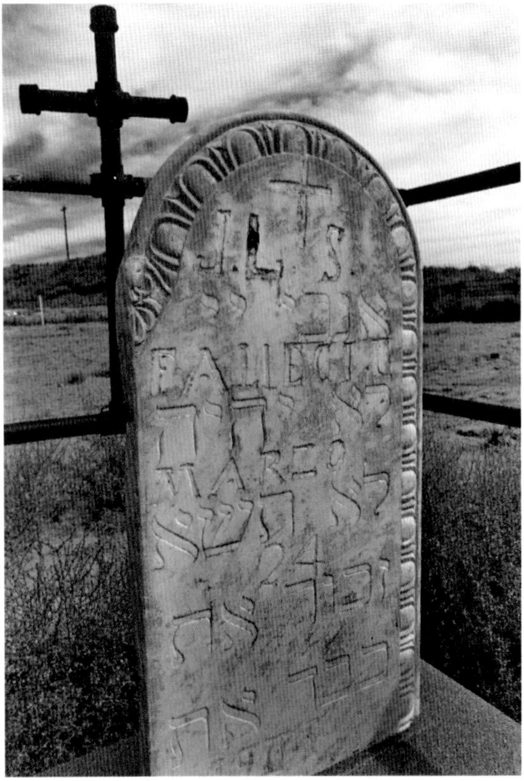

Left: The Five Commandments in Hebrew letters, Catholic cemetery in the Middle Rio Grande Valley, from New Mexico Crypto-Jews project. *Photo by Cary Herz, 1994. Courtesy Palace of the Governors [NMHM/DCA]. No. HP.2008.22.31.*

Below: Image with nine-point menorah and St. Joseph, San Pedro Cemetery, Santa Fe County, 1994. *Photo by Cary Herz. Courtesy Palace of the Governors Photo Archives [NMHM/DCA]. No. HP.2008.22.79.*

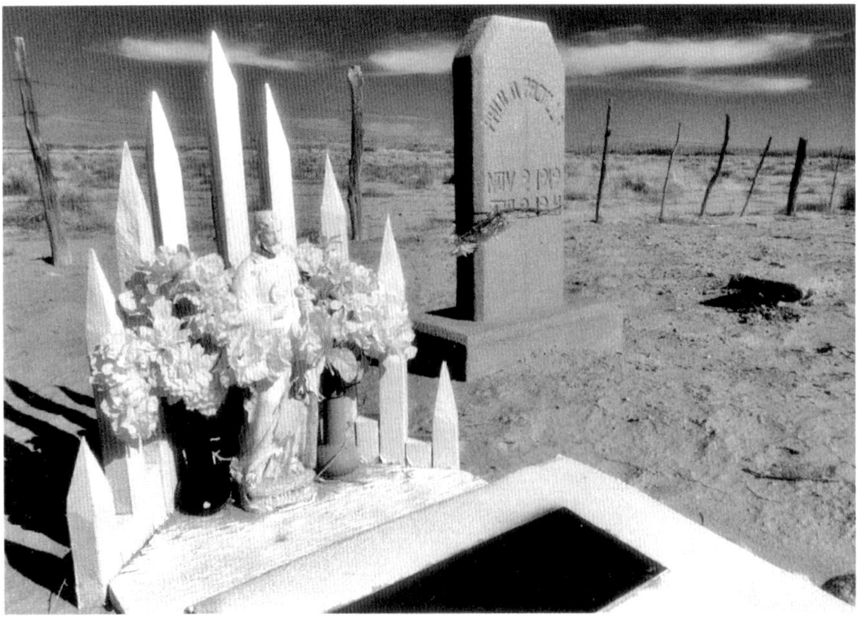

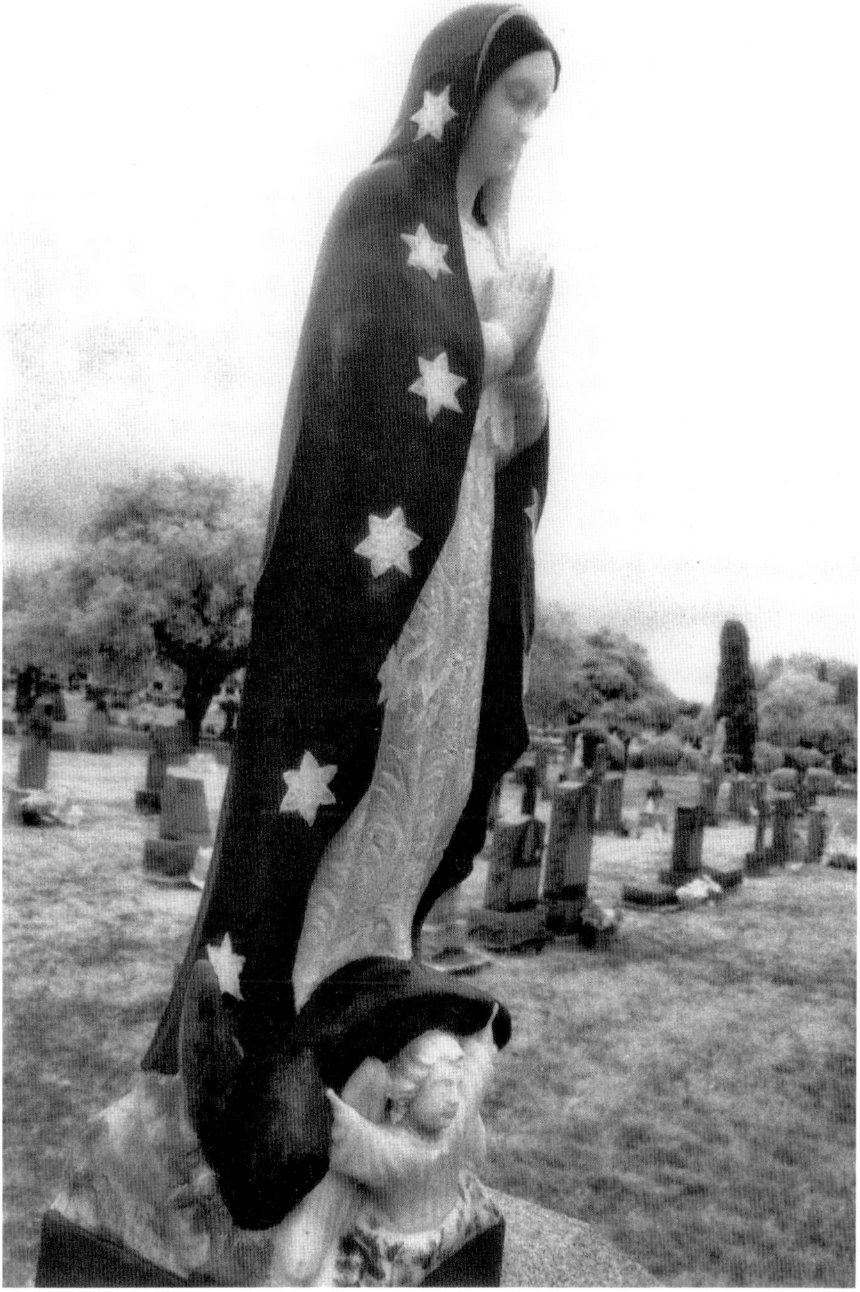

Our Lady of Guadalupe with a Star of David cloak at a cemetery in San Antonio, Texas, circa 1990s. *Photo by Cary Herz. Courtesy Palace of the Governors Photo Archives [NMHM/DCA]. No. HP.2008.22.80.*

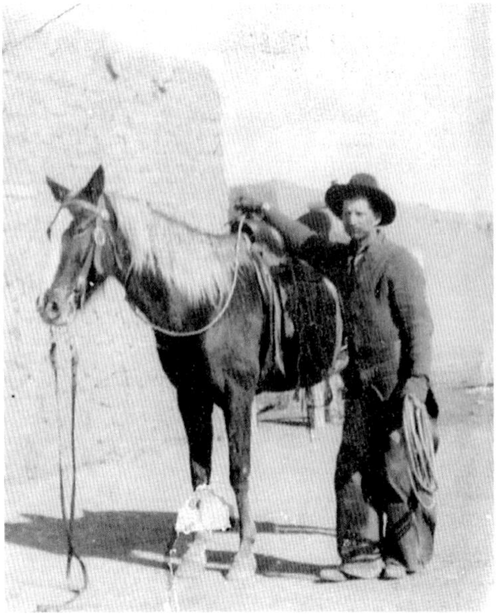

My grandfather Martín Pacheco carried the DNA J2 haplogroup indicating our Sephardic Jewish ancestry. *Courtesy Pacheco family archives.*

Genographic Project of National Geographic's website. One was for me, and the other two were for my father and my aunt Beatriz, my mother's only living sibling. My father's DNA results indicated that his family was definitely of Jewish origin. According to the Genographic Project, all males carry the Y chromosome, so my grandfather Martín Pacheco passed on the J2 marker to my father. The research stated that people of the J2 haplogroup began their journey around 8500 BC in ancient towns such as Jericho, known then as Tell es-Sultan. Stan Hordes went on to tell me that while researching his book he discovered a citation in the *Diccionario sefaradi de sobrenombres* of a famous Jew with the surname Pacheco who had worked for the sultan in Morocco and also served as ambassador to The Hague in the Netherlands in 1604.

I was never able to verify my mother's Jewish heritage, since only males carry both the Y and X chromosomes, making them easier to identify. However, her surname, Ortiz, means "light" in Hebrew. Surnames on both sides of my family also include Rodríguez, García, Córdova and Martín, all of which were names listed as Jewish victims of the Mexican Inquisition. So it's likely that I have Jewish roots on both sides of my family. As the years have passed, I continue to be intrigued by the topic and have learned that many zealous Spanish Catholics have Jewish origins. This makes sense to me, since I was raised in a devout Catholic home.

The settlement of New Mexico's Ashkenazi Jews from Germany and other European countries began with the merchants who traversed the Santa Fe Trail from 1848 to 1871. Many chose Santa Fe at the end of the trail as their new home. Growth for this community stagnated in 1878 when the railroad bypassed Santa Fe in favor of Las Vegas sixty miles to the northeast. Las Vegas became a major commercial hub, with a large Jewish community that ran mercantile businesses. In 1881, the Montefiore Cemetery was created, one of the first Jewish cemeteries west of the Mississippi. Three years later, Congregation Montefiore was established, and its members built the first Jewish temple in New Mexico in 1886. The congregation dissolved in 1955 because of a decrease in the number of Jewish residents.

Since their arrival, the Jewish spirit of community collaboration has spurred their involvement in all civic affairs. One of the most significant contributions to the city occurred during the construction of the Cathedral Basilica of St. Francis of Assisi in Santa Fe. In need of financial assistance to complete the construction, Archbishop Jean-Baptiste Lamy sought financial help from the Jewish merchants. In gratitude for their assistance, the doors of the main entrance bear an inscription in the ancient Hebrew Tetragrammaton of YHWH, the Hebrew name for God, which is articulated as Yahweh.

An interesting side note underscoring the close relationship between the Jews and Catholics in Santa Fe was the 2013 funeral for Rabbi Leonard A. Helman. It was held at the cathedral, probably the first time in recent history that a Jewish rabbi had a funeral at a Catholic church. Throughout the years, Hellman had attended major religious holidays at the cathedral. He appreciated the Christian iconography, music and ceremonial rituals. Helman's final request was that his funeral be held at the cathedral. In a fitting farewell, his coffin was carried through the doors bearing the word "God" written in the language of his faith.

In the 1930s, a small group of business owners in Santa Fe started a branch of B'nai B'rith, which means "sons of the covenant" in Hebrew. The oldest Jewish service organization in the world, it was started in 1843 on New York's Lower East Side. During the early days in Santa Fe, the group met in stores, libraries and churches. As the decade wore on and new people arrived in town to work on the Manhattan Project, the Jewish community grew substantially. It was then that the members of B'nai B'rith formed a committee to organize a congregation. On December 5, 1946, the Santa Fe Jewish Temple was established. In attendance were Julius Cans, Dan Taichert, Marcel Pick, Marcia Hertsmark, Louis Rubinstein, Albert Kahn and Emil Pick. By 1949, there were some thirty families, and the organization became the Santa Fe Jewish Temple and Community Center. The temple opened in 1956, and later that year, a Jewish section was added at Memorial Gardens Cemetery. Architect John Gaw Meem, who is famous for his Pueblo Revival buildings throughout New Mexico, designed the building on Barcelona Street. It retained that name until 1970, when it was renamed Temple Beth

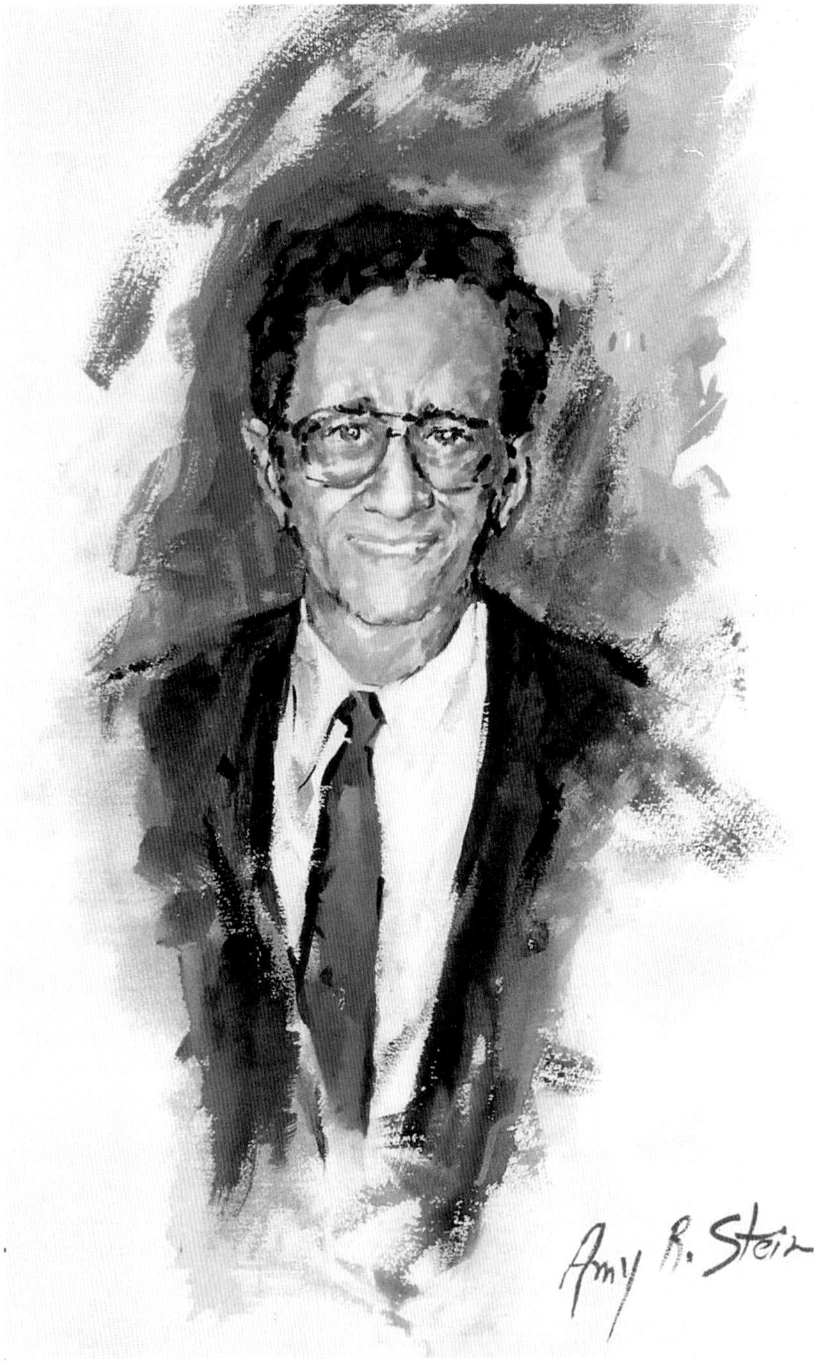

A painting of Rabbi Leonard A. Helman by artist Amy Stein.

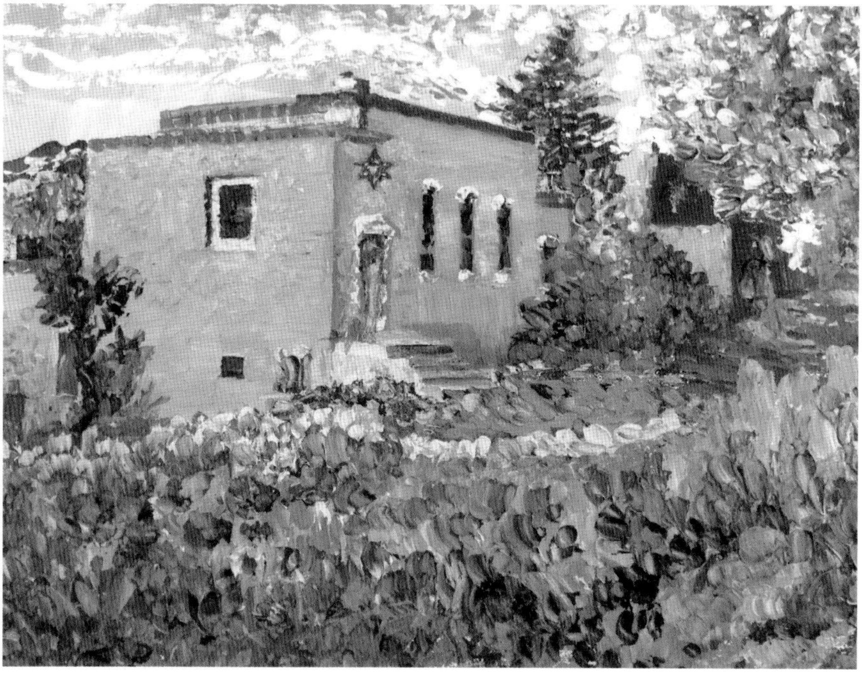

A painting of Temple Beth Shalom by Tommy Macaione. *Courtesy Raphael Shapiro.*

Shalom, which means "house of peace" in Hebrew. Today, the congregation counts close to four hundred families among its members, and in 1987, a new building was added. The first structure is now used as a preschool and library. The Las Vegas Torah, the oldest in New Mexico, is one of the major features of the library.

Since the late 1800s, Santa Fe's Jewish community has grown to include many followers from other parts of the world. Currently, there are five congregations that include Reform, Orthodox and Progressive Judaism. Some of the descendants of the early settlers have provided their own personal histories. Marian Silver is the only surviving member of the original founders of Temple Beth Shalom, Santa Fe's largest congregation. She was born in Santa Fe in 1932 to Pauline and Barney Petchesky. As she recalls:

> *When I was growing up there were about ten Jewish families in Santa Fe. My father had been trained as a cantor, but there were no rabbis back then. The Baptist church let us use their basement for Sunday school. I was confirmed at Temple Albert in Albuquerque, where most of the Santa Fe families traveled for major religious ceremonies and holidays. The rest of*

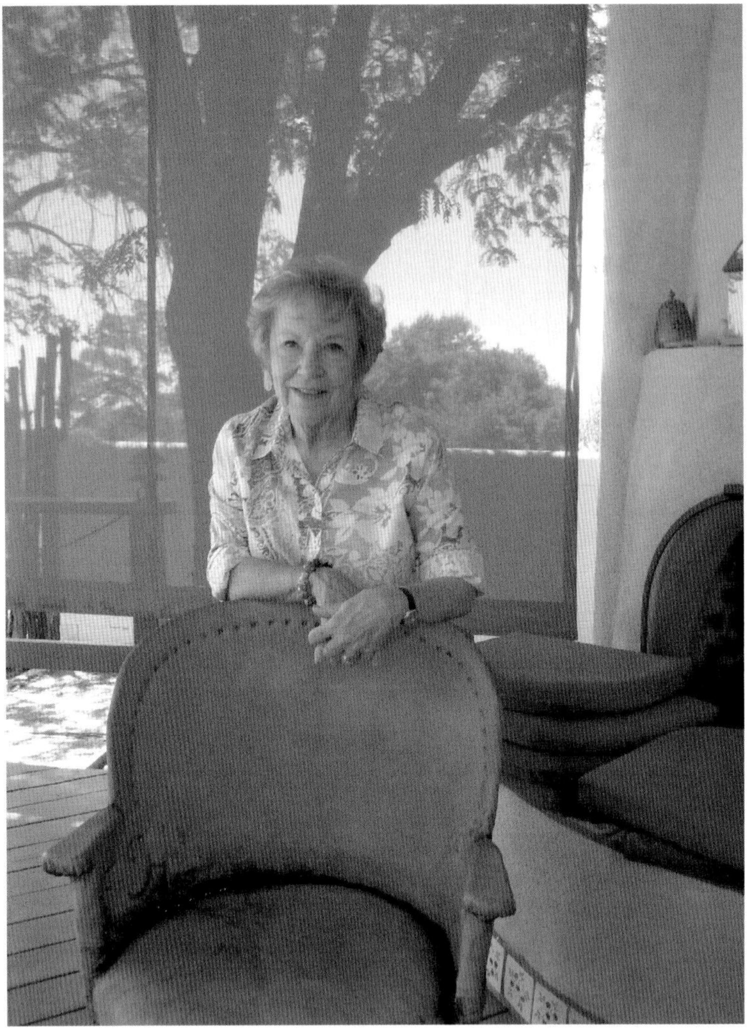

Marian Silver, the last remaining member of the original board of Temple Beth Shalom. *Photo by Ana Pacheco.*

> *the time we met in each other's homes. I married my husband, Abe Silver, in 1951 at a service held at the home of my grandmother Johanna Blatt.*

Kathy Kahn Mahon was born in Santa Fe in 1948. Her great-grandfather Ludwig Kempenich was one of the four founders in 1897 of Temple Albert, now Congregation Albert, in Albuquerque. As she recalls, "My parents tried, as had many others before them, to take us to Albuquerque for

Sunday school, but it was just too far. That's one of the reasons my parents, grandparents, aunts, uncles and other families in the community ended up founding Temple Beth Shalom."

Barb Bell Lamont, who was also born in 1948, added:

> *My mother, Leah Kellogg, was the first woman president of Temple Beth Shalom, where she served three terms. The energy and effort of the founders was monumental. Their drive to have a place of their own that allowed them to worship, to enjoy each other's company and to raise children with a Jewish identity was paramount. The pride in the building and grounds was shared by all the members. In the early days, the men were often out trimming the junipers, shoveling snow and fixing the toilets. How lucky we were then to have a great neighbor, the pastor of the Immanuel Lutheran Church, living next door to us. He and his family were great friends and supporters of our temple.*

Temple Beth Shalom was home to Santa Fe's best-known rabbi. Leonard A. Helman came to New Mexico in 1974, when he was forty-eight years old, and served as a rabbi until his death in 2013. He left an indelible mark in local history. As Lance Bell, born in 1966, recalls:

> *Rabbi Helman put Judaism on the map here in our City Different. Many of the original Jewish families, including founding families of Temple Beth Shalom, helped start Congregation Beit Tikva because of our love for Rabbi Leonard Helman. We have been referred to by some as "Helman disciples." Whether it was at a wedding or funeral, Rabbi Helman had special verbiage and life messages that he was so good at delivering. Attending his funeral in the magnificent Cathedral Basilica of St. Francis of Assisi was a special memorial that was fitting for Santa Fe royalty.*

Congregation Beit Tikva started at a Passover Seder in April 1995. The group met in a private home every Friday night for services after the first Seder. That summer, Rabbi Helman took charge of the congregation. The group quickly grew large enough that Leah Kellogg approached the Lutheran Church of the Servant and asked to rent space on Friday nights, where they continued to worship for the next ten years. During the High Holy Days, when attendance grew, services were held at the Capital Christian Church and Presbyterian Church. In 2005, Beit Tikva built its own temple on Old Pecos Trail and, more recently, added offices and a kitchen.

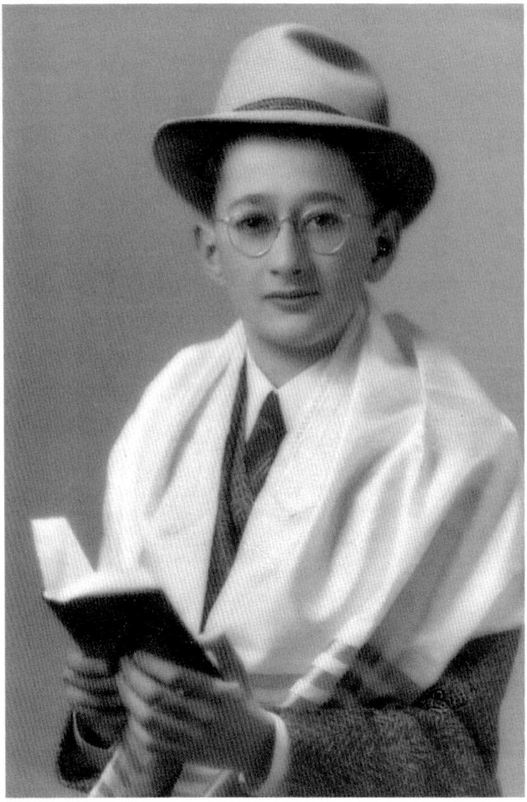

Left: Leonard A. Helman as a rabbinical student. *Courtesy Leonard A. Helman.*

Below: An outdoor service for the Beit Tikva congregation. *Courtesy Beit Tikva.*

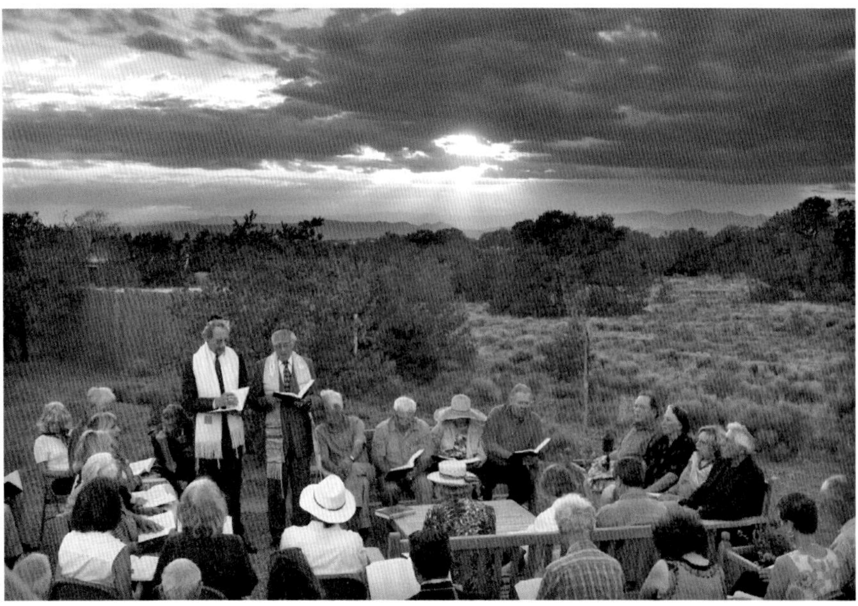

Malka Drucker began as a lay leader at Temple Beth Shalom in 1992. She was ordained as a rabbi in 1998 after completing her studies at the Academy for Jewish Religion in New York. Upon her return to Santa Fe, she served at both Temple Beth Shalom and Beit Tikva. In 2002, Drucker spearheaded HaMakom, Santa Fe's first progressive Jewish congregation. As she says:

> *There was a need for a more liberal approach to our faith while, at the same time, honoring the traditional ritual expression. We also wanted to be a*

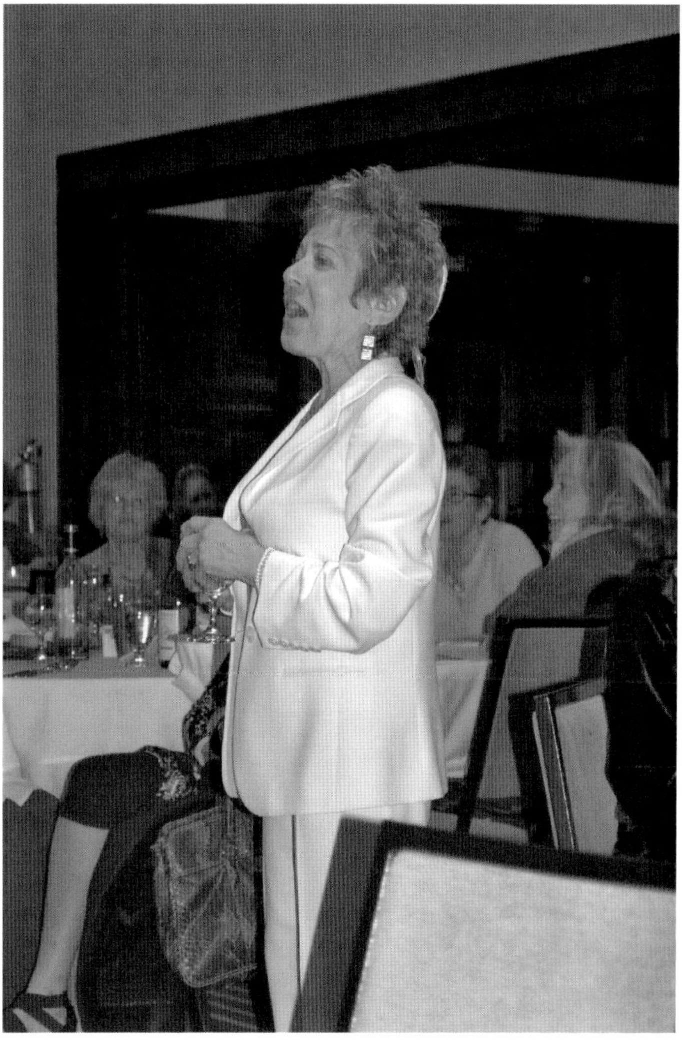

HaMakom rabbi Malka Drucker. *Photo by Victoria Lee.*

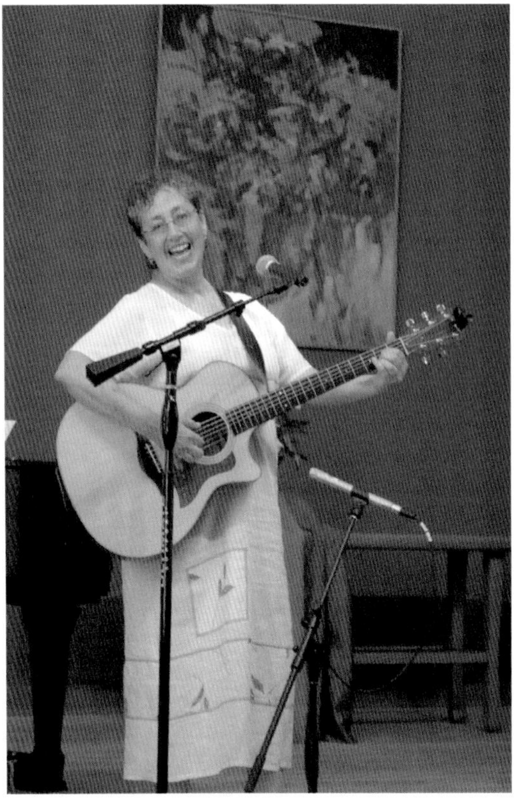

Left: HaMakom cantor Cindy Freedman. *Photo by Victoria Lee.*

Below: A member of HaMakom dancing with Torah scroll. *Photo by Victoria Lee.*

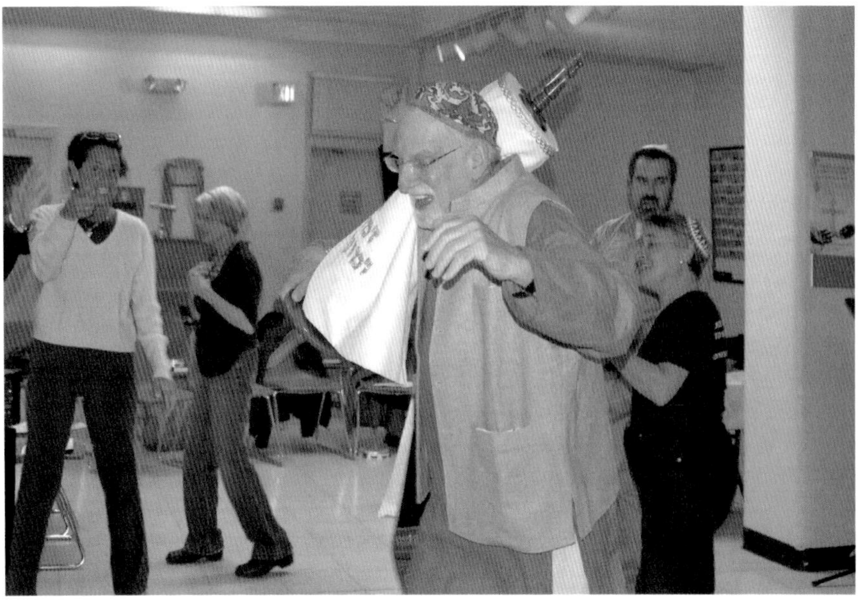

laboratory for a new Jewish practice that incorporated new technologies, such as meditation and chanting, along with a familiar order of service, to bring the tradition alive in the twenty-first century. We welcome all who long for connection to their inner lives. HaMakom: The Place for Passionate and Progressive Religion holds services at the Universalist Unitarian church.

Chabad, the largest and fastest-growing segment of Judaism, came to Santa Fe in 1997 under the direction of Rabbi Berel Levertov, who came from Brooklyn, the headquarters for Chabad's four thousand worldwide centers. Santa Fe's Chabad Center has about 150 members and offers the only full-service Hebrew school in town. As Rabbi Levertov states, "Our goal is to help Jews live a more Jewish life and inspire people in general to live a more meaningful, purposeful life. We feel very welcome as Jews. Santa Fe is so accepting of all denominational beliefs. I love how a Chassidic rabbi

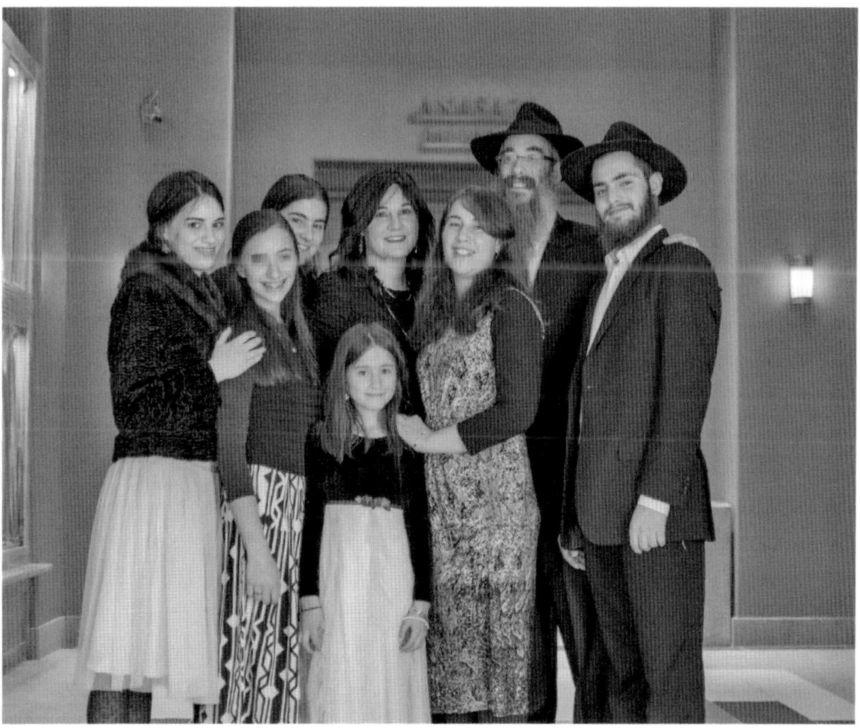

Celebration at the Chabad Jewish Center's eighteen-year anniversary gala. *Left to right, front row*: Mussi, Sara, Rivka and Cirel; *back row*: Devorah Leah, Esther, Rabbi Berel and Mendel Levertov. *Courtesy Chabad.*

from Brooklyn has been so welcome and embraced, to become part of the fiber of this wonderful place!"

The Kol BeRamah Torah Learning Center began in 2007. In the Orthodox tradition, it is committed to fostering Jewish growth and learning throughout northern New Mexico. The center is led by Rabbi Ron Wittenstein, who moved to Santa Fe from Jerusalem in 2014. After completing his rabbinic studies, he was ordained Kollel Darchei Hora'ah under the auspices of Rabbi Mordechai Eliyahu, who was the chief Sephardic rabbi of Israel from 1983 to 1993.

Chapter 5

Spiritual Inroads to the Ancient City

Divine Providence brought a jolt of spirituality to Santa Fe during the second half of the nineteenth century. Just as the Spanish explorers believed themselves to be superior when they arrived, the Anglo-Saxons who colonized the eastern seaboard thought they were entitled to claim America as their own. Per the 1845 Manifest Destiny decree, they believed they were following a preordained path laid out for them by God as they pursued a westward expansion.

It began, somehow, when they ignored the historical fact that the Spaniards were the first ones to land in America in 1598 in San Elizario, Texas, not the English at Plymouth Rock. Their arrogance grew as they acquired land and political strength through the Revolutionary War, the War of 1812 and the Louisiana Purchase. The popular phrase of that era, "Go west, young man, go west," spurred the settlers onward and westward in the pursuit of what they thought was their right and duty in fulfilling their destiny. The only thing standing in the way was the hundreds of Indian tribes spanning the continent. This posed a dilemma for the U.S. government, which was embroiled in a vicious cycle with the Indians: they signed treaties, gave money for the land, broke the treaties and took back the money.

On August 8, 1846, General Stephen W. Kearny and his army entered Santa Fe, and by the following morning, the American flag flew atop the roof of the Palace of the Governors, declaring a new government. As a result of the Mexican-American War, a third of Mexico's territory was handed over to the Americans as part of the Treaty of Guadalupe Hidalgo.

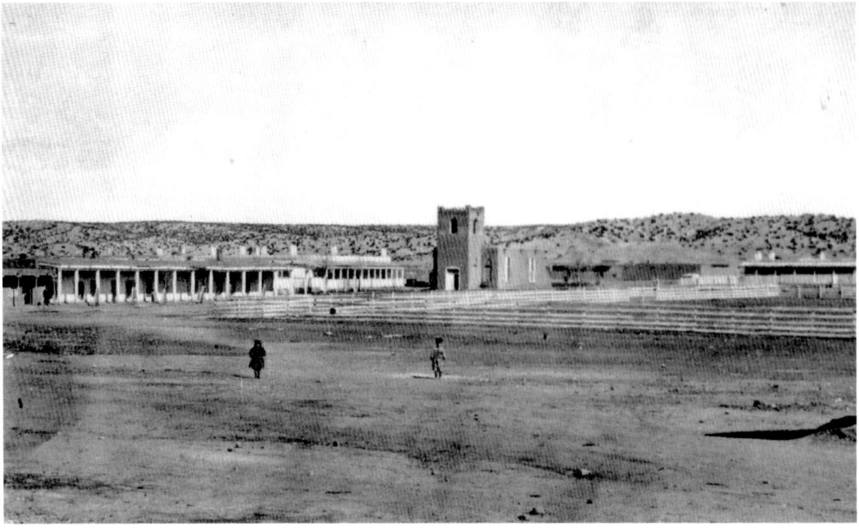

The American First Baptist Church at Fort Marcy in 1854. It was purchased by the First Presbyterian Church in 1867. *Courtesy First Presbyterian Church of Santa Fe.*

The floodgates of old European-based religions opened, and Santa Fe was to be transformed. Since the first arrival of the Spanish settlers, and through the Mexican era, Catholicism was the only religion. In fact, the Mexican constitution of October 4, 1824, stated, "The religion of the Mexican nation is and will permanently be the Roman Catholic, Apostolic religion."

The first Protestant church was the Baptist church built at Fort Marcy at the behest of the wives of the soldiers who needed a place to worship. Reverend Hiram Walter Read was the first preacher assigned by the Home Mission Board of New York. He arrived in Santa Fe by wagon train on July 12, 1849, having been summoned by the territorial military governor, Colonel John M. Washington, to be the first Protestant chaplain of Santa Fe. When the thirty-year-old Yankee arrived with his wife, Anna Alzin, they brought the first melodeon (reed organ) via the Santa Fe Trail. It was to be an itinerant stop for Read, who had been appointed as a Baptist missionary to preach to the forty-niners, the gold-rush miners of California. Read accepted the chaplaincy, which grew to be the New Mexico–Arizona Baptist mission.

The December 1849 Home Mission Society's periodical reported, "With a population of 1,000 souls in the Territory, uninstructed in gospel truth by a single protestant preacher, with nearly a thousand imploring him to remain, and many Mexicans favorably disposed to study the religion he preaches, it is our duty to acquiesce in the overruling of guidance of the divine hand."

It's not clear how long the Baptist work continued in Santa Fe, but the historical record shows that the property was sold by the Home Mission Society to the Presbyterians on May 4, 1869. The church and property were sold for $300, at which time the Home Mission withdrew its support from a number of missionaries in the New Mexico territory. After the missionaries left, there wasn't any active representation of the Baptist faith for the next fifty years.

With the departure of the Baptist Church, Catholicism flourished under the strong influence of Archbishop Jean-Baptiste Lamy. St. Michael's College and Loretto Academy educated the young men and women, while the Sisters of Charity, who relocated from Cincinnati, ran St. Vincent Hospital and orphanage. Although there were about three hundred Protestant Americans in Santa Fe at that time, the Baptist, Episcopal, Methodist and Presbyterian faiths had all failed to establish missions.

Documents show that a plea was sent out for representation in the territory, and God answered with the arrival of Presbyterian minister Reverend David F. McFarland. With the Catholic Church having a two-hundred-year head start, he knew a difficult task lay ahead. He also learned that the Baptists had invested $20,000 in Santa Fe and had given up a hopeless effort to establish a church in the community. Within months of his arrival, McFarland purchased the rundown church with a collapsed roof and boarded-up windows. He conducted his first service at the Council Chamber at the Palace of the Governors three days after his arrival, on Sunday, November 25, 1866, with forty people in attendance. Three weeks later, he began a school for children in his home. The following year, his wife, Amanda, arrived to take charge of the school, and she dove into assisting at community events. During the course of the next year, McFarland and his followers petitioned to organize a Presbyterian church in Santa Fe. On December 14, 1868, the Presbyterian Church of Santa Fe was organized, which, under the auspices of the Synod of Kansas, included other churches in New Mexico. Sunday services were held at the refurbished Baptist church until 1882, when a new church was built on the former grounds of Fort Marcy at Grant and Griffin Streets, which is its current location.

Reverend McFarland performed a marriage ceremony for Catherine McCarty and William Antrim on March 1, 1873, in the sanctuary of the church. It was a second marriage for Catherine, who had been widowed nine years earlier. Her two sons, Henry and Joe, stood witness at the ceremony. After her first husband died in New York City, she had taken the boys west, where she met William Antrim. Catherine had severe, advanced

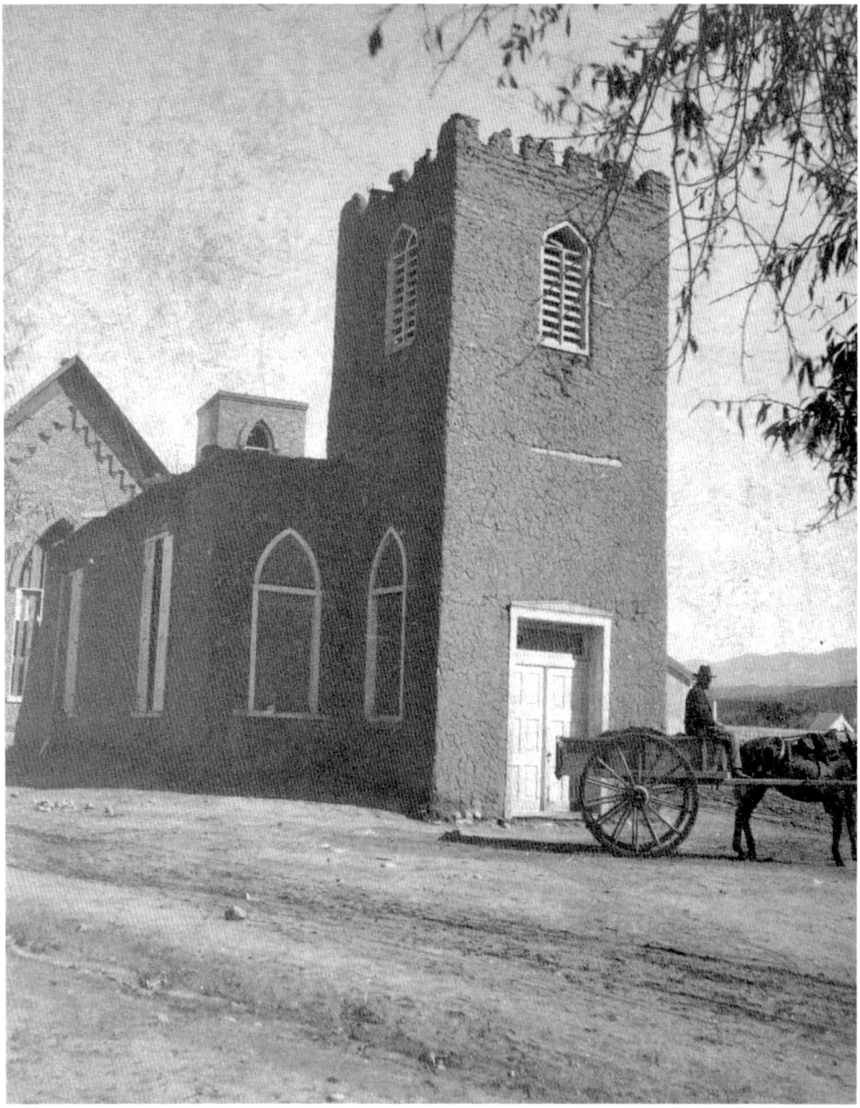

The First Presbyterian Church, Santa Fe, New Mexico, 1875. *Courtesy Palace of the Governors [NMHM/DCA]. No. 074552.*

tuberculosis, and she knew that her new husband loved the boys and would care for them if anything happened to her. After the wedding, they moved to the drier climate of Silver City. She prayed that her sons would lead a Christian life. She died a year later, when Henry was fifteen. He was close to his mother, and her death led him to a life of petty theft and pranks around

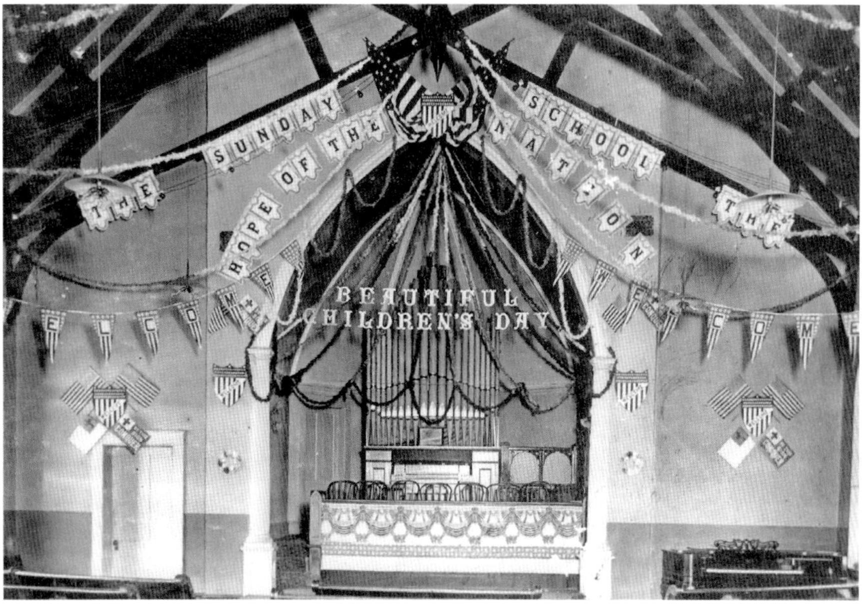

A 1907 interior photo of the chapel of the First Presbyterian Church. *Courtesy First Presbyterian Church of Santa Fe.*

town. After stealing clothes from a Chinese laundry, he was incarcerated but escaped through the jailhouse chimney. That was the beginning of his life as a criminal in New Mexico and Arizona, where he became known as Billy the Kid.

In failing health, McFarland and his wife relocated in 1874 to San Diego, where they established a teaching academy. As his health improved, McFarland was called to serve at the Nez Perce Indian reservation in Idaho, where he died in 1876. The Santa Fe Collegiate Institute that he had started continued to grow. Charity Ann Gaston was brought in to teach in 1867. She stayed two years and then left to go to the Fort Defiance Indian Reservation, where she married John Menaul. They continued their work together at New Mexico's Laguna Pueblo, and the couple's educational legacy is evident today at Menaul School and Library in Albuquerque.

The Presbyterian mission to educate and spread the word of God expanded when Matilda Allison arrived in 1881 and started a boarding school for girls called the Santa Fe Industrial and Boarding School for Mexican Girls. In 1905, the Mary James Missionary Boarding School for Boys opened. The school building was later purchased by the St. Germain Foundation and is used as the I AM Sanctuary. In 1928, the

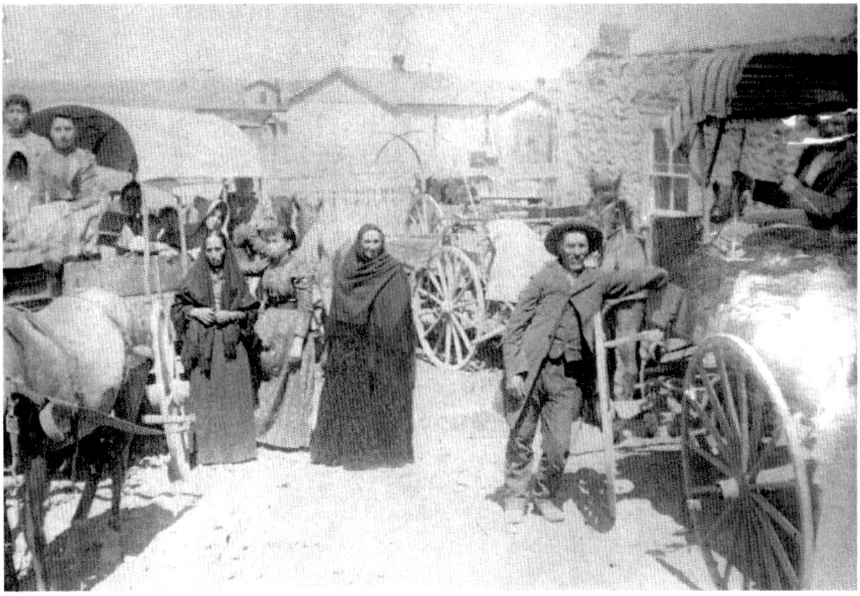

Children arrived by wagon train to attend the Santa Fe Industrial and Boarding School for Mexican Girls. *Courtesy First Presbyterian Church of Santa Fe.*

two schools merged and became Allison-James, a coed junior high school primarily serving Hispanic boys and girls from the Presbyterian mission day schools in the mountains of northern New Mexico. It was in operation through 1958.

The missionary Gabino Rendón was responsible for recruiting the large Spanish population of northern New Mexico. He was the first New Mexican Hispanic ordained a Presbyterian minister, and he presided over the Spanish-speaking congregations in the region for more than sixty years during the nineteenth and twentieth centuries. He was also the first person of Spanish descent to be elected moderator of the Presbyterian Synod of New Mexico.

Rendón was born to a Catholic family in Las Vegas, New Mexico, on February 18, 1864. As was the Spanish custom, he was named in honor of a saint, San Gabino. His father, who was a *cibolero* (buffalo hunter), allowed his son to attend the Presbyterian mission school. That was Rendón's first introduction to hymns and scripture taught in his native language. In 1885, when he was twenty-one, Rendón became a member of the church. He started a mission school in Las Vegas and was ordained in 1899 as the first pastorate in Pueblo, Colorado. In 1900, he moved to Santa Fe and started the Spanish Presbyterian Church, which is now called Westminster Presbyterian Church. Rendón was the chaplain at the Allison-James School and supervisor of Hispanic evangelist churches in northern New Mexico. Through the determination and commitment of Rendón, Allison, McFarland and the others, the capital city has been home to the First Presbyterian Church of Santa Fe for 150 years.

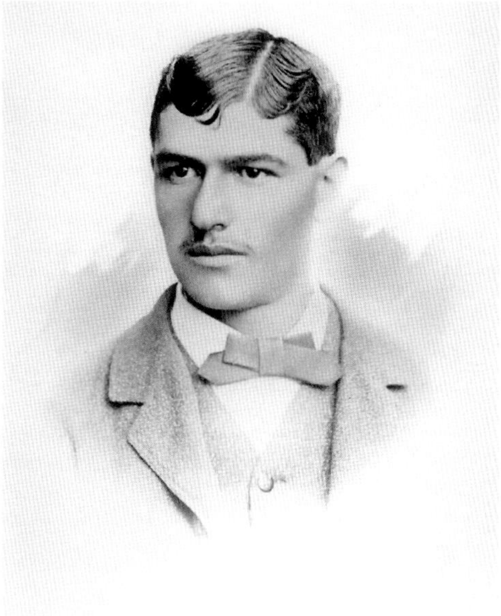

Gabino Rendón, the first person of Spanish descent to be elected moderator of the Presbyterian Synod of New Mexico. *Courtesy First Presbyterian Church of Santa Fe.*

Holy Faith of Santa Fe is the oldest Episcopal church in New Mexico. It was founded in 1863, with lay people conducting services. Some of the early worshippers were the Anglo soldiers and officers stationed in Santa Fe during the Civil War. Bishop Josiah Cruickshank Talbot was the first to arrive, followed by the Reverend John Woart and Reverend J.A.W. LaTourette, who were chaplains at Fort Union and Fort Garland, respectively. Within five years, the small congregation had become the Parish of the Good Shepherd. The name was later changed to the Church of Holy Faith to reflect the English translation of Santa Fe. The following year, L. Bradford Prince began raising money for the building of the church, which was completed in 1882. Prince became the governor of New Mexico in 1889, and church-related functions often took place in the reception room at the Palace of the Governors. He would also conduct services when there was no pastor. His wife, Mary C. Prince, often assisted at these church functions.

Holy Faith Church was one of the first dressed-stone buildings at the time, with the rocks coming from a quarry in the community of Galisteo, southeast of Santa Fe. Many renovations have taken place since then, including work done by renowned architect John Gaw Meem. The church received financial assistance from the Jewish community, and a Star of David was etched into the stained-glass window at the entrance of the church in gratitude for its generosity. The church's organ, which was installed in 1961, is the largest of its kind in northern New Mexico.

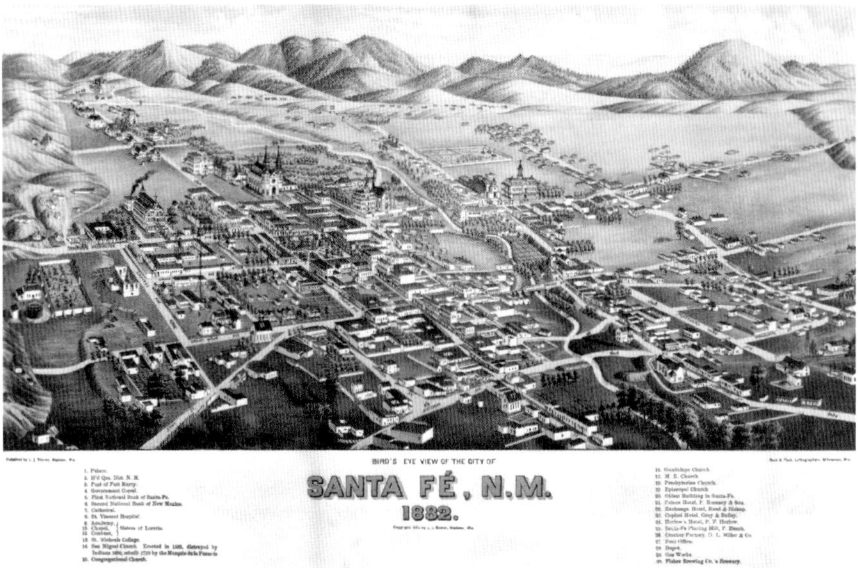

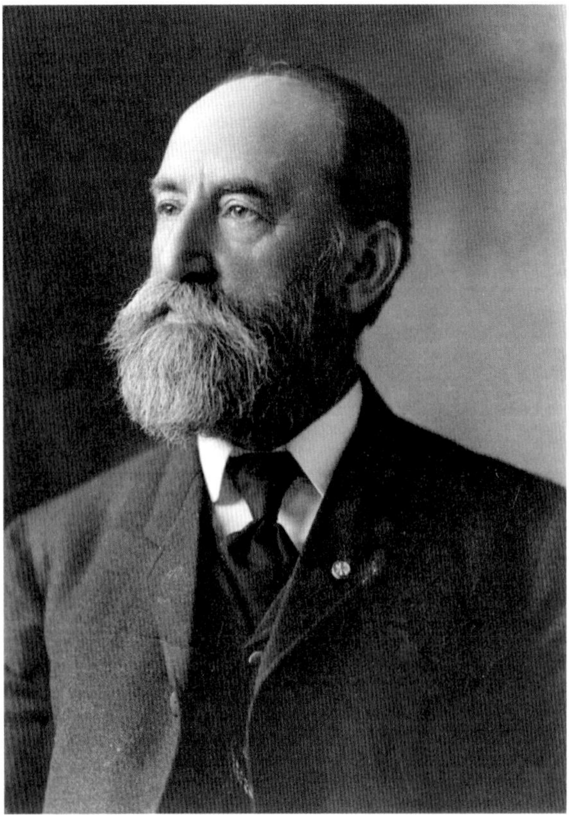

Above: An 1882 bird's-eye view of Santa Fe featuring the following religious establishments: Cathedral Basilica of St. Francis of Assisi; Sisters of Loretto Convent and Academy; St. Michael's College; San Miguel Mission Church; Congregation Church; Our Lady of Guadalupe Church; Methodist Church; First Presbyterian Church; and Holy Faith Episcopal church. *Courtesy Palace of the Governors [NMHM/DCA]. No. 023306.*

Left: L. Bradford Prince, governor of New Mexico Territory, 1889–93. *Courtesy Palace of the Governors [NMHM/DCA]. No. 050444.*

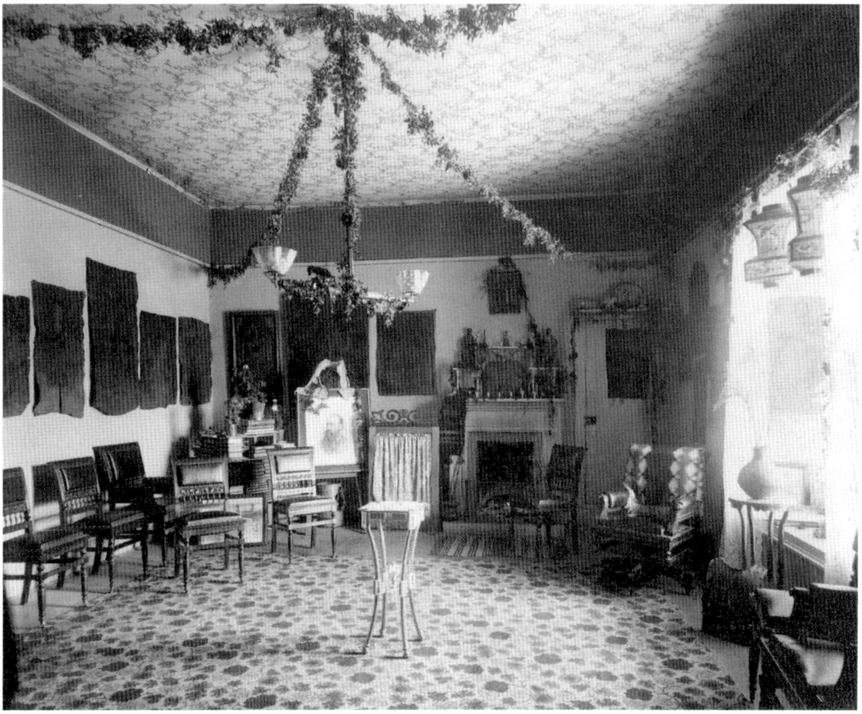

Above: Palace of the Governors interior while occupied by Governor Prince, 1893, Santa Fe, New Mexico. *Photo by Wyatt Davis. Courtesy Palace of the Governors [NMHM/DCA]. No. 016658.*

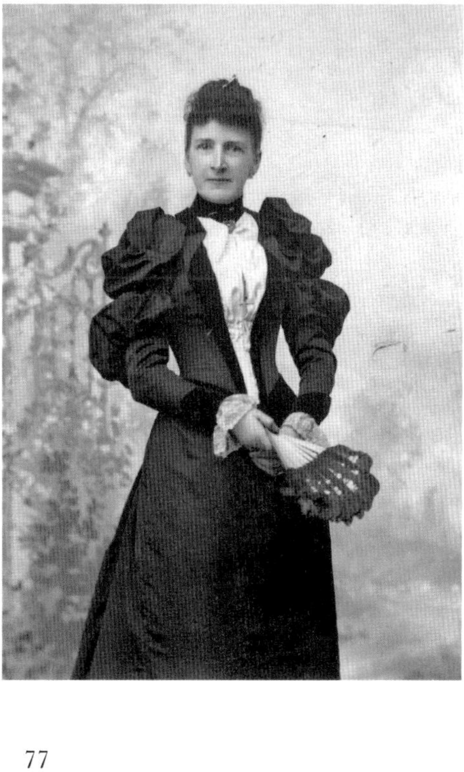

Right: Mary C. Prince (Mrs. L. Bradford Prince), circa 1890, by Herman Wunder Studio. *Courtesy Palace of the Governors [NMHM/DCA]. No. 010354.*

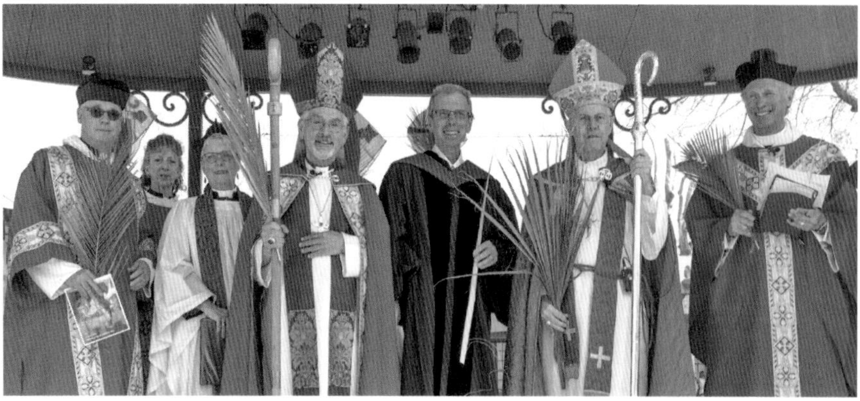

The 2015 Palm Sunday celebration on the Santa Fe Plaza. *Left to right*: The Reverend Jim Gordon (Episcopal), Alice McSweeney (Episcopal), the Very Reverend Peggy Patterson (Episcopal), Bishop Michael Vono (Episcopal Diocese of the Rio Grande), Reverend Harry Ebberts (pastor, First Presbyterian Church), Archbishop Michael Sheehan (Roman Catholic) and Father Kenneth J.G. Semon (rector, the Church of the Holy Faith [Episcopal]). *Photo by Timothy Roberts.*

Throughout its history, Holy Faith has been known for its ecumenical leadership and collaboration with other faiths.

In October 1850, Methodist minister Reverend E.G. Nicholson arrived in Santa Fe from Independence, Missouri, and preached his first sermon to a small congregation that consisted of military personnel and their families. It was a short-lived ministry because the headquarters of the army soon relocated. Three years later, Nicholson returned, accompanied by Reverend Walter Hansen of New York and Reverend Benigno Cárdenas, a former Catholic priest. By 1865, the Colorado Conference of the Methodist Episcopal Church had sent Reverend John L. Dryer to New Mexico. A local Presbyterian minister allowed him to assist at the pulpit, where he delivered Methodist-Episcopal sermons. Dyer conveyed his support for establishing a church to the district superintendent. In 1872, Reverend Thomas Harwood was appointed the superintendent of the Methodist Mission in New Mexico, and Reverend H.H. Hall became the pastor in 1880. A small adobe church was built on West San Francisco Street and was dedicated on April 17, 1881, by the Reverend David H. Moore. As the congregation grew, it moved to a building on Johnson Street. On June 24, 1906, a new church opened on Don Gaspar Avenue. That church was home to the Methodists for the next forty-eight years. In 1963, they moved to their current location on Córdova Road, adding more buildings as the congregation grew to include two thousand members. In

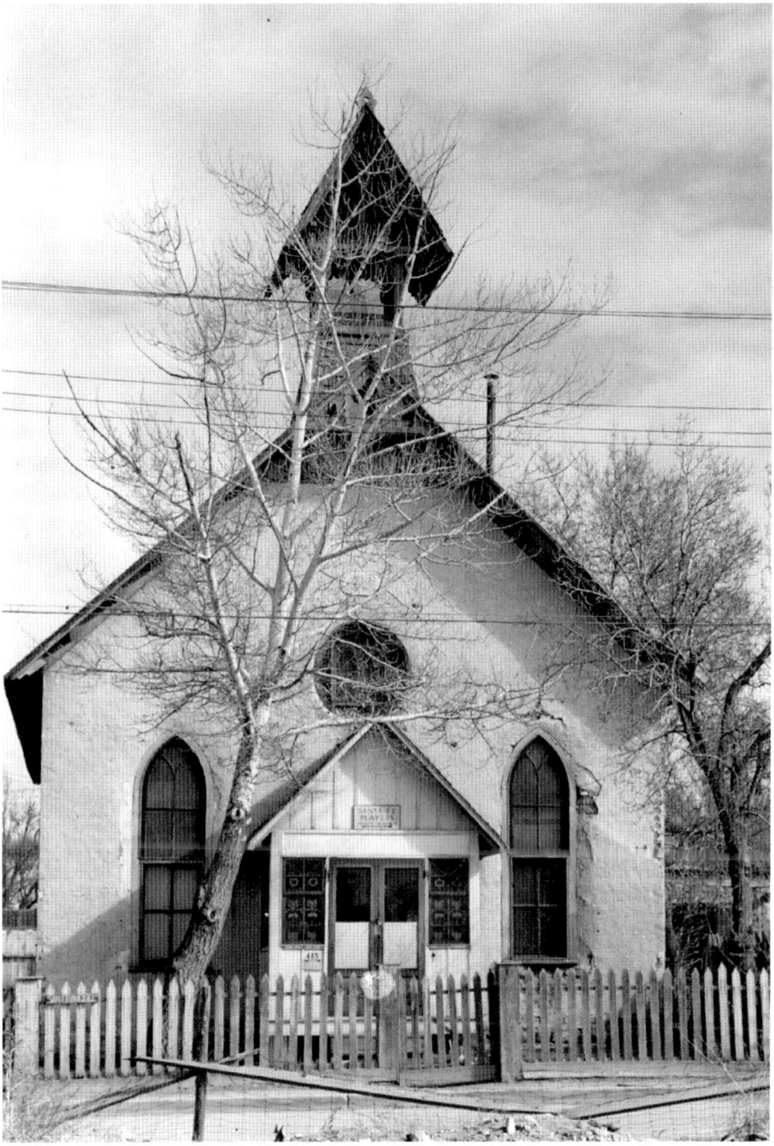

The old Methodist church on San Francisco Street, circa 1935. *Courtesy Palace of the Governors [NMHM/DCA]. No. 041834.*

1968, the church merged with the Evangelical United Brethren Church and became St. John's Methodist Church.

As with other Protestant missions that first came to Santa Fe, the Methodist Mission of New Mexico disseminated its message through education. The

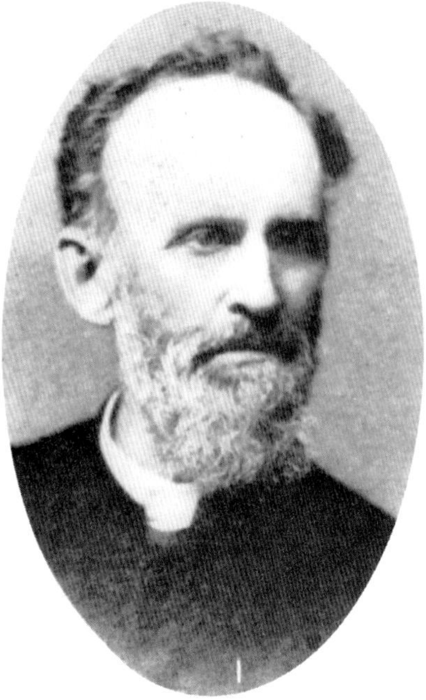

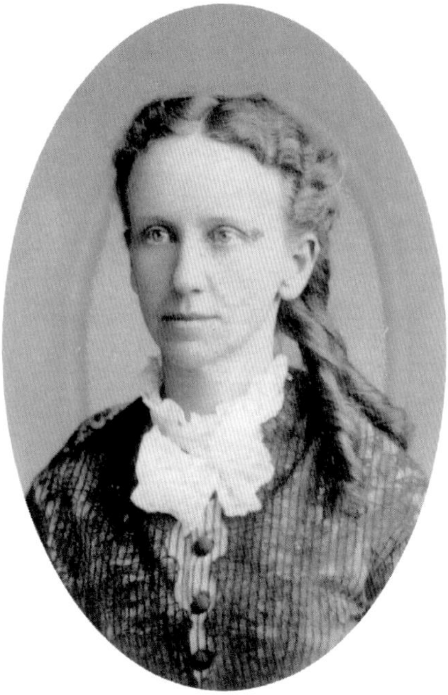

Left: The Reverend Thomas Harwood, New Mexico's district superintendent when St. John's Methodist Church was built in 1880. *Courtesy St. John's Methodist Church.*

Right: Mrs. Emily Harwood of St. John's Methodist Church, who established schools in northern New Mexico and Albuquerque in the 1880s. *Courtesy St. John's Methodist Church.*

Reverend Thomas Harwood and his wife, Emily, began schools in northern New Mexico and Albuquerque. The McCurdy Ministries was founded in Española in 1912 by Millie Perkins, a United Brethren deaconess. They started the first medical clinic, nursing program and hospital. A century later, in 2012, they began the McCurdy Charter School, which serves kindergarten through twelfth grade. The ministries also set up a preschool, after-school camps and a mental health program.

As the fervor of Manifest Destiny established a foothold throughout the West, the existence of the traditional religious values and practices imported from Europe came under siege during the spiritual movement known as the Second Great Awakening. Showing discontent with traditional dogma and responding to the need to adapt to a new environment, the movement began in the early part of the nineteenth century and, by the millennium, had transformed the religious landscape of America. Several new denominations grew out of this movement, including the Church of Jesus Christ of Latter-Day Saints.

When Joseph Smith, the founder of Mormonism and the Church of Latter Day-Saints, was still a teenager, he began to report Divine visitations. In 1823, the angel Moroni directed him to a box buried on Camorah Hill in Manchester, New York. In the box Smith discovered a 1,400-year-old book that contained the history of God and was believed to be a relic of a lost tribe of Israel. The translated book became the Book of Mormon, the pillar of their beliefs, published in 1830. Soon after, Mormon missionaries were sent to Missouri to preach their gospel to Native Americans. The church grew quickly to sixteen thousand members, and their first temple was built in Kirtland, Ohio.

The Latter-Day Saints movement suffered great persecution, and Smith and his brother Hyrum were killed in Nauvoo, Illinois, in 1844 by an angry mob while they were incarcerated on their way west to Utah. Brigham Young, the president of the Quorum of the Twelve Apostles, became the next prophet of the Latter-Day Saints.

The Mormons' first arrival in Santa Fe was during the Mexican-American War of 1846–48. The Mormon Battalion is the only religion-based unit in the military history of the United States. The volunteer unit consisted of 560 men who were led by Mormon company officers. At the time, they were seeking government aid for their migration west after the murder of their leader in Nauvoo. Brigham Young devised the effort as a way to get them to Utah while creating positive public relations. Each man was paid forty-two dollars for a year of service. The Mormon Battalion was part of General Kearny's army. In 1996, a restored monument to the Mormon Battalion was erected, replacing the 1940 memorial that had been razed when the portion of Interstate 25 from Santa Fe to Albuquerque was widened.

The first Mormon Santa Fe Ward was opened on December 14, 1896, under the direction of Apostle John W. Taylor. Missionary work was soon established in the remote villages of northern New Mexico. In 1905, William Kyle Shupe and his wife, Martha Stover, moved to Santa Fe and were most likely the first Mormons to live for any length of time in Santa Fe. Shupe was a sales manager for the Singer Sewing Machine Company. In 1912, the year of New Mexico's statehood, the small Mormon settlement of Carson, just west of Taos, was established. It was associated with the unsuccessful struggle to create the settlement of Mariana, a Mormon community near Abiquiu. On April 1, 1907, the Colorado Mission expanded and changed its name to the Western States Mission, which included the area known as the Santa Fe Stake. The Durán family became the first permanent Latter-Day Saints residents of Santa Fe. Rebecca Ann Chávez was born on October 14, 1888,

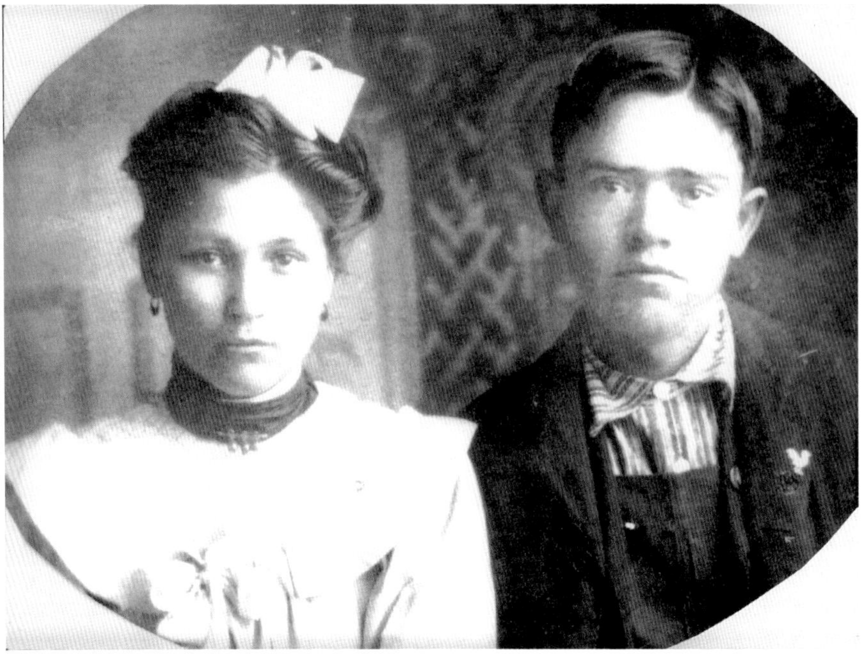

A 1903 photo of Rebecca Ann Chávez and Guillermo Durán, the first early permanent Latter-Day Saints residents of Santa Fe. *Courtesy Church of Jesus Christ of Latter-Day Saints, Santa Fe, New Mexico.*

in Manassa, Colorado. Her family fell on hard times, and she was sent to live with a Mrs. Flowers, who ran a boardinghouse. When the boardinghouse closed a year later, Mrs. Flowers took a job running a mess hall for a lumber company in Tres Piedras, New Mexcio, and Rebecca Ann went with her. That's where Rebecca Ann met Guillermo Durán, and they married in 1903. Durán was baptized and converted to Mormonism. Three years later, three more members of his family were baptized in the Rio Grande, just below the Otowi Bridge on the road to Los Alamos. His brother Richard Durán later became the branch president of the church in Española. There was no chapel in Española, so the family would conduct Sunday school at home one week and the following week at the home of Guillermo and Rebecca Ann in Santa Fe. One of the first orders of business for the Mission District was to have the Book of Mormon translated into Spanish. The project was completed in 1929, and the Zion Publishing Company of Independence, Missouri, printed 10,671 copies to aid the Durán family in their missionary work.

During the 1920s and 1930s, money was scarce, and it was a trying endeavor to keep missionaries in the field. James Byron Barton and his

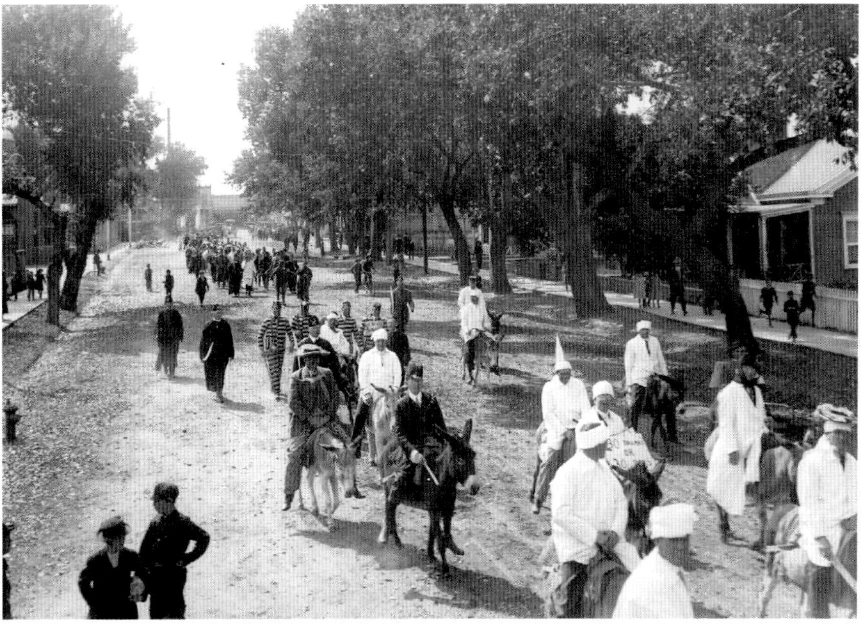

A procession of Masons and Shriners in 1911 on Washington Avenue, preparing to lay the cornerstone for the Scottish Rite Temple. *Photo by Jess Nussbaum. Courtesy Scottish Rite Temple.*

wife and five children moved to Santa Fe from Ogden, Utah, in 1934. Barton was named branch president for Santa Fe and began holding church services in his home. As word got out, families from the outlying areas began to attend the church, and other Mormon families moved to town. By 1946, there was an enclave of Mormons living in the Casa Solana area in the north part of town, and they began to hold services at the First Christian Church. In 1960, they built a chapel on Barcelona Street, and in 1985, the Mormon community had grown large enough that it was divided into two wards: the Santa Fe Ward and the Camino Real Ward. Today, the Temple of Jesus Christ of Latter-Day Saints is located on Rodeo Road and houses a library of the history of the Mormons' foothold in the West and throughout the world.

Like the Mexican War of 1846–48 that brought a new breed of spirituality to Santa Fe, the Civil War brought Freemasonry. In 1909, Harper Cunningham, a former private in the Union army and attorney general of Oklahoma, arrived in Santa Fe. A member of the Freemason organization, he began work on establishing a chapter of the Masons. Although Freemasonry is not a religion, the Masons believe in a Supreme Being and work for the

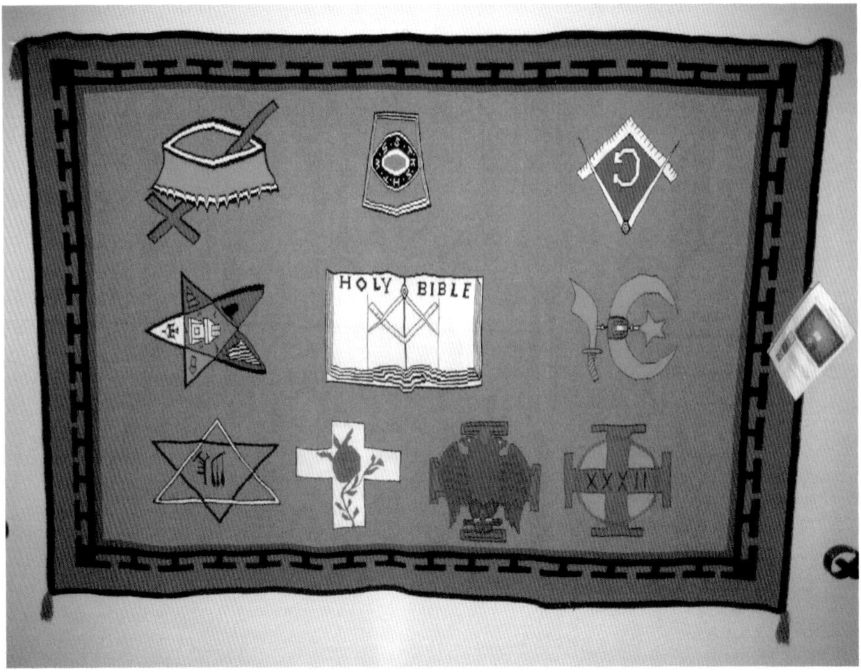

A wall hanging of Freemason imagery at the Scottish Rite Temple. *Photo by Ana Pacheco.*

betterment of society. In Santa Fe, they have supported the work of hospitals and clinics and work with children with dyslexia.

Masonry began in England 1717 and in Scotland in 1770. During this era, the old-world authority regulated the exchange of religious ideas. Wanting to break from the past, Masons sought ecumenism and religious tolerance. They didn't agree with the sectarian divisions that have caused dissension among many organized faiths. To become members, all have to claim allegiance to something bigger than man himself.

Many people believe that Masonry symbolism is represented on the back of the dollar bill. The design for the great seal of the United States, which features an eye and a pyramid, was introduced by Benjamin Franklin, who was a Mason. On July 4, 1776, the seal was created by an order of the Continental Congress under the direction of Benjamin Franklin, Thomas Jefferson and John Adams. The seal was used as a government stamp for official business until 1935. During the Great Depression, at the behest of Franklin D. Roosevelt and Henry A. Wallace, both Masons, the great seal appeared on the back of the dollar bill. The Latin sentence surrounding the unfinished pyramid states, *Annuit Coeptis* (Providence Has Favored

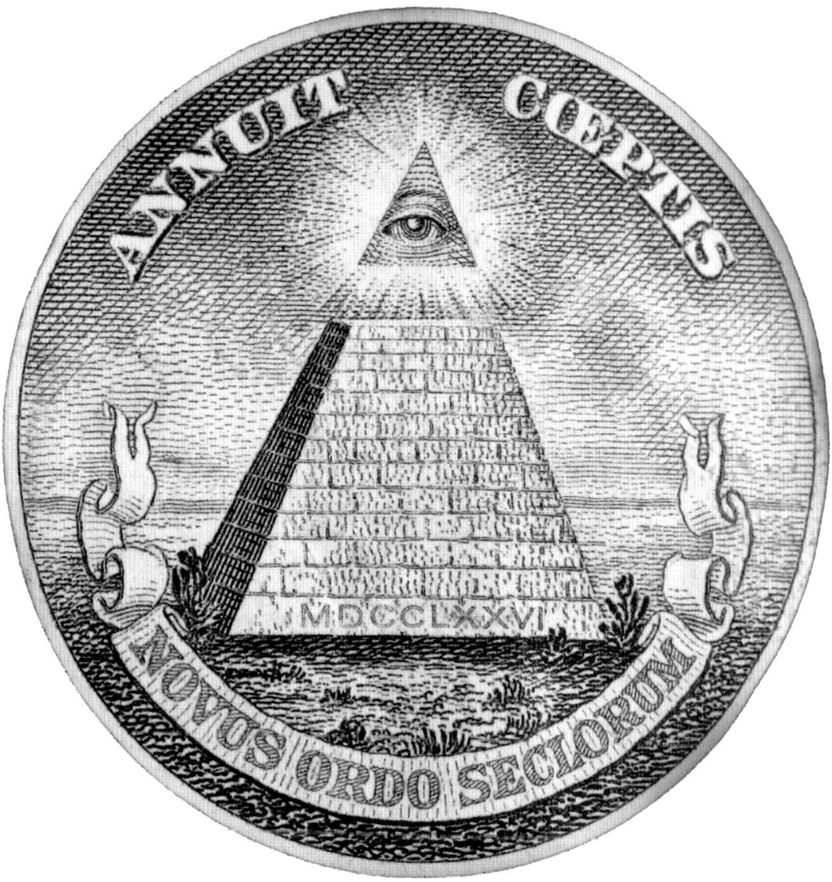

The great seal of the United States on the back of the dollar bill. *Courtesy Shutterstock images.*

Our Undertakings) and *Novus Ordo Seclorium* (A New Order of the Ages). That symbolism correlated with Masonry ideals; the pyramid is a worldly achievement that's incomplete without the blessing of Providence. During the Renaissance, occultists viewed ancient Egypt as the source of primal, ageless wisdom transcending nations and dogma. The eye and the pyramid sought to achieve that ideal.

Harper Cunningham died in 1911, one year before the Scottish Rite Temple was built. The building was erected in 1912 at Paseo de Peralta and Washington Avenue, where it stands today. Built to resemble the Alhambra in Spain, where Santa Fe's name was christened by Queen Isabel, its pink façade has always stood apart from the rest of Santa Fe's architecture

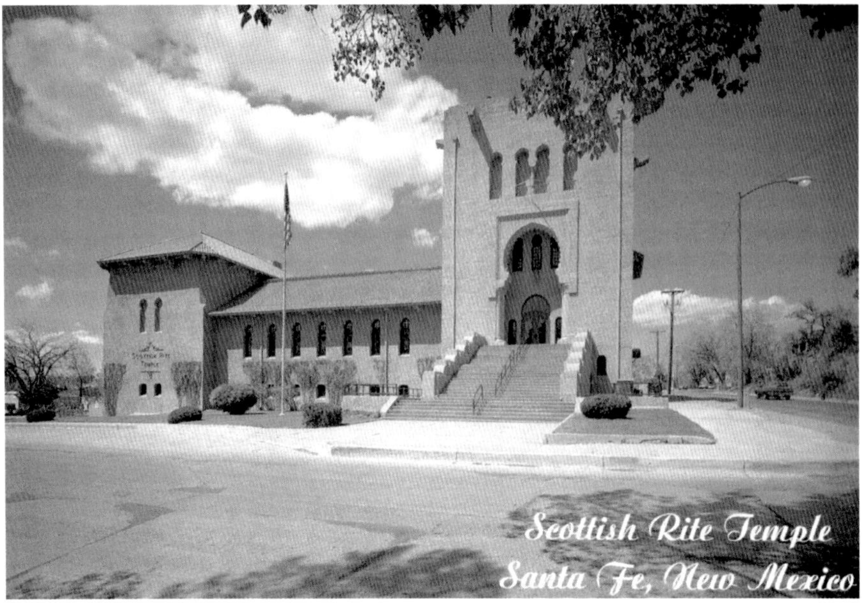

A postcard of the Scottish Rite Temple in Santa Fe. *Courtesy Scottish Rite Temple.*

and has been referred to by many as the Pepto-Bismol building. Although Cunningham never got to see his dream realized, many well-known New Mexicans continued his work, including Richard Henry Hanna, a New Mexico Supreme Court justice, and Edgar Lee Hewitt, the founder of the Museum of New Mexico. Harper Cunningham and his wife, Eva, are buried beneath the stairs of the temple entrance.

It took half a century, but under the leadership of Dr. E.B. Atwood, the corresponding secretary of the New Mexico Baptist Convention in Albuquerque, the First Baptist Church, Santa Fe was formed on August 20, 1917, with twenty-three members. The momentum grew out of evangelistic meetings held in a tent that were the first tent revivals in Santa Fe's history. For ten days, they held services in a large tent that was borrowed from the Baptist state office on a lot located at Manhattan and Don Gaspar Avenues. At that time, there were a number of Baptist families living in Santa Fe, but they didn't have a church. They would worship at other Protestant churches but never joined them. During these tent meetings, the First Baptist Church of Santa Fe was organized. Immediately following, the first baptism of church member Kenneth Euler by Dr. Atwood took place at a pond on East Buena Vista Street owned by Mrs. D.L. Miller. Their enthusiasm and hard work came to a grinding halt the following year with the worldwide influenza

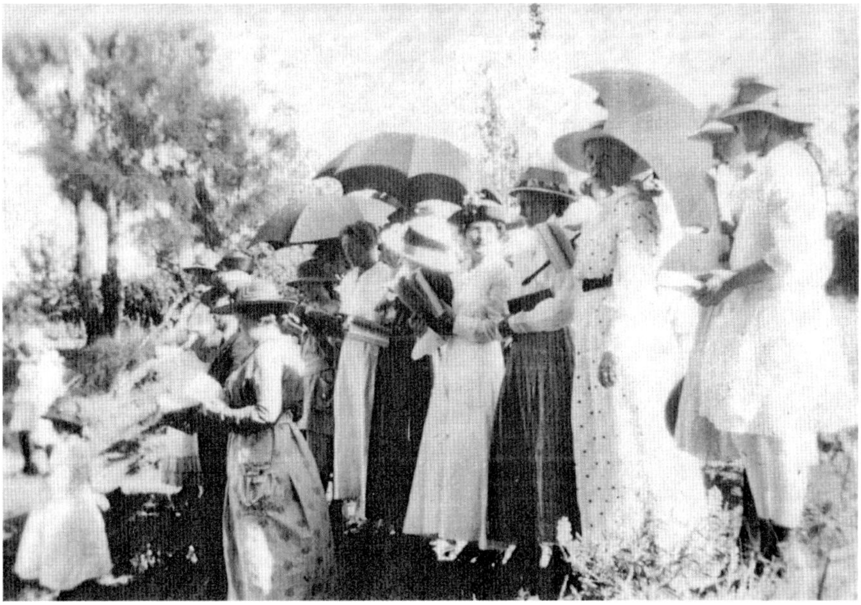

The first baptism, of church member Kenneth Euler by Dr. Atwood, took place in 1917 at a pond on East Buena Vista Street owned by Mrs. D.L. Miller. *Courtesy First Baptist Church of Santa Fe.*

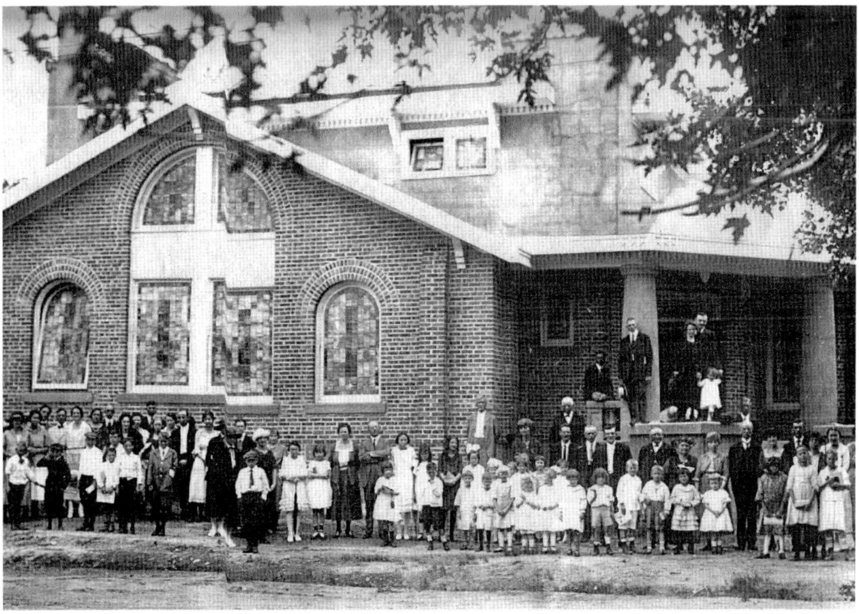

A 1921 photo of the First Baptist congregation in front of their first church at the corner of Don Gaspar and Manhattan Avenues. *Courtesy First Baptist Church of Santa Fe.*

outbreak of 1918. Many of the churches in Santa Fe closed during that time. World War I also took many pastors and young men from the state.

On August 7, 1921, on the very lot at Manhattan and Don Gaspar Avenues where the congregation first met in a tent, the First Baptist Church of Santa Fe was dedicated. The church persevered and grew throughout the Great Depression, the Dust Bowl and World War II. In 1955, the site of its present location on Old Pecos Trail was purchased. The church was dedicated on December 11, 1960, and additions to the church were built in the 1970s. In 2017, the First Baptist Church will celebrate one hundred years in Santa Fe.

Chapter 6

A Gentler Way

At the beginning of World War I, a group of Lutheran pacifists found their way to Santa Fe. Their objection to that war followed a long history of their Christian social consciousness based on the teachings of the gospel. In the fall of 1914, the first recorded Lutheran worship services in Santa Fe took place, with five adults in attendance. This initial service and subsequent services were conducted by Lutheran Church–Missouri Synod traveling missionary Reverend Carl F. Schmid, pastor of Immanuel Lutheran Church in Albuquerque.

Regular weekly services for the Immanuel Lutheran Church began in 1915, including afternoon services for inmates and staff conducted at the state penitentiary. Although the church began with great enthusiasm, services held between 1915 and 1929 became intermittent. It wasn't until the early 1930s that regular weekly services, sponsored by the permanent founding members of the congregation, resumed. Consistency and growth finally produced a congregation that was incorporated in 1938, with weekly services held in the members' homes. From 1940 to 1948, the congregation rented facilities for Sunday and midweek activities in Sena Plaza, on Palace Avenue. Early names associated with the congregation are the Rogers, Kahre and Gust families. Various Lutheran ministers of Lutheran Church–Missouri Synod congregations in northern New Mexico served the Immanuel congregation initially until the first permanent pastor of the congregation, Reverend Theo G. Schoech, was installed in 1938, following the congregation's organization. The current building at 209 East Barcelona was dedicated in February 1949.

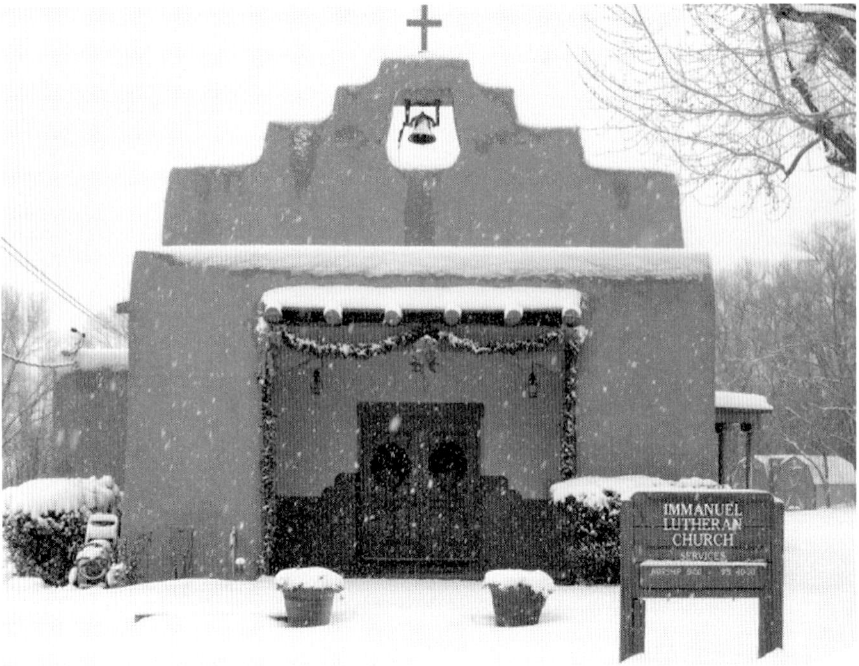

The Immanuel Lutheran Church on Barcelona Street at Christmas. *Courtesy Immanuel Lutheran Church.*

In the late 1950s, the first mission of the Rocky Mountain Synod of the Evangelical Lutheran Church in America began a property search to build the Christ Evangelical Lutheran Church. In 1964, it purchased a six-acre plot that was originally part of the Spanish land grant of Sebastian De Vargas. On June 19, 1966, it held a formal dedication. The congregation currently resides on Arroyo Chamiso. Later, the Rocky Mountain synod built a second church, Christ of the Servant, on Legacy Court off Rodeo Road.

The Lutheran Church, the third-largest Protestant denomination in the United States, was founded in the sixteenth century by Martin Luther, a German monk who began the Protestant Reformation. Luther took a defiant stance toward the Roman Catholic Church, contending that it was corrupt. He adamantly disagreed with the practice of making donations to the church in order to limit the amount of time an individual would spend in Purgatory. Luther did not trust the Catholic hierarchy, and the basis of Lutheran doctrine continues with the Bible as the one true source of religious teachings. On October 31, 1517, Luther posted his Ninety-five Theses on the church door of the castle of Wittenberg,

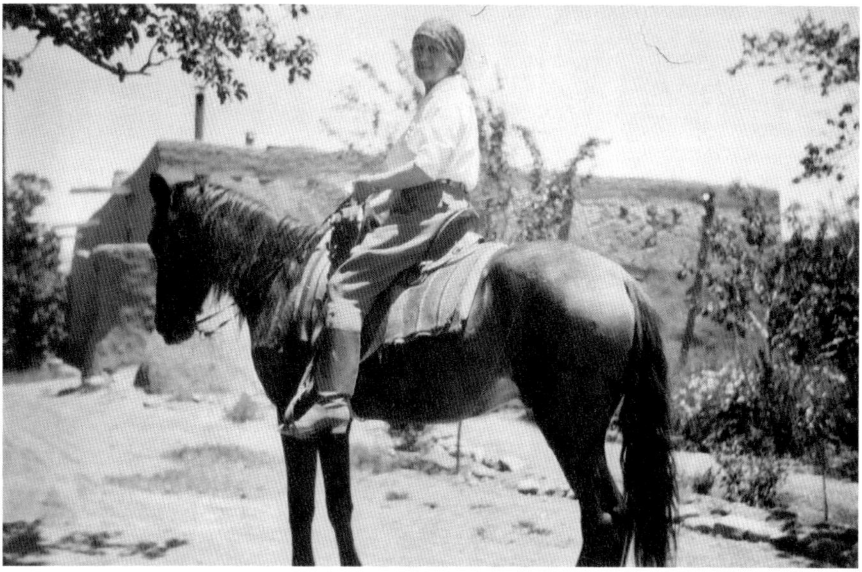

Olive Rush on horseback in the garden at 690 Canyon Road, Santa Fe, New Mexico, circa 1930. *Courtesy Palace of the Governors [NMHM/DCA]. No. 019270.*

challenging the practices of the Catholic Church that led to the start of the Protestant Reformation.

After World War I, Santa Fe had become a refuge for the war-weary and those in search of a second chance at life. From 1880 through 1940, people suffering from tuberculosis, as well as soldiers who suffered from mustard-gas poisoning, came to New Mexico for its pristine air and dry climate. In fact, the State of New Mexico promoted its sixty sanitariums in magazines throughout the country. Santa Fe's Sunmount Sanitarium is currently located on the grounds of the Carmelite Monastery. The well-known artists Will Shuster and Carlos Vierra came to Sunmount to convalesce. These men were two of the first artists whom Olive Rush met when she came to Santa Fe in 1920. Like most artists, Rush was drawn to Santa Fe's tranquil landscape and ever-changing light. Her arrival brought Quakerism and the "inner light" to Santa Fe.

Born in 1873 in Fairmount, Indiana, Olive Rush came from a long line of Quakers, who were followers of the seventeenth-century religious leader George Fox. They were known as the "Children of Light," referring to the light or inspiration of the "inner Christ." The Quakers believe that it is only when one silences all human thought, desires and activities that Christ can be heard. Their gatherings, largely characterized by long periods of silence, were sporadically broken by the utterances of members when led by

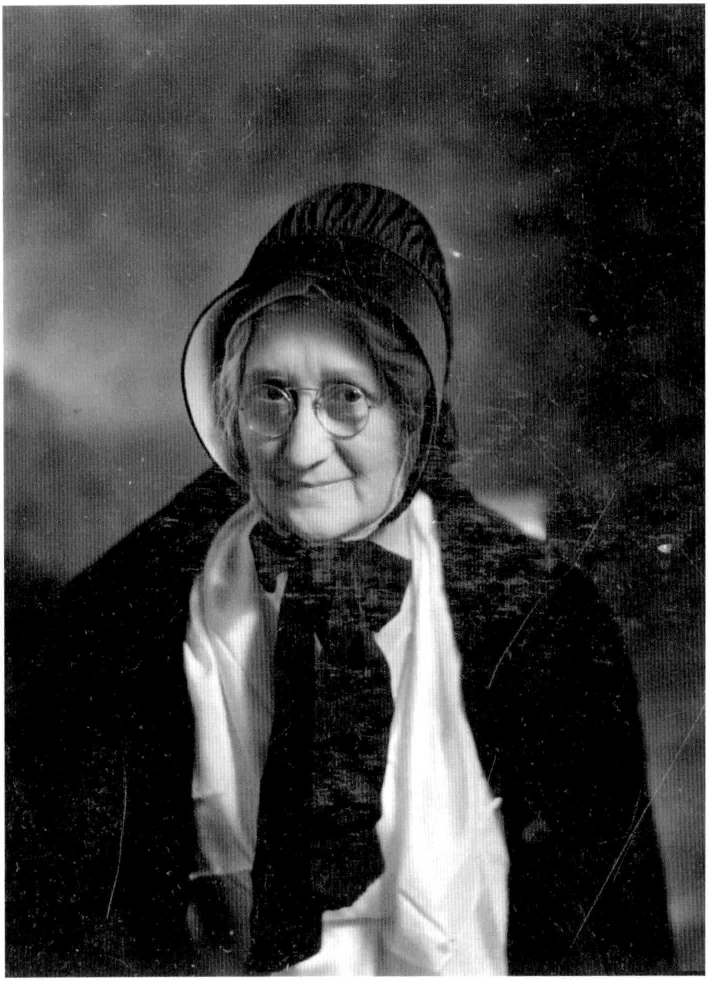

Artist Olive Rush, Santa Fe, New Mexico, 1932. *Photo by Will Connell. Courtesy Palace of the Governors [NMHM/DCA]. No. 059744.*

Divine inspiration. When under the influence of the Spirit, the speaker would tremble and quake, therein gaining the name "Quakers" from outside observers. Today, the self-named Religious Society of Friends identifies this type of worship as a form of meditation. It differs from Buddhist meditation in that during the prolonged silence, one or more members will break the silence with a message of guidance from within. A Quaker meeting has no preordained minister; ideally through the silence and contemplation, the word of God will be transmitted to the Friends.

The first Quaker missionaries to arrive in America in 1652 were Elizabeth Harris and her followers, who came from England. Since the Quakers were pacifists, the Puritan colonists quickly banished them from Virginia and Massachusetts. They dispersed to outlying areas and gained a foothold in Rhode Island, the first colony to codify freedom of religion into law. William Penn founded the first Quaker colony in 1681 in Pennsylvania, where thousands of Friends migrated prior to his death in 1718. Unlike the early colonists, the Quakers maintained good relations with the Native American populations. These relationships, along with the fact that they spoke out against slavery, caused great dissension with their neighbors. From 1758 to 1784, at every documented meeting of the Friends they voted to ban slavery. Standing apart from the culture at large, America's first liberals fought for basic human rights and the equality of women.

Quaker Susan B. Anthony co-founded the National Women's Suffrage Association in 1869, which led to the passage of the Nineteenth Amendment in 1920, giving women the right to vote. Her work, like that of the Friends who followed, has been at the forefront of antiwar demonstrations beginning with World War I. They initiated the "conscientious objector" status so that men of conscience were excluded from having to go to war. Their emphasis on pacifism and nonviolence during the civil rights movement became a hallmark of protests led by Dr. Martin Luther King. In 1947, the Friends were awarded the Nobel Peace Prize, and in 1987, they performed this nation's first gay marriage.

An advocate of social justice, Olive Rush began the first Religious Society of Friends in her home on Canyon Road. For many years the sign "Torture Is Wrong" was placed at the entrance to the meeting place, but it has been removed, adhering to the regulations in Santa Fe's historic district. Since her death in 1966, the Quaker heritage that Rush embodied has become an integral part of Santa Fe. Today, the Friends take an active role in local and international social justice initiatives. Both the Canyon Road Meeting House and the South Santa Fe Worship Group on Calle Ensenada contribute to various community programs in the area. They sponsor speaker presentations throughout the year that are open to the community. In addition, they play an active role in immigration issues, support local homeless shelters and provide advocacy and volunteer activities for the state's prison population. As pacifists they are compelled to actively resist taxes, which support the U.S. military budget, and to oppose the development and proliferation of nuclear armaments while protesting the practices of torture and the death penalty.

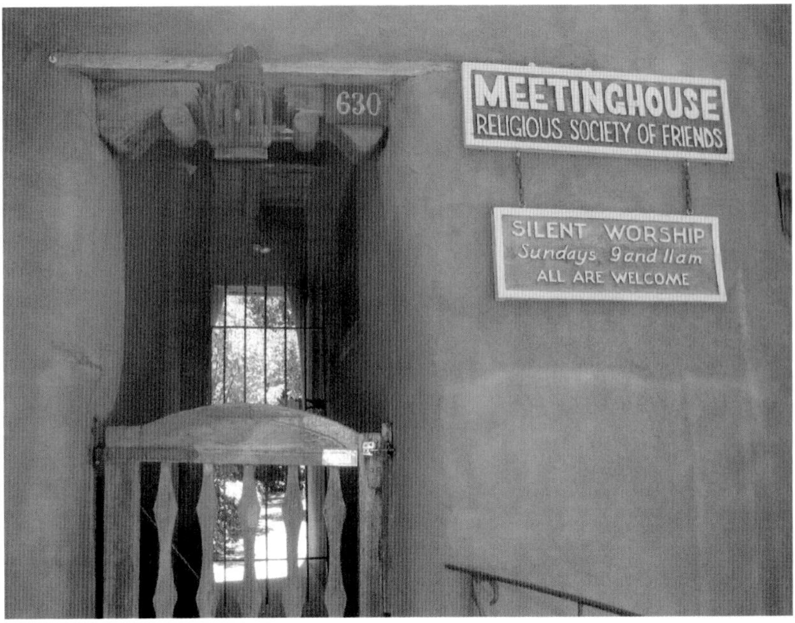

The meetinghouse of the Society of Friends on Canyon Road. *Photo by Ana Pacheco.*

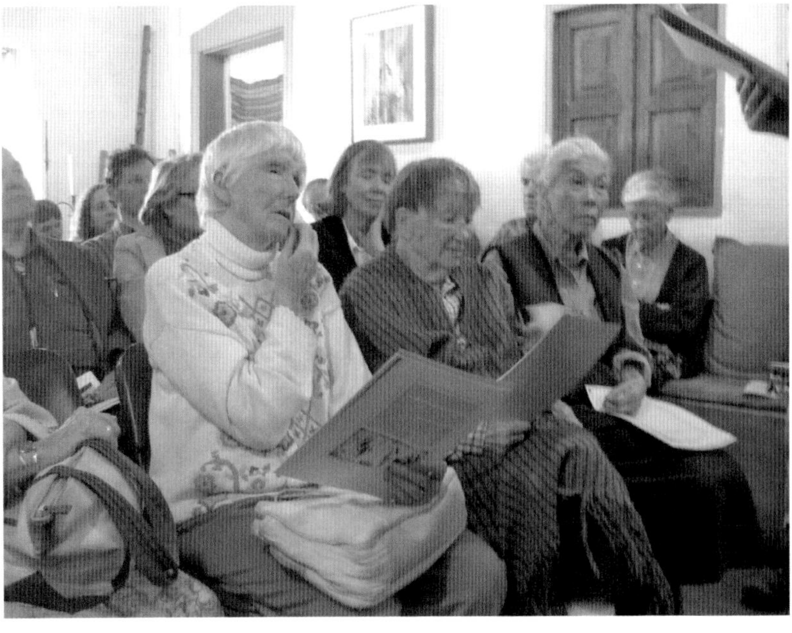

Members at a service of the Society of Friends on Canyon Road. *Courtesy the Society of Friends.*

The Unitarian Universalism congregation in Santa Fe was formed in 1952 when a group of religious liberals from Santa Fe and Los Alamos held their first meeting at the La Fonda Hotel. A representative from the American Unitarian Association in Boston was brought in to advise the group on the steps necessary to form the Santa Fe Fellowship. For the next several years, the group met in rented offices, and in 1968, the members purchased and renovated an old house that became their first church. Ten years later, as their membership grew, they purchased the Mormon Church on Barcelona Street. Since then, they have remodeled and expanded the church.

Unitarian Universalism has an open-minded theology that incorporates democratic ideals and the evolution of science. The church is closely related to the Congregational Church (aka the United Church of Christ) that was formed by Protestant Christians who arrived on the *Mayflower.* Followers of both the Unitarian Universalism tradition and the Congregational–United Church of Christ have been active in the abolition of slavery, environmental education, health reform and many other socially conscious efforts. Above all else, the mandate of both traditions is to share in the journey toward more meaningful lives with all people regardless of religion, race or sexual orientation.

The first recorded work of the Congregational Church (United Church of Christ) in Santa Fe is a letter, dated 1856, that a representative of the "American Missionary Society (AMA)" stationed here wrote to the AMA board in Massachusetts. He wanted their financial support to buy a printing press to produce tracts, simple brochures, for the citizens and U.S. soldiers in northern New Mexico. His focus wasn't salvation but slavery or, more precisely, its abolition. The AMA, founded by the Congregational Church and other Christian denominations, was the country's main antislavery organization. Although the Roman Catholic Church had abolished the practice of slavery centuries before, U.S. Protestant churches throughout the South supported the buying and selling of human lives. Congregational Christians offered a different understanding of the Christian faith. The man, whose name is lost to history, had been sent by the Congregational Church to New Mexico to help make sure the newly acquired U.S. territory remained free.

After the Civil War, the Congregational Church, through the AMA, sent both clergy and laypeople to the South to start churches and schools for the newly freed African Americans. Education had always been a part of Congregationalism, back to the founding of Yale and Harvard, because people were not truly free without education. In the 1870s, the AMA also started both a church and a Congregational college in Santa Fe. The first "University of New Mexico," it was housed in the Victorian-style building that still stands across from the train station. Like Oberlin and other Congregational colleges, the school was coeducational and interracial to serve people often denied access to higher education, including women.

Unfortunately, due to lack of funding, both the Congregational church and college closed by the 1890s. It wasn't until the 1970s that the Congregational tradition, now known as the United Church of Christ, reappeared in Santa Fe. With help from the national denomination, the United Church of Santa Fe was organized by Reverend Martha Baumer. (The UCC was the first Christian denomination to ordain women, starting in 1853.) The small congregation met first in El Gancho restaurant and then at St. Michael's High School before purchasing its current site at the corner of Arroyo Chamiso and St. Michael's Drive, near Christus St. Vincent Hospital.

From the beginning, the church has been true to its heritage of "living its faith in the world." During its first decade, the United congregation helped start the Prison Family Center, Habitat for Humanity, Esperanza Shelter for Battered Families and St. Elizabeth Shelter for the Homeless. That commitment has continued to the present day. United's partnership with Salazar Elementary School, started in 1995, has become the city-wide Communities in Schools. In 1994, the church became the first Christian congregation in Santa Fe to be "open and affirming" of LGBT persons. From the beginning, the congregation has cared for creation, with both sustainable practices and advocacy for environmental issues.

The church is equally committed to being an intergenerational community, with programs for all ages, including a two-year "Rite of Passage to Adulthood" for teens. Similarly, music is a central part of the church's ministry, and on any given Sunday, the congregation sings classical and traditional Anglo-Protestant hymns, African American gospels and spirituals, global music and Spanish songs. Currently, the congregation numbers over four hundred adults, children and youth.

Chapter 7

Seeds of Dharma

On December 7, 1941, the psyche of Americans was forever altered by the Japanese bombing of Pearl Harbor. In response to the affront to our national security, the sleepy artist haven of Santa Fe became a military checkpoint, with hundreds of people passing through town to work on the Manhattan Project. The activity around the creation of the nuclear bomb brought the brightest minds from all over the world. Military personnel and scientists checked in at 109 East Palace Avenue, which was part of a set of offices located on Sena Plaza, named for Bernardino Sena, who arrived in Santa Fe in 1694 and was the progenitor of twenty generations in northern New Mexico with the Sena surname.

After a briefing, the scientists were sent up "the Hill" to Los Alamos, twenty-five miles northwest of Santa Fe. It was a covert community shut off from the rest of the world, where men and women toiled day and night, racing against the clock in their effort to bring an end to the war. Back in Santa Fe, Japanese American prisoners began to arrive. These people, who were considered of foreign enemy ancestry, were forcibly removed from other parts of the country, mostly the West Coast. Their arrival in Santa Fe was brought about through an executive order signed in 1942 by President Franklin D. Roosevelt. The Department of Justice purchased the Civilian Conservation Corps (CCC) camp that was previously used as part of FDR's plan to rejuvenate the economy, providing jobs for young men all over the country who came to be known as Roosevelt's "Tree Army." They built cabins at Hyde Memorial State Park in the Sangre

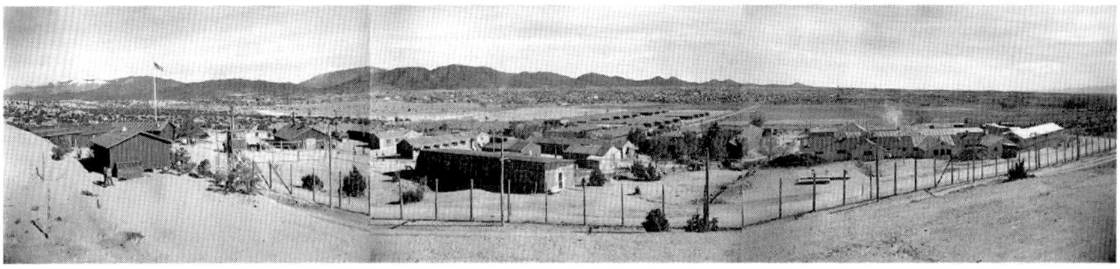

The Japanese internment camp in Santa Fe in 1942. *Courtesy manymountains.org.*

de Cristo Mountains northeast of Santa Fe, as well as the National Park Service building on the Old Santa Fe Trail. The newly transformed CCC camp became the Japanese internment camp, one of several opened throughout the country in areas considered to be of military importance to the safety of all Americans.

Within weeks, more than four thousand men were imprisoned at the camp. These so-called enemy combatants were teachers, journalists, businessmen and artists—the type of people the American government felt posed a threat because they were free thinkers. They were forced to leave their families, businesses and all ties to their communities. Along with these erudite prisoners were Buddhist "ministers" (teachers) who withstood the camp's privations through the teachings of dharma. This manifestation of spiritual awakening, alleviating the universal human experience of suffering, was taught by the Buddha twenty-five centuries ago. Through the enlightenment of dharma, the detainees sought patience, and it provided them the solace needed to abide such dire conditions. It was during this dark time in U.S. history, as we fought the country of the Rising Sun, that the seeds of Buddhism were planted in Santa Fe, although it would be another three decades before Buddhism took root. And just as the prisoners of the World War II Japanese internment camp endured oppression, this spiritual movement was born out of oppression.

In 1950, the People's Republic of China invaded Tibet, and by 1959, it had taken control of the country, ousting the Dalai Lama, who fled with 80 of his close followers to India. More than 87,000 Tibetans were killed and another 100,000 fled to India, Nepal and Bhutan. While taking control of the country, the new government imposed Chinese law and custom in the region, and all the Buddhist monasteries were closed. By 1962, 340,000 Tibetans had died during famines caused by the repression of the totalitarian regime. For the next twenty-five years, the people of Tibet lived under virtual martial law. It wasn't long afterward that the rest of the world began to take notice. Through the ongoing efforts of His Holiness

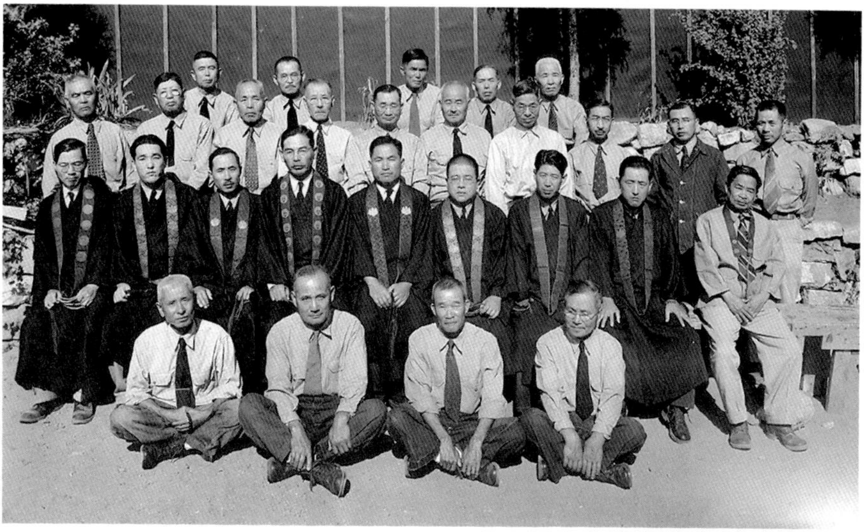

Buddhist "ministers" (teachers) in 1942 at the Japanese internment camp in Santa Fe. *Courtesy manymountains.org.*

the Dalai Lama, many Tibetans have been allowed to leave their beloved homeland in search of a better life.

Santa Fe's Project Tibet was founded in 1980 by Paljor Thondup, who fled eastern Tibet in 1959 at the age of twelve. After living in India and England, he received a scholarship to attend the College of Santa Fe. Thondup began the organization by opening an importing company that sold Tibetan weavings and rugs. Through the business, he was able to support fellow refugees in the United States and abroad while promoting Tibetan culture and preserving Mahayana Buddhism. On September 2, 1997, the Tibetan Association of Santa Fe was founded by a new wave of Tibetans who were part of an international diaspora, aided by the Immigration Act of 1990, which was designed by Congress to address the ongoing plight of the people of Tibet. In 1992, twenty-five refugees arrived in Santa Fe and were hosted by local families. Their community quickly grew as family members joined them. These Tibetans felt a profound obligation to keep their language, culture and religion alive. In 2002, the Phende Rigzod Khan Center on Hickox Street was opened by His Holiness the Dalai Lama. The center serves Santa Fe's Tibetan community and is the basis for the growth of the Mahayana tradition of Buddhism. Santa Fe is home to the four major lineages of this tradition: Nyingma on Alta Vista Street, Kagyu on Airport Road, Sakya on Upper Canyon Road and Gelug on Second Street.

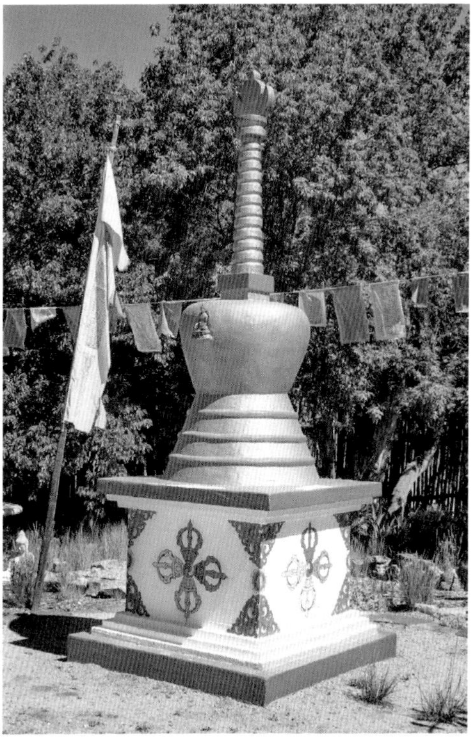

Left: The stupa at Project Tibet. *Photo by Lisa Law.*

Below: The Tibetan monks of the Drepung Loseling Monastery in India created a sand mandala at Seret and Sons in Santa Fe in the spring of 2015. During this ceremony, they disassemble the mandala to show the impermanence of things in this world. *Photo by by Lisa Law.*

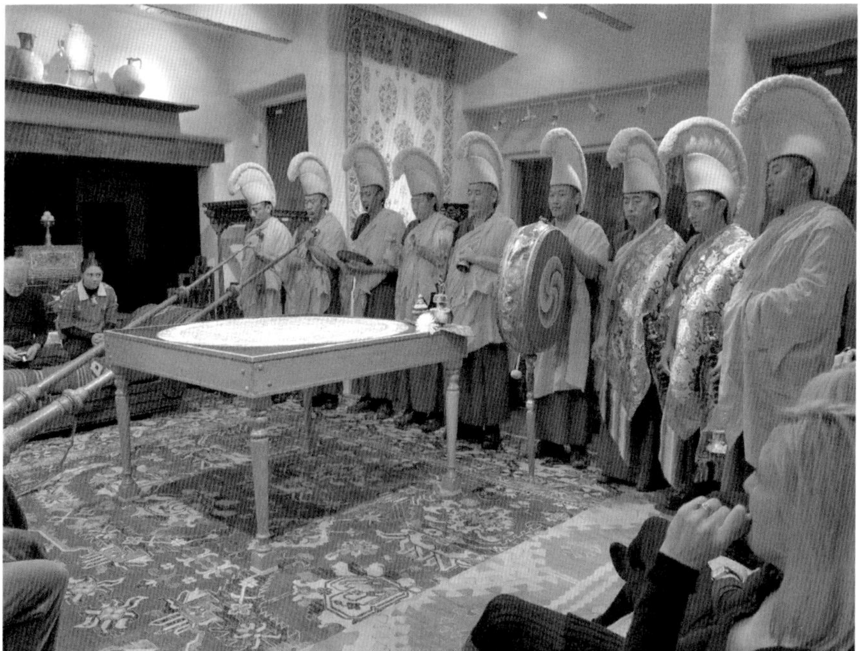

The Maha Bodhi Stupa, the first of its kind in the United States, was erected in 1973 on Cerro Gordo Road. The history of the sacred art contained in a *stupa* began in India during the fourth century. Stupas are believed to embody the living presence of an enlightened mind and to give the protection that comes from the wisdom and compassion taught by the Buddha. Under the inspiration of His Holiness Dudjom Rinpoche, the supreme lama of the Nyingma lineage of Tibetan Buddhism, the stupa was consecrated on the new moon in October 1973 as a Mahayana stupa for the welfare and happiness of its followers. In 1974, it was blessed by Chogyam Trungpa Rinpoche of the Kagyu lineage, and later a courtyard and *gompa* (temple) were built around the stupa, which today continues to be used as a retreat. Now known as the Cerro Gordo Temple, it's located in the hills north of Santa Fe. Throughout its history, it has been utilized by Zen, Vipassana and Vajrayana Buddhists groups, and it is an ongoing temple for dharma activities.

The Kagyu Shenpen Kunchab (KSK) Center was founded under the auspices of His Eminence Kyabje Kalu Rinpoche and a group of students in 1975. In 1981, they welcomed a resident teacher, the Venerable Lama

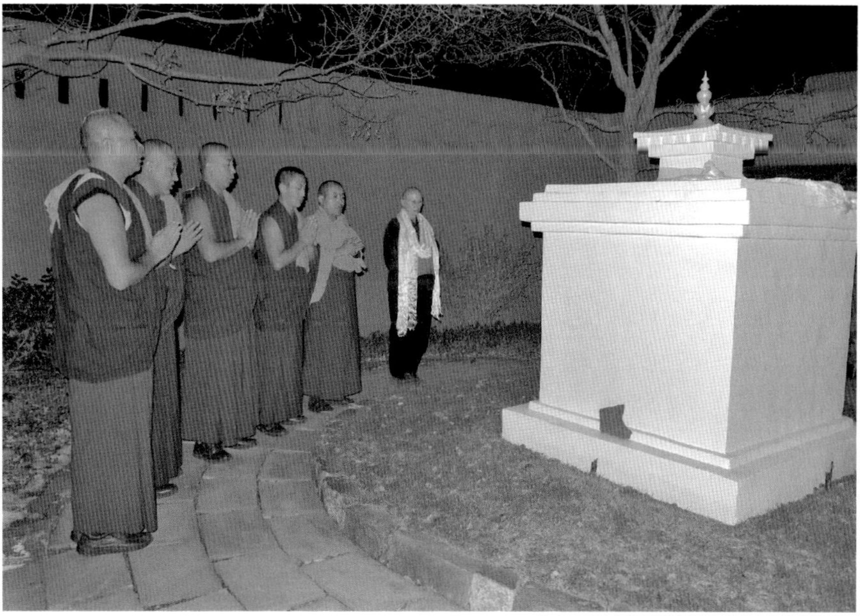

Erected in 1973, the Maha Bodhi Stupa is one of the oldest Buddhist stupas in North America. Roshi Joan Halifax shows the Tibetan monks of the Drepung Loseling Monastery in India the stupa on Cerro Gordo Road in Santa Fe in the fall of 2014. *Photo by Lisa Law.*

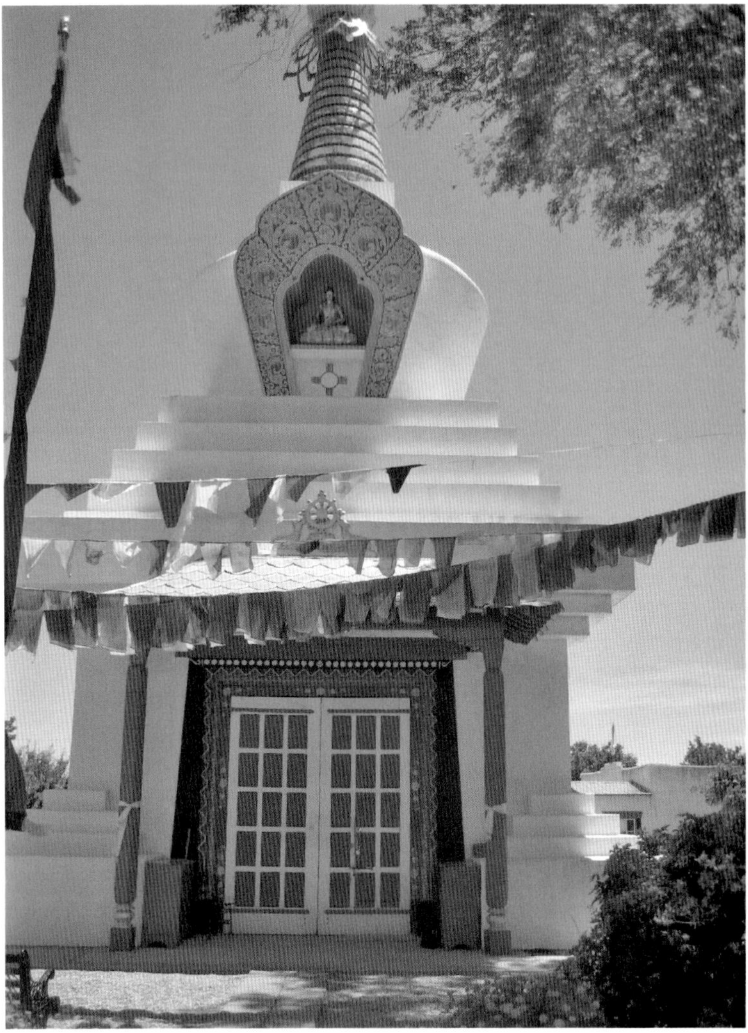

The Bodhi Stupa at the Kagyu Shenpen Kunchab Center on Airport Road is one of the largest stupas in the United States. *Photo by Ana Pacheco.*

Karma Dorje. The following year, construction of the Bodhi Stupa, one of the largest stupas in the United States, began, using a blueprint from India. A crystal that had been recovered from the cremation of Buddha Shakyamuni was placed at the tip of the spire, and the stupa was consecrated on November 14, 1986, by His Eminence Kalu Rinpoche. Since its completion, the stupa has been blessed by masters from all four of the major monastic traditions of Tibetan Buddhism, including His Holiness the Dalai Lama (Gelug), His Eminence Tai

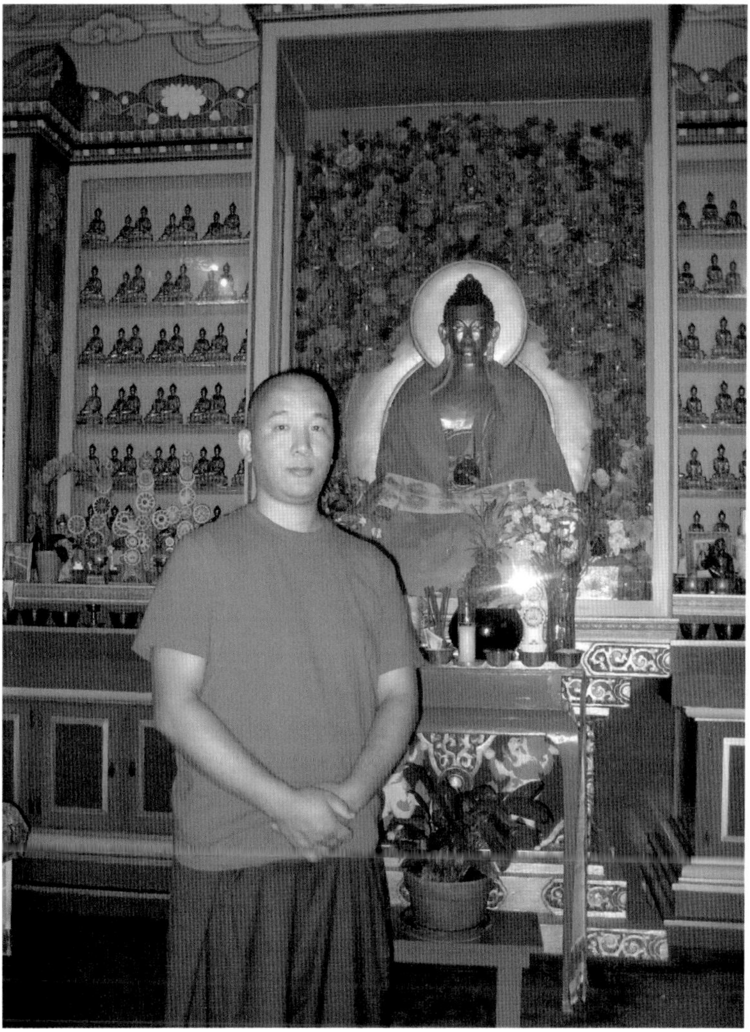

The Venerable Lama Mingma Sherpa in front of the statue of Buddha sculpted by Chagdud Tulku Rinpoche in the KSK stupa. *Photo by Ana Pacheco.*

Situ Rinpoche (Kagyu), V.V. Bokar Rinpoche (Kagyu), Nagpa Yeshe Dorje Rinpoche (Nyingma) and His Holiness Sakya Trizin Rinpoche (Sakya). The large Buddha statue in the shrine was sculpted by Chagdud Tulku Rinpoche. The KSK stupa and *gompa* on Airport Road are sites of worship for many followers and teachers of Tibetan Buddhism.

Geshe Thubten Sherab of the Thubten Norbu Ling Buddhist Center on Second Street began to study as a monk at the age of nine in Manang, a

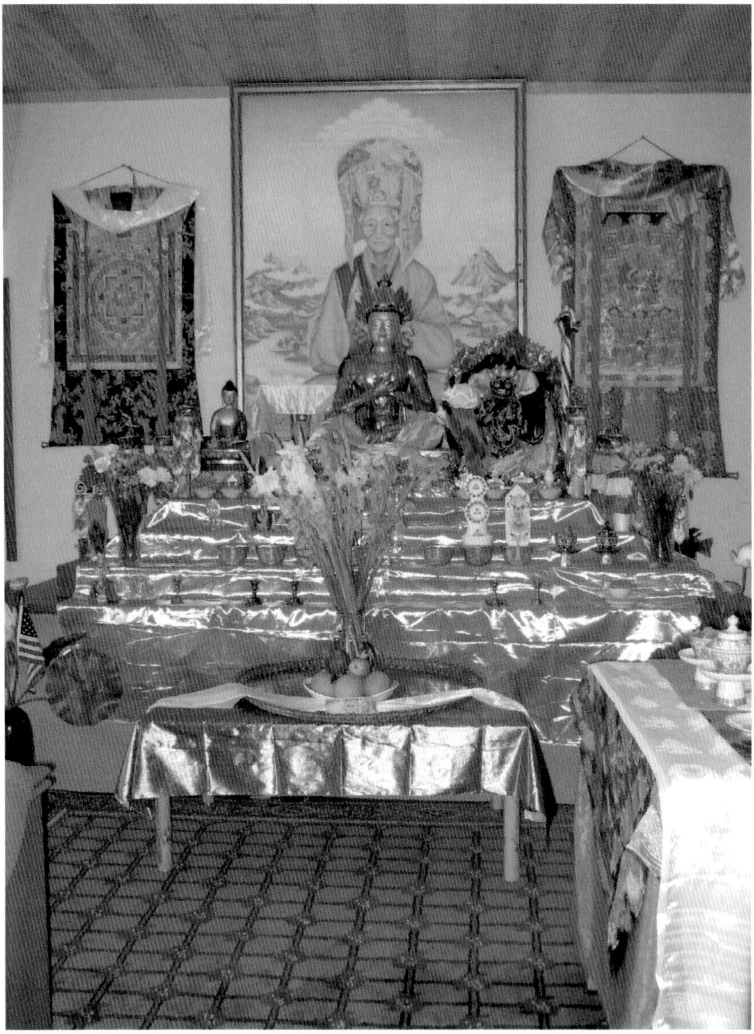

The KSK *gompa* (meditation center) on Airport Road. *Photo by Ana Pacheco.*

mountainous region in western Nepal. After years of studying and contemplation, he was appointed headmaster at the Kopan Monastery in Kathmandu, where he was also the acting abbot for four years. In 2001, he traveled to the Thubten Norbu Ling Center in Taos and to Santa Fe in 2010, where a second temple was built. For six months of the year, he serves as the teacher in residence at the Second Street gompa. Santa Fe has become a home of sorts for Geshe Sherab; as he says:

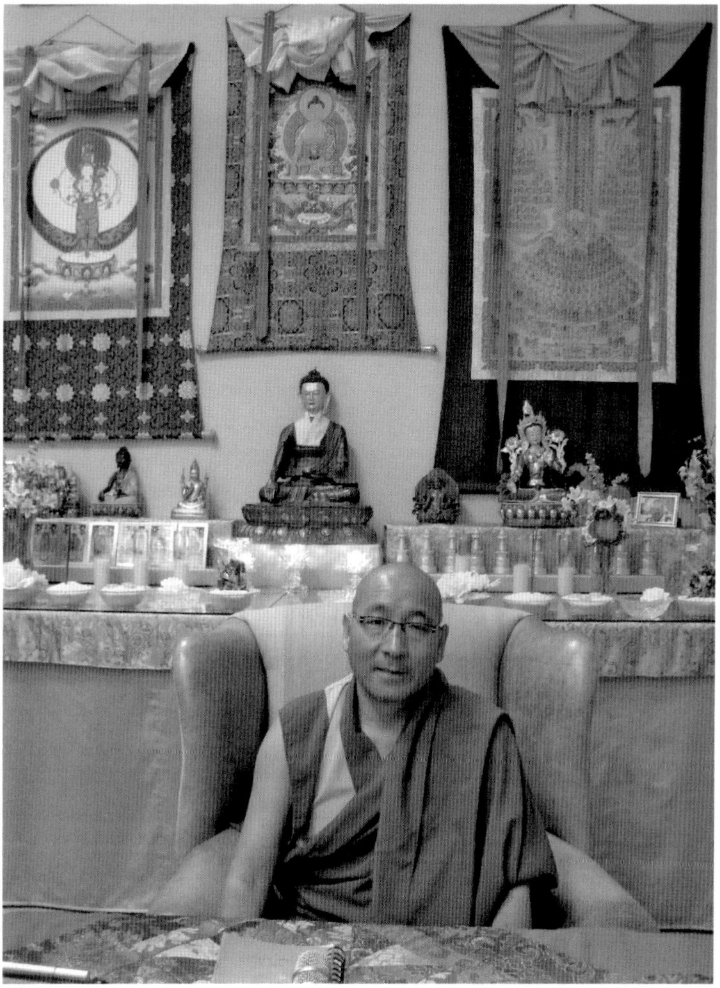

Geshe Thubten Sherab of the Thubten Norbu Ling Buddhist Center on Second Street. *Photo by Ana Pacheco.*

Santa Fe reminds me of Nepal, with the high altitude and mountains. The people are very accepting and spiritually minded; they don't look twice when they see a monk in a robe. They're open to alternative things and there is a strong Christian foundation. It's all very positive energy. In our teachings we include the teachings of Jesus and we have a deep respect for the humanity of Mother Teresa and the Virgin Mary. The prayer of St. Francis of Assisi is featured in the first volume of our book, the Essential Buddhist Prayers and FPMT Prayer Book.

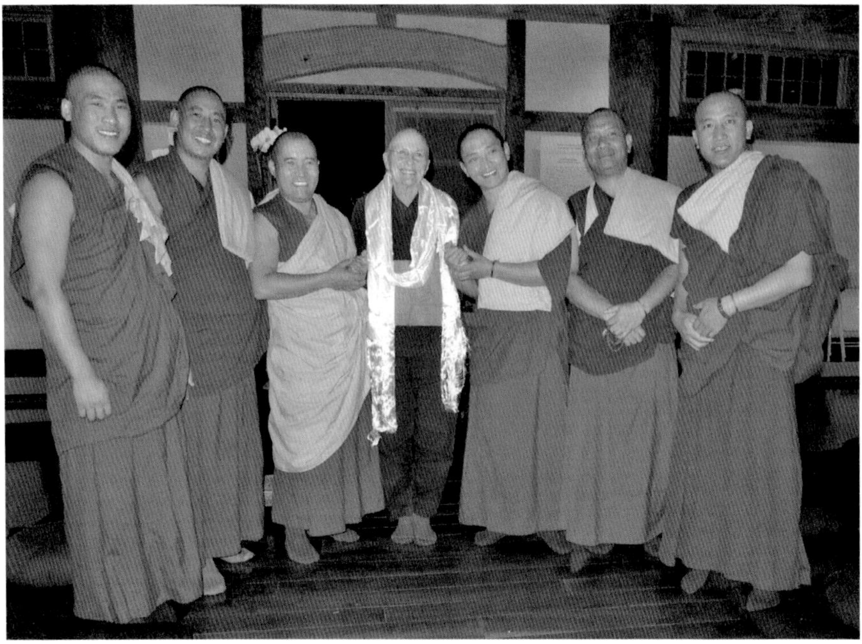

Tibetan monks from the Drepung Loseling Monastery visit Roshi Joan Halifax at the Upaya Zen Center in Santa Fe, New Mexico, in the fall of 2014 while they were creating a Buddha sand mandala at Seret and Sons. *Photo by Lisa Law.*

In 1990, Roshi Joan Halifax founded the Upaya Zen Center on Cerro Gordo, where this nation's first stupa was built. In 2001, she built the Circle of the Way Temple, with Mannenzan Dokanji at the center. The following year, she founded the Prajna Mountain Buddhist Order in the lineage of the Venerable Hakuyo Taizan Maezumi Roshi, Roshi Bernard Glassman's Zen Peacemaker and White Plum Asanga. Although the Tibetan lineages of Buddhism are the major focus of the Buddhism practiced in Santa Fe, Zen Buddhism also flourishes at this vibrant monastery in the hills of Santa Fe's east side. Upaya offers daily Zen meditation, weekly dharma talks, personal retreats, a residency program and special events year round.

Roshi Joan Halifax, who studied for a decade with Zen teacher Seung Sahn and was a teacher in the Kwan Um Zen School, is internationally known for her work on the process of dying. She created the Being With Dying professional training program, which combines science and spirituality to provide clinicians with the essential tools for sustaining their resilience and dedication while caring for the sick and dying.

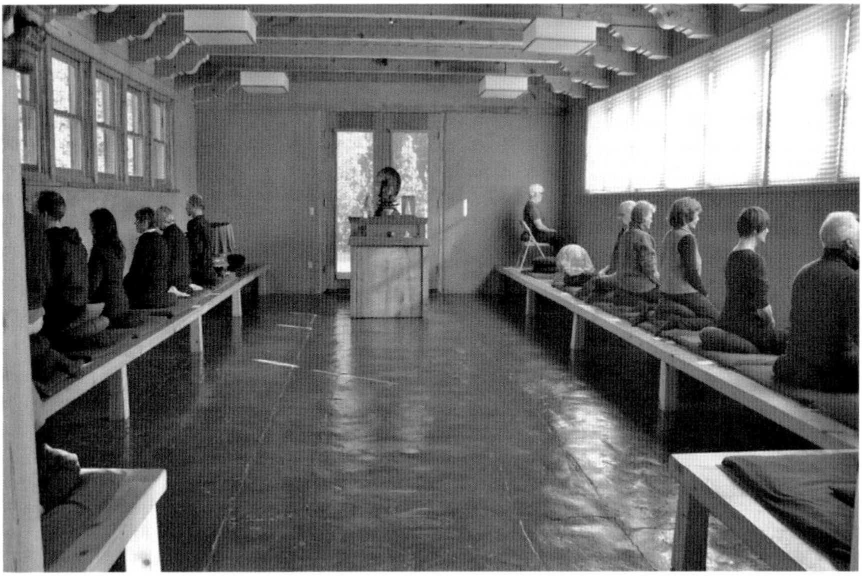

Meditation at the Mountain Zen Center. *Courtesy Mountain Zen Center.*

The Pema Khandro Ling Center, which opened on Luisa Street in Santa Fe in 2008, offers Nyingma, in the tradition of the oldest school of Tibetan Buddhism. Gochen Tulku Sang-ngag Rinpoche is the founder and spiritual leader. He was born into one of the oldest families in Tibet. As a teenager, he was imprisoned for nine years by the Chinese government. After his incarceration, he made it his mission to speak out against oppression throughout Europe and the United States. Gochen is a master stupa builder, and he established the Turquoise Leaf practice center for Tibetan nuns in Nepal. He also built the Garden of One Thousand Buddhas, north of Arlee, Montana. Thousands of people annually flock to this peace garden, which is surrounded by the ongoing construction of the Buddha sculptures. Gochen visits frequently to oversee the project. During the rest of the year, he teaches in Santa Fe and around the country. Like Geshe Sherab of the Thubten Norbu Ling Buddhist Center, he is reminded of his native Tibet by Santa Fe and has chosen the city as his permanent home.

Other Buddhist centers in Santa Fe include the Mountain Cloud Zen Center, Diamond Way and the Santa Fe Vipassana Sangha.

Chapter 8

Freedom of Religion

In 1946, when the prisoners of the Japanese internment camp had been freed, the First Amendment's right to practice freedom of religion also became a part of Santa Fe history. That year, in a stunning victory, the Supreme Court rendered a 5–4 landmark decision in the *United States v. Ballard*, which exonerated the I AM faith for practicing its beliefs. Like the Japanese American citizens who were unwillingly brought to Santa Fe in 1942, the founders of I AM had also moved to town that year, and they, too, were persecuted for being different.

During World War II, paranoia was entrenched throughout the country, and the government kept a close eye on several far-right sects that had sprouted on the West Coast. So it's no wonder that the followers of I AM came under scrutiny. Their beliefs stemmed in part from theosophy, a movement that was started in the United States in 1875 by Helena Blavatsky, which includes mysticism and reincarnation as part of its foundation. They're also considered one of the first New Age religions, with the use of colors and light embedded in the foundation of their practices.

In 1930, Guy Ballard, an engineer from Chicago, had a vision of St. Germain while hiking on Mount Shasta in California. This ethereal figure surrounded by light provided revelations to Ballard that had been kept secret for many centuries. The teachings of St. Germain became the basis of the I AM doctrine.

Count St. Germain was an eighteenth-century European courtier, diplomat, philosopher and musician who dabbled in mysticism. He was a

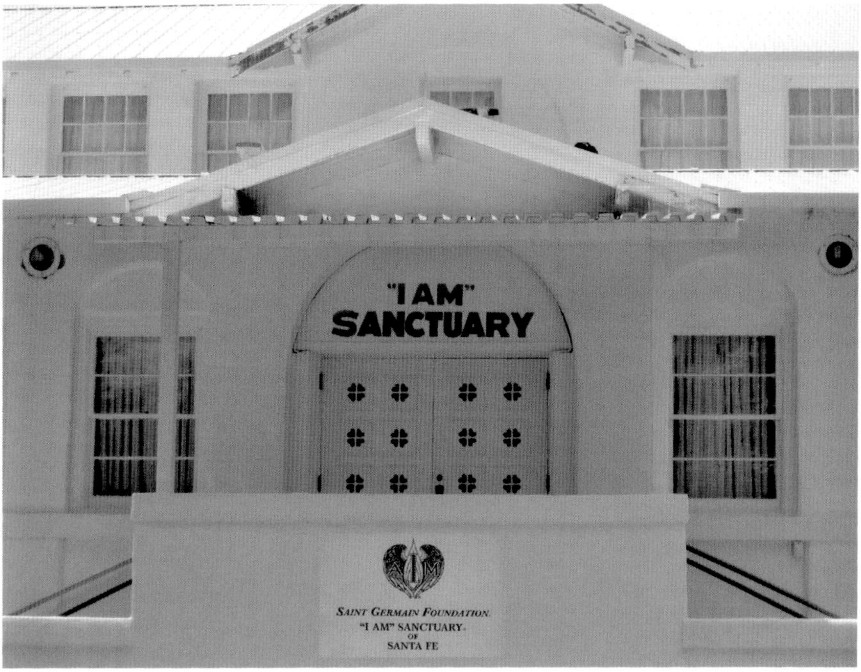

The St. Germain I AM sanctuary on Old Taos Highway. *Photo by Ana Pacheco.*

popular figure during the nineteenth century, and he spoke many languages and traveled among the European elite. His persona caught the attention of early Theosophists, and his legacy is incorporated in other spiritual groups.

After his first encounter with St. Germain, Guy Ballard and his wife, Edna, embarked on spreading this newly shared doctrine from Mount Shasta. They held lectures and classes and began the St. Germain Press, publishing books and articles on the tenets of I AM. These included the premise of I AM, which is that God is found within each individual. In the book *The Magic Presence*, written by Ballard under the pen name of Godfré Ray King, he stated, "The purpose of this book is to reveal to the individual the whereabouts of his own Divine Self—God, the Mighty 'I AM' presence, that all who desire may return to their Source, receive their Eternal Inheritance, and feel once again the Divine Self."

The Circles of Color have a meaningful role in I AM beliefs. Through the different rays of color surrounding an individual, the accumulated good of all previous embodiments from previous lives is discovered. The Violet Consuming Flame can help believers rid themselves of discord and imperfection, so I AM followers are frequently garbed in shades of purple.

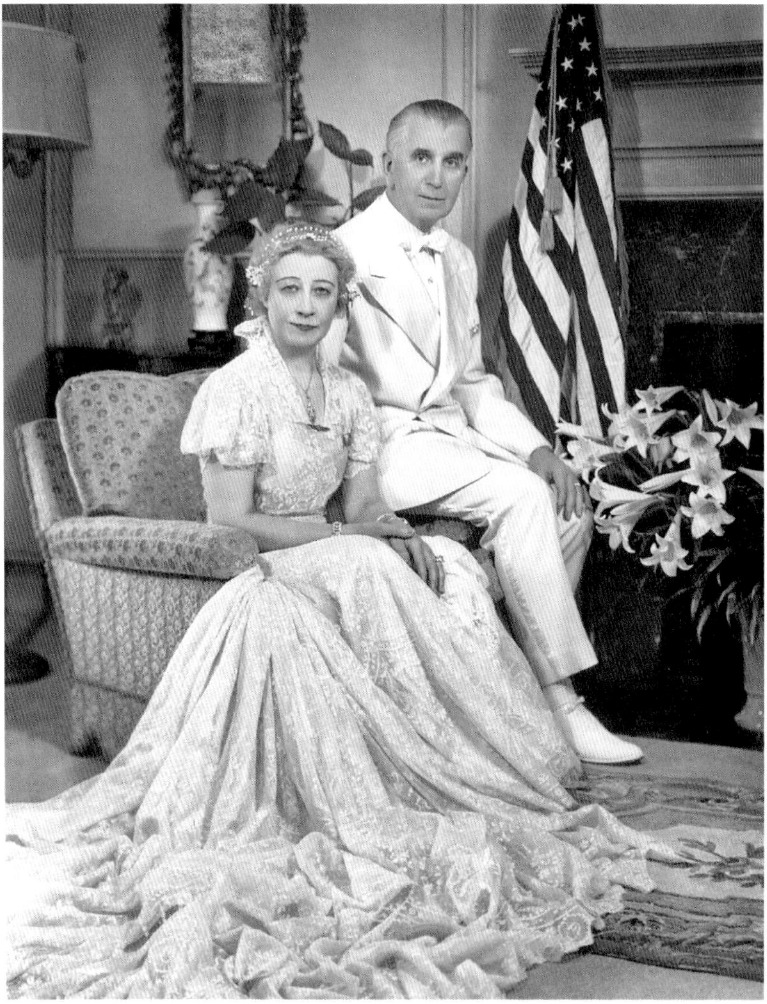

A 1930s photo of Guy and Edna Ballard in Chicago. *Courtesy St. Germain Foundation.*

Re-embodiment is another important tenet of I AM. There are many ascended masters in their beliefs, including St. Germain, Jesus, Guy Ballard (known as Beloved Godfré), Edna Ballard (known as Beloved Lotus), Beloved Mary, Archangel Michael, the Great Divine Director, Beloved Cyclopea, Beloved Goddess of Light, Beloved Rose of Light, Lord Maha Chohan and Beloved Victory.

Guy Ballard was born in 1878 and became one of the ascended masters of the Great White Brotherhood after leaving this world. His previous embodiments have included George Washington, the first president of the United States; King Richard I of England (Richard the Lionheart), 1157–1199; and the Roman centurion Aemilius, who witnessed the crucifixion of Jesus Christ. He later became the governor of the Island of Britain with Adina, who also witnessed the crucifixion. They also had been the son and daughter of the great king St. Germain, who ruled civilization seventy thousand years ago in what is now the Sahara Desert.

Edna Ballard was born in 1886 and became a messenger for St. Germain and the ascended masters of the Great White Brotherhood. Her previous

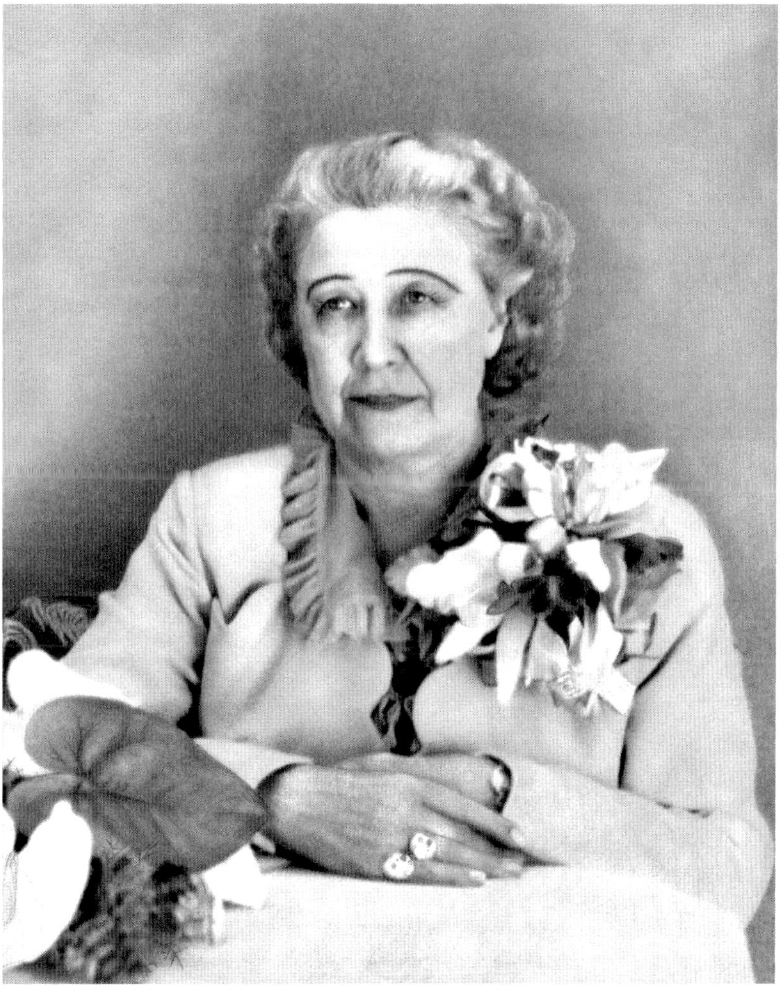

Edna Ballard wearing a violet suit in the 1940s in Santa Fe. *Courtesy St. Germain Foundation.*

embodiments were Joan of Arc from 1412 to 1431, who as a girl led the French army; Benjamin Franklin, one of the founding fathers of our nation; and Adina of the Island of Britain. She attained the Victory of the Ascension on February 12, 1971; Guy Ballard ascended in 1939. The Ballards ascended as the Twin Rays when they passed on, he as the Ascended Master Godfré and she as the Ascended Lady Master Lotus.

After Guy Ballard's encounter with St. Germain, he and Edna set off on an ambitious course, spreading the word of the ascended masters in Chicago during the 1930s. Through public appearances and lectures, which included a great deal of patriotism, they attracted many followers. America was headed into World War II, so their message resonated with the public.

The couple also began the St. Germain Press, with several thousand discourses dictated to Guy Ballard by St. Germain. These discourses, disseminated through the U.S. mail, are what caused the U.S. government to revoke the movement's tax-exempt status in 1941, stating that it did not recognize the movement as a bona fide religion. The group had been charged with eighteen counts of mail fraud for sending information on its spiritual practices through the mail. This accusation became an exercise in testing our Constitution's Bill of Rights and the freedom of religion. The presiding judge instructed the jury not to judge the validity of I AM beliefs but, rather, to respect others and their choice of worship and spirituality. The conviction was overturned in 1946, but it wasn't until 1957 that their right to use the mail to carry their message was restored.

Guy Ballard died in 1939, and Edna Ballard and her son, Donald, moved to Santa Fe in 1942. They began the I AM Sanctuary on the Old Taos Highway in the building formerly used by the Presbyterian Mary James Missionary Boarding School for Boys. During that time, with both the Manhattan Project and the Japanese internment camp in town, their presence didn't go unnoticed, but as always, Santa Fe's "live and let live attitude" prevailed and allowed the group to worship in peace and privacy.

Within a few years, I AM had four hundred members in Santa Fe, among them new converts and people who had followed them to live in town. Edna Ballard passed on in 1971, but Santa Fe's I AM Sanctuary continues with a smaller congregation. There are I AM temples and sanctuaries all over the world. The St. Germain Foundation Worldwide Headquarters is in Schaumburg, Illinois. It maintains an I AM Temple in downtown Chicago. Since 1950, the group has held annual conclaves at its Mount Shasta location, where it sponsors the I AM COME! Pageant on the life of the Beloved Jesus Christ, which is open to the public.

Chapter 9

The Age of Aquarius

A change in the celestial constellation brought the fifth-largest religion in the world to Santa Fe. In astrology, the transition of the earth moves approximately every 2,150 years. Though accounts differ as to when our planet moved out of the Piscean age, the hippie movement in the late 1960s is credited with ringing in the Age of Aquarius. It was an era of transition filled with global turmoil combined with the proliferation of efforts in self-discovery. Yogi Bhajan, the leader of Sikh Dharma International, recognized that the higher consciousness that the hippies were trying to reach through drugs could be achieved by practicing Kundalini yoga. In teaching this practice during that anxiety-ridden era, he also introduced Sikhism to the western hemisphere.

In 1968, Lisa Law, the American photographer best known for documenting the history of the counterculture of the 1960s, attended Yogi Bhajan's yoga classes at the East West Cultural Center in Los Angeles along with her husband, Tom, and a group of friends. They became smitten with the yogi and helped him move into his new ashram in Hollywood on the corner of Melrose and Robertson at Jules Buccieri's furniture store. Buccieri and the singer-songwriter Johnny Rivers sponsored his trip to the United States from Canada, where he was teaching yoga at the University of Toronto. The group invited the yogi to come teach in Santa Fe at the 1969 Summer Solstice celebration at Aspen Meadows in Tesuque, six miles north of Santa Fe. Dawson Hayward, who had already been exposed to Yogi Ji's teachings, was one of the participants in the gathering. He then offered his

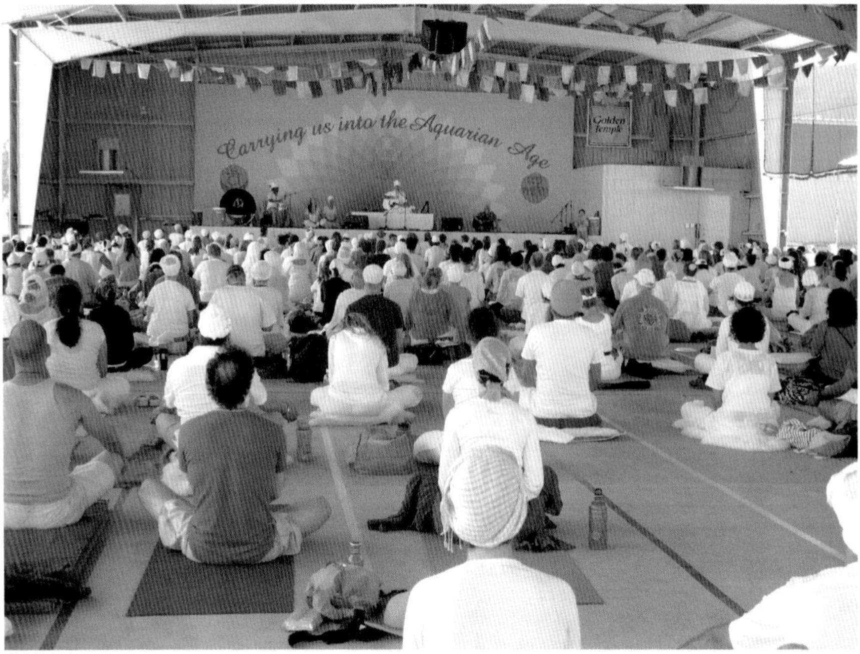

A Sikh summer solstice celebration at Guru Ram Das Puri site in Española, New Mexico. *Photo by Lisa Law.*

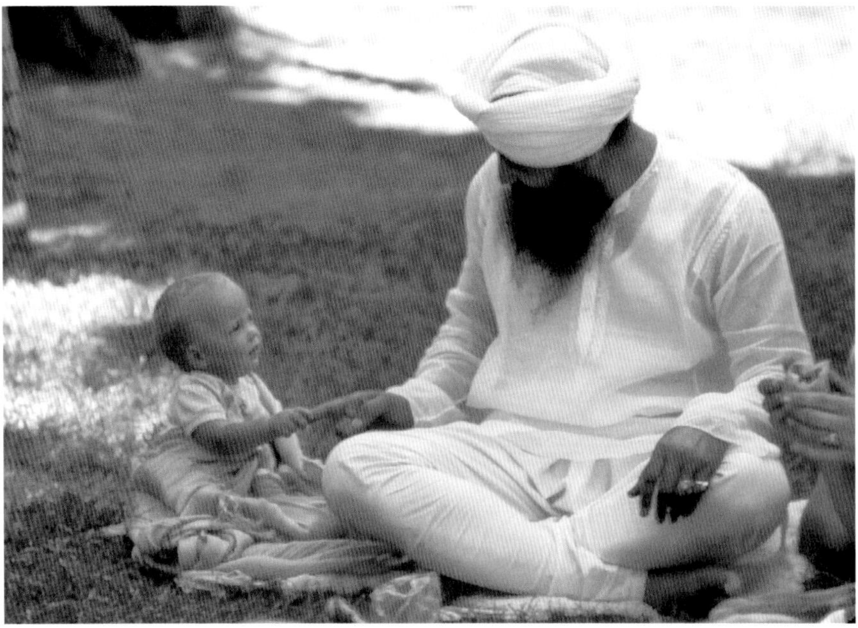

A toddler communicating with Yogi Bhajan at the Holy Man celebration at the University of Colorado in Boulder, July 1970. *Photo by Lisa Law.*

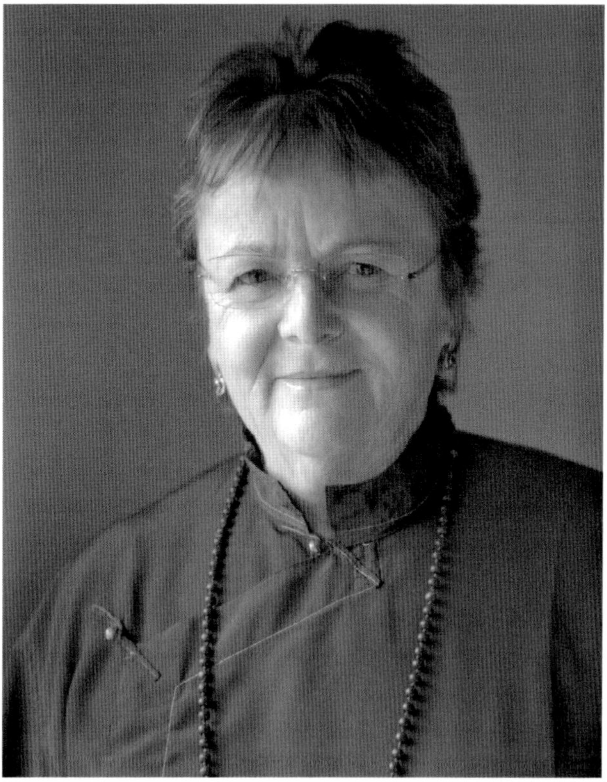

Right: The photographer and historian Lisa Law. *Photo by Pilar Law.*

Below: Yogi Bhajan teaching Kundalini yoga in 1969 at the Hog Farm and Friends Summer Solstice celebration in Aspen Meadows, Tesuque, New Mexico. *Photo by Lisa Law.*

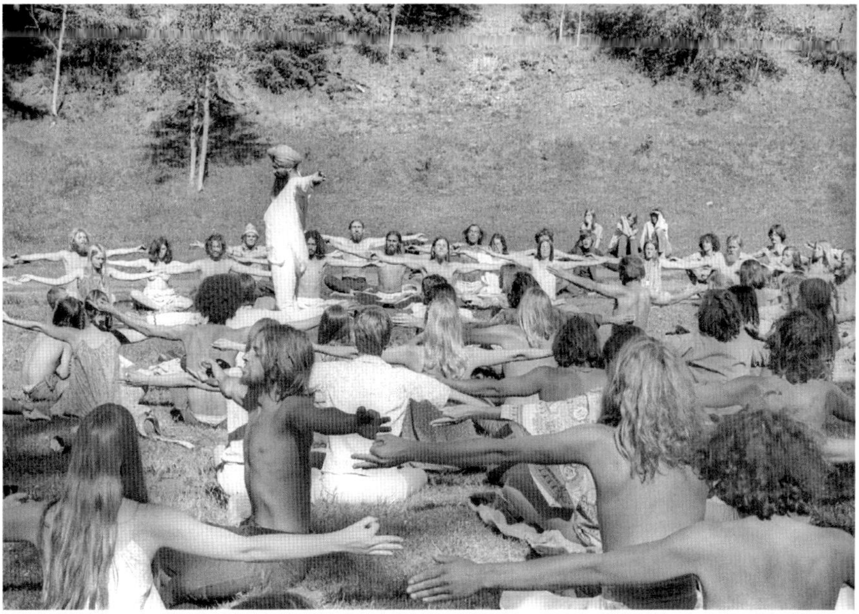

twelve-acre piece of land as an ashram for the yoga teachings in Santa Fe. Within a year, yoga was being taught by newly trained teachers to a small group of inspired students. Yogi Bhajan would frequently fly out to Santa Fe to teach; he fell in love with New Mexico and decided to make it his home. He moved to Española in Santa Fe County, where the ashram spiritual center and Sikh Dharma International are located today.

Yogi Bhajan's birth name was Siri Singh Sahib Bhai Sahib Harbhajan Singh Khalsa Yogi Ji. He was born on August 26, 1929, to a wealthy Sikh family in Kot Harkarn, Gujranwala District, in the province of Punjab now known as Pakistan. His father, Dr. Kartar Singh Puri, was a medical doctor in the area who also served as the doctor at the Sacred Heart Catholic School run by nuns in the village of Dalhousi, where Yogi Bhajan received his early education. His wife, Dr. Bibiji Inderjit Kaur, remembered a story told to her by her husband during his days at the Catholic school. "The Mother Superior of the school was very fond of him, and sometimes even changed the rules for him," she recounts. "On one occasion he was brought before the Mother Superior for punishment because he had failed to come to chapel when he heard the bell ring. Mother Superior asked him what he was doing, and the young Harbhajan said he was meditating on the beach. He then told her that when he heard the bell ringing, it was so beautiful it caused him to meditate deeply on the Divine. He said, 'Mother, if you do not want us to meditate, then please do not ring that bell.'"

While young Harbhajan Singh received his academic education and studied Christian philosophy from the nuns, he was simultaneously educated in Sikh teachings at home, primarily by his paternal grandfather, Bhai Fateh Singh, and other Sikh tutors and family members. When he was just eight years old, Harbhajan Singh began his yogic training with a teacher known as Sant HazaraSingh, who proclaimed him to be a master of Kundalini yoga when he was sixteen.

The British occupation of India ended in 1947, and a partition was declared establishing Pakistan as a Muslim state, dividing the Punjab culture of the country. With the country split in two, Pakistan to the north and India to the south, millions of people were displaced. Harbhajan Singh's education was interrupted, and at age eighteen he assumed the responsibility of leading his village of seven thousand people 325 miles on foot to their new home in the city of Amritsar, the home of the Golden Temple. From that time forward it has become "the home in the heart" of every Sikh. Considered by Sikhs to be the holiest place on earth, it is a temple made half of marble and half of gold, sitting in the middle of a sacred pond that has been revered from time immemorial for its mystical healing properties. Prayer and chanting of God's name continue at the Golden Temple day and night. There, as in all Sikh *gurdwaras*, or temples, Sikhs work together to ensure that everyone—regardless of race or faith or any earthly distinction—is given food in the free community kitchen. It is there that millions of Sikhs come to be healed and refreshed from their wearying travels so that they can begin their lives anew.

After graduating from college with a degree in economics, Singh began his government service with India's Internal Revenue Department.

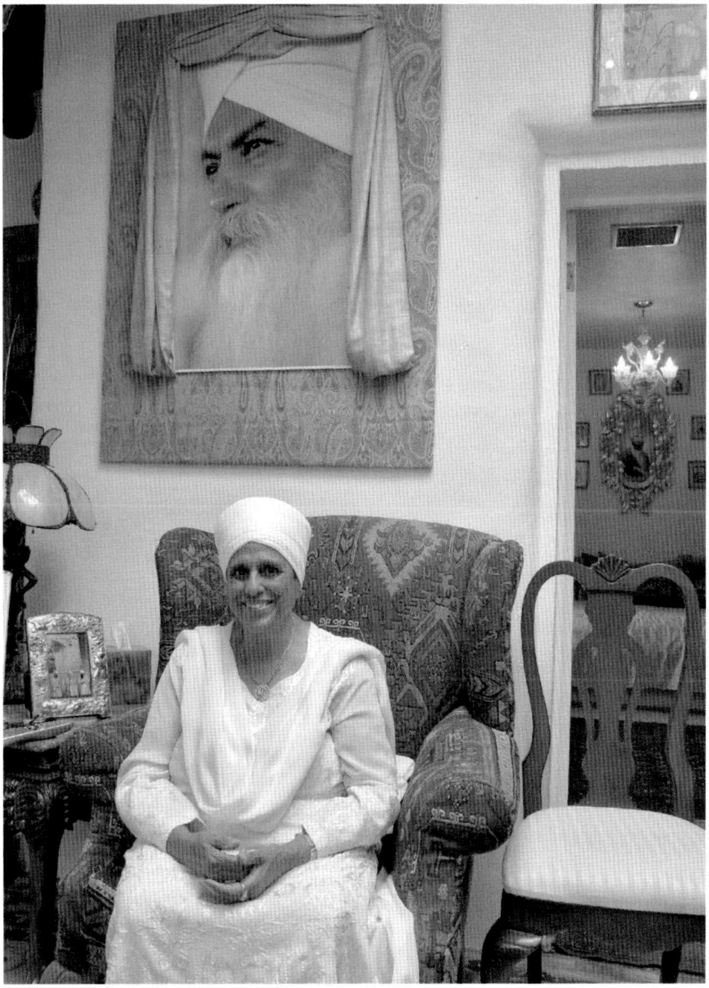

Dr. Bibiji Inderjit Kaur, the widow of Yogi Bhajan, at Yogiji's Guru Ram Das's ashram ranch in Española, New Mexico. *Photo by Lisa Law.*

Shortly thereafter, he moved to the Customs Service and became head of customs at Palam International Airport, now known as New Delhi's Indira Gandhi Airport.

In 1952, he married Bibiji in accordance with family and Sikh tradition. The couple had three children: two sons, Ranbir and Kulbir Singh, and a daughter, Kamaljit Kaur. His wife now serves as the *bhai sahiba* (owner) of Sikh Dharma International.

Bibiji remembers the early days of their marriage:

> *That's when my husband began his highest spiritual education as he washed the floors of the Golden Temple each morning, beginning at 1:00 a.m. We rode to the temple together on our motorbike for four years. During that time he told me that it was only by washing the sacred floors of the Golden Temple that he received the true understanding of the power of spiritual grace. He learned that only through humility will the guru's grace truly manifest in our lives on earth.*

Siri Singh Sahib Bhai Sahib Harbhajan Singh Khalsa Yogi Ji (Yogi Bhajan) became an American citizen in 1976. Under his guidance, the Sikh community in northern New Mexico grew, attracting people from all over the world. In 1971, Sikh Dharma was officially acknowledged as a religion in the United States. In recognition of his work in spreading the universal message of Sikhism, he was named the siri singh sahib, chief religious and administrative authority, for the western hemisphere. As he traveled the world spreading Sikh Dharma, he caught the attention of many world and spiritual leaders, including Pope Paul VI, Pope John Paul II and His Holiness the Dalai Lama. Sikhi, popularly known as Sikhism, began in the sixteenth century in Punjab. Sikhi comes from the word *sikh*, meaning disciple or learner. The founder of Sikhism was Guru Nanak, who shared his message of integration and universalism and traveled to Bengal and Assam during the first half of the sixteenth century. He continued on his mission to Ceylon, Kashmir, Ladakh and Tibet. As he grew older, his two sons, Sri Chand and Lakshmi Das, carried on his work.

An interesting aspect of the belief of Sikhism and its integration in the West is highlighted on the wall of the Gurdwara at the Hacienda de Guru Ram Das (ashram) at the Sikh Dharma community in Española. The following narrative on Our Lady of Guadalupe was documented by the Marian scholar Jacqueline Dunnington:

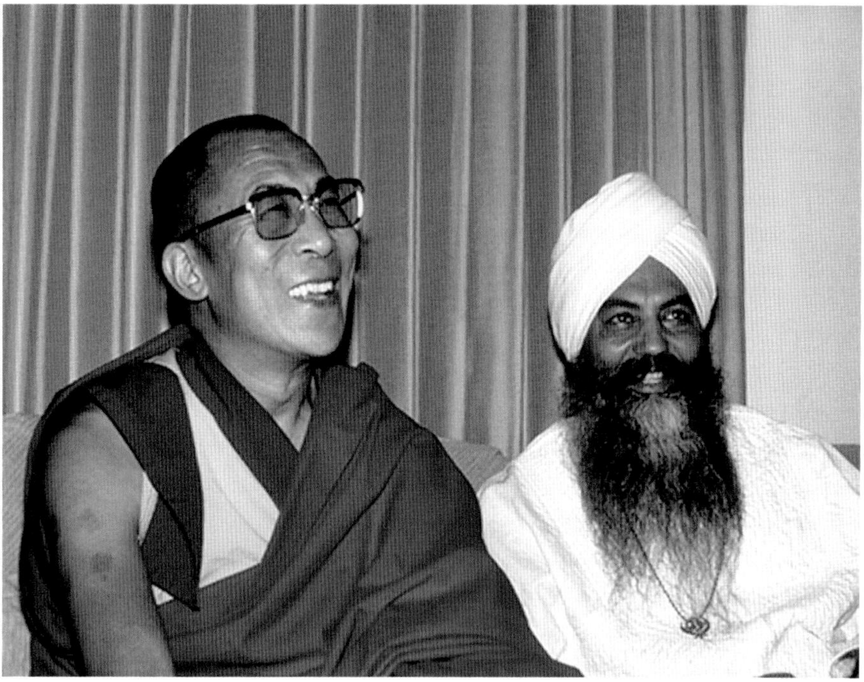

Yogi Bhajan with His Holiness the Dalai Lama. *Courtesy Sikh Dharma International.*

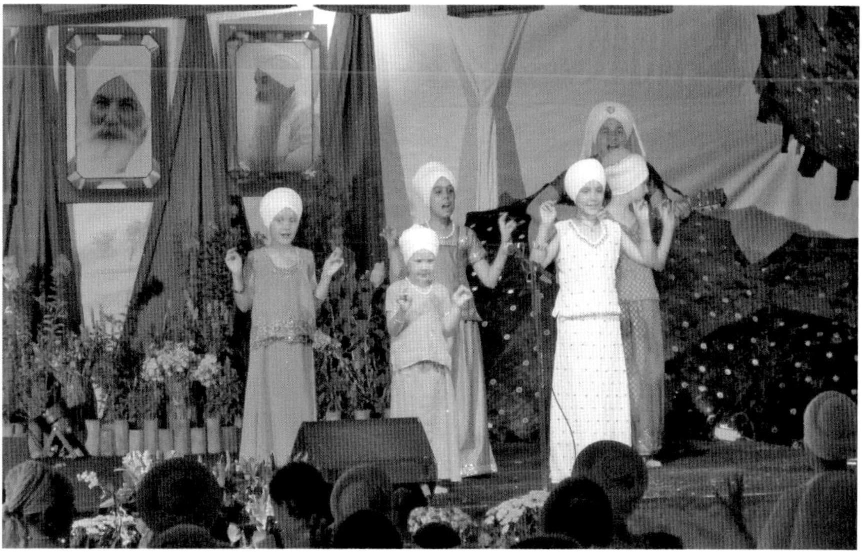

A group of Kalsa children singing and dancing at Yogi Bhajan's guru Ram Das's Ranch House in 2013 in Española, New Mexico. *Photo by Lisa Law.*

In 1973, muralist Edward O'Brien became enthralled with Sikhism and the representation of the feminine principal in Sikh Dharma. He realized that Shakti represented Our Lady of Guadalupe. At the center of the Adi Shakti is the two-edged sword—the feminine principle—surrounded by the circle representing God on either side, as well as spiritual and temporal sovereignty, to be in this world but of the spirit at the same time. So, Our Lady is in the center of the mural as the feminine principle. She stands on the crescent in front of two swords representing Sikhism.

O'Brien was impressed that this universal principle was the same in both the east and west. In his mural, the same concept from both ends of the world become one. On the right side of the mural is the Golden Temple of the Sikh faith of India. On the left side is the Basilica in Mexico. The image of Don Diego's shawl is filtered and projected in the Adi Shakti. On the left is Yogi Bhajan bringing Sikh Dharma to the western hemisphere. On the right is the American Sikh bringing Sikh Dharma to the west. So Adi Shakti, after being blessed by Guadalupe, is being reintroduced into eastern culture.

The twelve astrological symbols frame the mural, showing the all-encompassing effect of the universe and its influence upon man's life. At the top there are four sections showing the universe in creation and repose, and showing life taking form, from the cellular world to the creation of man. Here the universe is seen in macrocosm and microcosm and in the past, present and future, showing God's continuous involvement with creation.

The basic structure of the mural is established by two equilateral triangles forming a six-pointed star, with one triangle rising from the earth toward the heavens, the other bringing energy down to earth. The center depicts the western symbol, Our Lady of Guadalupe, combined with the eastern symbol, the Adi Shakti. This combined symbol represents the Universal Mother for all humanity through the purity and power of the feminine principle. It takes form as it comes from eternity, through the sphere of sound, down through the color spectrum, into physical form. Above her shoulders are two eastern goddesses, Saraswati and Bhagwati, representing the aspects of beauty and balance in the life of a God-conscious being.

On both sides of the Adi Shakti are portraits of the ten Sikh gurus, and to the side of each one is a miniature painting detailing a virtue from a significant event in the life of each guru. The left side of the mural represents the formation of Sikh Dharma in the western hemisphere. Yogi Bhajan is depicted with no pillow of rest behind him, showing the time and work spent in preparing the destiny of this country. His foot rests on the United States, symbolizing his mission of coming to this country to train teachers and inspire many to a new way of life. The right side represents the activity and projection of Khalsa over the next five thousand years. The man represents a Sikh man of the future with attributes of Guru Ram Das. The pillow behind symbolizes the widespread popularity in the east and the prophecy that generations would return to the Indian continent to teach and to prosper for the next five thousand years. Next to this figure is the Golden Temple with its nectar tank in the foreground.

The last scene painted by O'Brien was of the Lady of Guadalupe appearing to Don Diego and telling him of her mission to crush the evil serpent for the misunderstanding and abuse of mankind. Her image is imprinted on his poncho to prove her presence and her intentions to the Catholic Church, and in the painting this is filtered through the Adi Shakti symbol to show the universality of her mission.

On May 1, 1975, one week after he completed the mural, O'Brien died of a heart attack in the ashram. Yogi Bhajan said of O'Brien and his work, "When beyond the faith, in interfaith, God is seen and recognized, that is where man rises above the clouds and sees sunshine. With this Christ consciousness, Ed O'Brien worked with the Sikh Dharma and predicted and

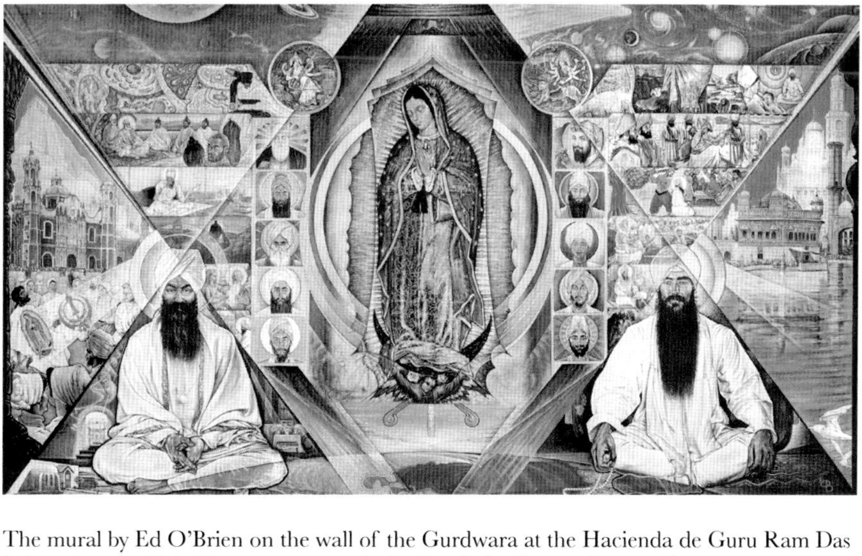

The mural by Ed O'Brien on the wall of the Gurdwara at the Hacienda de Guru Ram Das (ashram) at the Sikh Dharma community in Española. *Courtesy Sunstone Press.*

depicted, through the mural, the future events of the world, through which mankind will be grateful."

Yogi Bhajan died of heart failure at his home in Española on October 6, 2004. His vision to spread Sikhism throughout the western hemisphere flourishes today, with more than two hundred books in print about Sikh Dharma. And Kundalini yoga, which brought the yogi to New Mexico in 1969, continues to provide its followers with a higher state of consciousness in the Age of Aquarius.

Chapter 10

Fellowship in Christ

Santa Fe has a myriad of Christian churches and organizations. One of many such organizations in town, the Barnabas Institute/Center for Christian Community, lists eighty-three active churches, sixteen of which are Spanish-speaking. This chapter is meant to provide a sampling of the diversity within the Christian community. Many of these churches fall into what is called the sister-church category of American-made Christian faiths because their beliefs often overlap. The three main faiths are Pentecostal, Evangelistic and Charismatic. The main tenet for all three is guidance from the Holy Spirit. Pentecostal ideas began to surface in Protestant churches in 1860 in Pennsylvania when Dennis Bennett, an Episcopal priest, announced that he had spoken in tongues. That was the beginning of the Charismatic faith, the fastest-growing segment of Evangelical religion. Believers who have received the blessing of the Holy Spirit can speak in tongues, known as glossolalia, an emotionally charged form of speech that is often unintelligible to the listener.

The Fruit of the Spirit Ministry is one of Santa Fe's Charismatic churches. In addition to its regular services, it holds an annual tent revival at the Rodeo Grounds. The first instances of people motivated by the Holy Spirit to speak in tongues began in the late 1960s and early '70s in Santa Fe, Albuquerque and Las Vegas, New Mexico. The Charismatic movement swept through several Catholic churches and sparked the beginnings and growth of denominational and nondenominational churches, including Capital Christian Church and other ministries still in existence today.

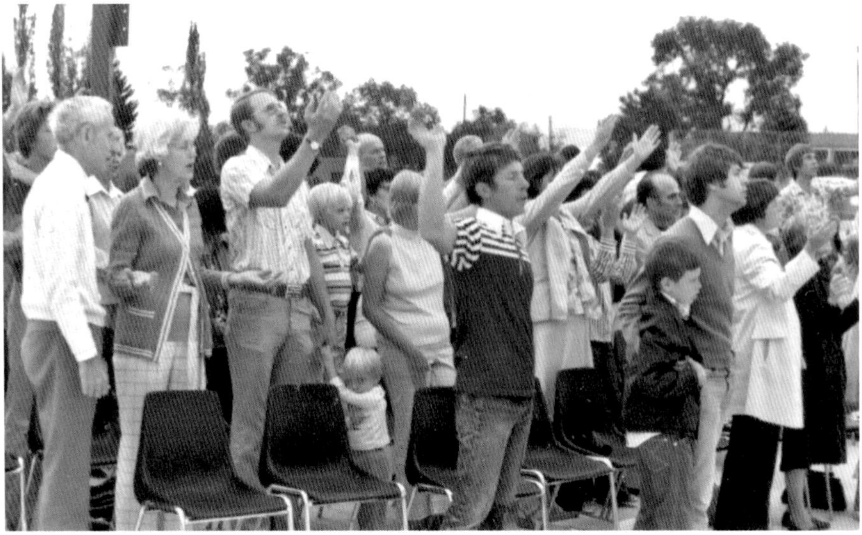

The Capital Christian Church congregation in 1978. *Courtesy the Light at Mission Viejo.*

Capital Christian Church was founded in 1974 with Wade Pope as its first minister. Some of the earliest members were new converts and people from traditional denominations looking for a place where Christians of various religious traditions and backgrounds could worship and share Christ together. By 1976, it had 125 members, with Pastor Pope having performed two hundred baptisms during that period. By 1977, the membership had reached 382, and services were being held in the Santa Fe Women's Club. As the church continued to grow, the Capital Christian School was built in 1985. In the 1990s, members purchased property near the Rancho Viejo subdivision with the expectation of moving the church and school there, allowing room for expansion. In 2006, both the church and school moved into the new facility. The church took on a new name, the Light at Mission Viejo, and the school closed in 2014. Today, the church supports a local homeless ministry and collaborative missions in Israel, India, Mexico and Albania. In 2008, it began La Luz en Santa Fe, a Spanish-language branch, to cater to the large Spanish-speaking community.

The First Assembly of God, the largest Pentecostal church in America, arrived in Santa Fe in 1959; its first church was on Jefferson Street, and it later moved to Apache Avenue. Today, Santa Fe's Pentecostal community includes New Beginnings and the First Assembly, as well as the River of Life in Española. America's Pentecostal movement began to grow in the 1950s

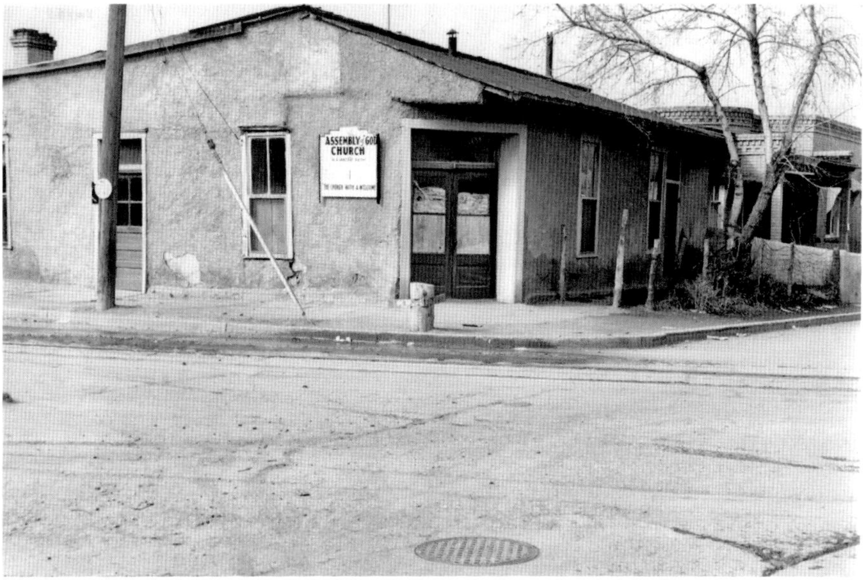

The Assembly of God Church, Jefferson Street at San Francisco Street, Santa Fe, New Mexico. *Photo by Margaret McKittrick. Courtesy Palace of the Governors [NMHM/DCA]. No. 030188.*

through the work of the evangelist Oral Roberts, who has been credited with bringing the Holy Spirit movement to the forefront. He founded the Full Gospel Business Men's Fellowship, which used the Holy Spirit to help businessmen. The Santa Fe branch of this fellowship was started in 1970 by Rudy Rodríguez, the publisher of the *Santa Fe News*. Rodríguez and charter member Dr. Victor Hendren remain active in the organization today.

Another charter member of the Full Gospel Business Men's Fellowship was Belarmino "Blackie" González, who died in 2008. After having had a spiritual awakening in 1984, González launched Son Broadcasting, KCHF TV-11 in Santa Fe, the first full-powered VHF Christian television station in the United States. The station broadcasts award-winning original programs like *God Answers Prayer*, *Israel in Focus* and *The 700 Club.* In 2014, the Israel Ministry of Tourism gave the station its Ambassador of Goodwill award, stating, "Son Broadcasting is a powerful force and instrument in New Mexico in advancing Jesus." In 2005, González wrote a book, *Miracles on La Voz de Cristo Rey*, about his Christian awakening. In the foreword to the book, Oral Roberts wrote, "The miracles that God has given Blackie González are unbelievable to the unbeliever, but very believable to those who believe in God's Holy Spirit."

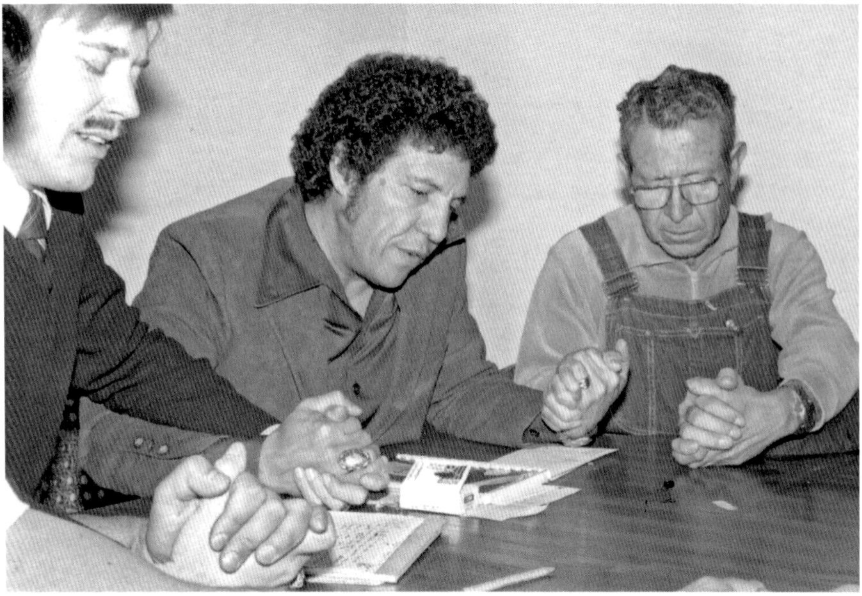

Belarmino "Blackie" González (center) in 1984, the founder of Son Broadcasting, KCHF TV-11 in Santa Fe, the first full-powered VHF Christian television station in the United States. *Courtesy KCHF TV.*

Other Christian organizations in Santa Fe include Shalom Ministries, which has operated a prison ministry in the Santa Fe area since 1972. Perhaps one of the largest Christian groups with the mission of helping others is the Salvation Army, which has had a presence in New Mexico since its arrival in Albuquerque in 1890. The Salvation Army, founded in 1865, is an international religious and charitable movement and a branch of the Christian church that is organized and operated on a quasi-military basis. Its membership includes the clergy, soldiers, members of various activity groups and volunteers who serve as advisors, associates and committed participants in its service function.

The motivation of the organization is love of God and a practical concern for the needs of humanity. This is expressed by a spiritual ministry from the Gospel to help all people regardless of race, color, creed, sex or age. The Salvation Army came to Santa Fe in 1974 and set up shop in a converted garage and single-wide mobile home on a property at 525 West Alameda Avenue, where it is still headquartered today. There it began to identify the physical needs of people and established a corps (church) to meet the spiritual, social, physical and psychological needs of the community. It also began a children's ministry to teach Bible lessons through songs, puppets

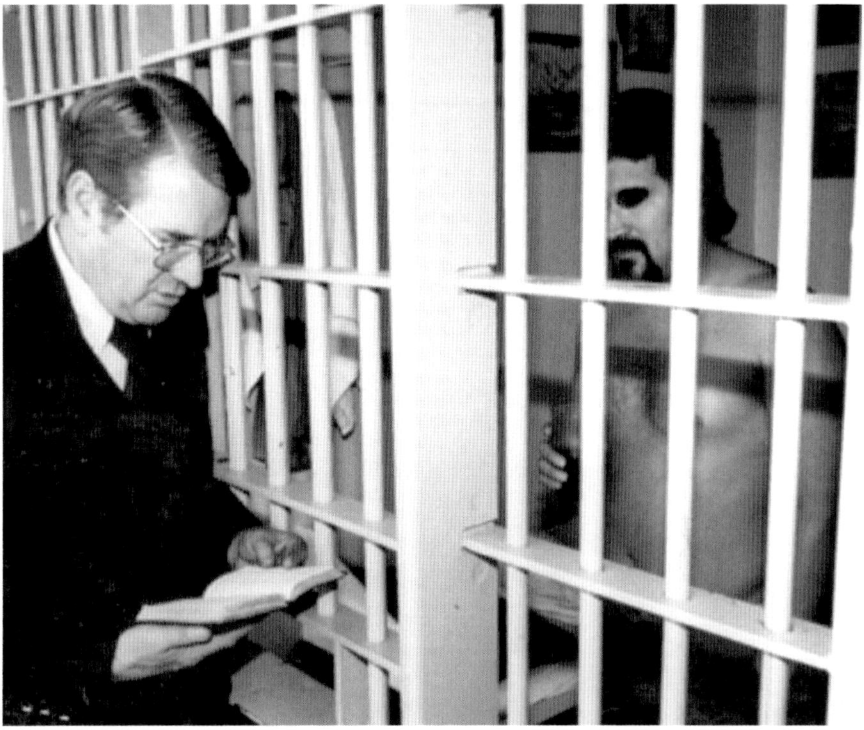

Above: The Shalom prison ministry that began in 1972. *Courtesy the Light at Mission Viejo.*

Right: Members of the Salvation Army in Albuquerque, New Mexico, circa 1890. *Courtesy Center for Southwest Research, University Libraries, University of New Mexico. No. 000-119-0352.*

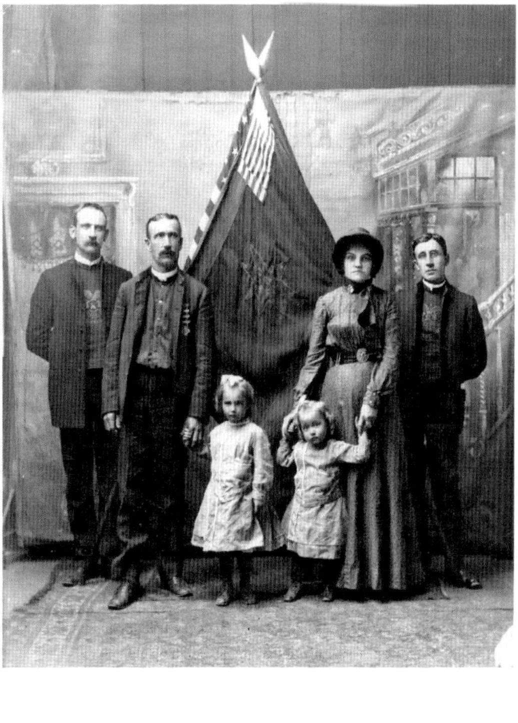

and prayer. The mobile home was used for other children's meetings, a weeklong vacation Bible school conducted during Easter week and Bible studies. Christmas toys were given to struggling families, and residents in care facilities and jails also received gifts. A weekly Bible study was conducted in the city jail. Over the past forty-two years, the ministry's motto, "Heart to God and Hand to Man," has resonated with the community of Santa Fe.

Gideon International is the oldest association of Christian business and professional men in the United States, founded as a missionary arm of the church in 1898 by John H. Nicholson and Samuel Hill. Both men were Christians who did a lot of business travel, and they formed an association to get Bibles into hotel rooms across the country. They held their first meeting the following year on May 31, 1899, and named their organization Gideon, from the biblical reference in the Book of Judges verses six and seven. Called the Bible Project, it was adopted nationally in 1908, and the First Presbyterian Church became the first sponsor to pay the cost of printing the Bibles. More than a century later, Gideon International has a presence in more than 190 countries. The Bible and the New Testament are printed in more than ninety languages, and close to two billion Bibles have been distributed in hotels, jails, schools, hospitals, nursing homes, colleges and medical offices around the world. Gideon's work in Santa Fe, which continues today, began in 1968. Two of the original board members, Jack Horne and Nina Beaty, are still living.

In addition to the numerous Catholic churches in Santa Fe, the surrounding area includes Catholic institutions revered by many. El Santuario de Chimayó, known as the Lourdes of North America, is located twenty-eight miles north of Santa Fe. It was built in 1816 and has been designated a National Historic Landmark. Many miraculous cures have been attributed to this shrine, and every year on Good Friday, thousands of pilgrims make the journey on foot to the holy shrine. There they seek the healing powers of the *tierra bendita* (holy dirt) found in the *pozito*, the little hole containing the holy dirt that has miraculously cured many people of all types of illnesses.

Our Lady of Guadalupe Abbey, located in the Pecos River Canyon twenty-five miles east of Santa Fe, is an Olivetan Benedictine Monastery. Established in 1948, it served as a center of the Catholic Charismatic Renewal from 1969 to 1985. Today, the monastery continues to draw spiritual seekers for prayer and contemplation. Another Benedictine monastery that people seek out is the Monastery of Christ in the Desert, seventy-five miles northwest of Santa Fe. It was founded in 1964 by the monks of Mount

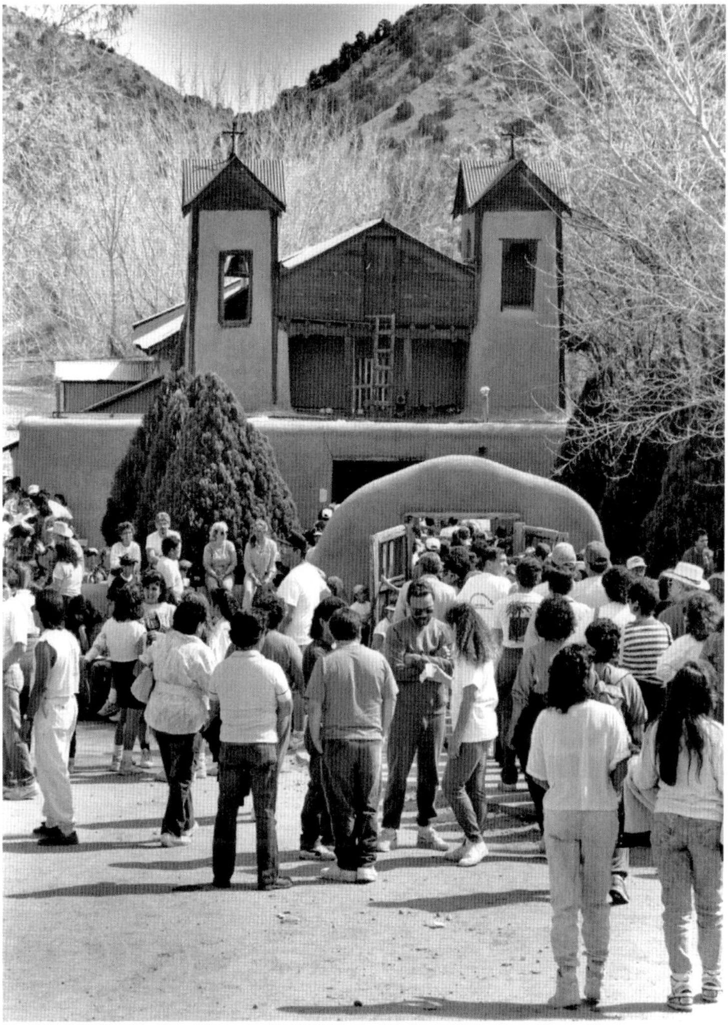

Good Friday pilgrims at the Santuario de Chimayó, 1990. *Photo by Larry Beckner. Courtesy Palace of the Governors [NMHM/DCA]. No. HP.2014.14.1146.*

Saviour Monastery in New York State. From its beginning, the monastery has followed the contemplative Benedictine life.

The foundation of KSWV AM 810 (Qué Suave Radio) began in 1991 with the owners, George and Celine Gonzales, who wanted to spread the word of God. Every Sunday at 8:00 a.m., the Mass is broadcast live from the Cathedral Basilica of St. Francis of Assisi. The rosary is heard Monday through Friday at 9:30 a.m., and *La Palabra de Dios* (the Word of God) is

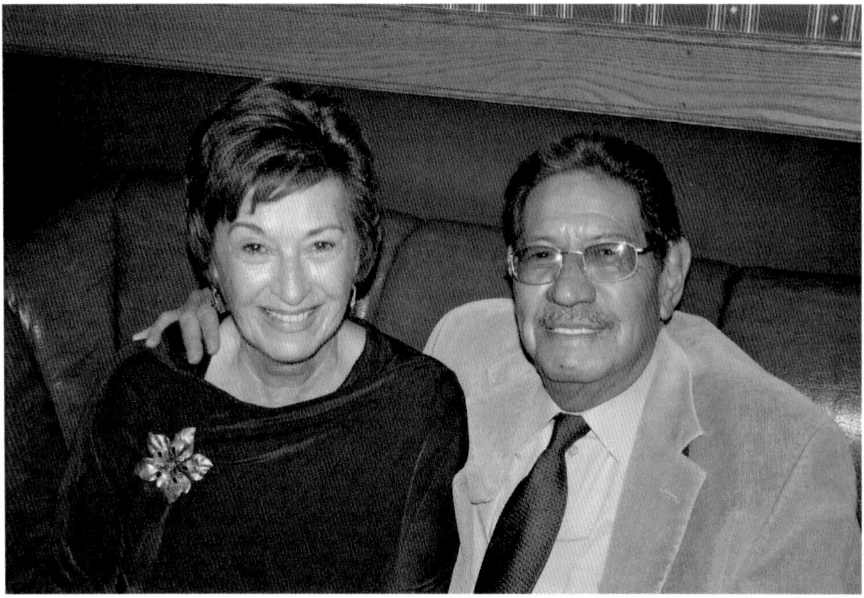

Celine and George Gonzales, owners of Qué Suave (KSWV), broadcasting Christianity to the heart of old Santa Fe. *Courtesy KSWV.*

heard twice hourly at fifteen and forty-five minutes after the hour. Christmas on Qué Suave Radio is a special time of celebration of the birth of the Lord and Savior Jesus Christ. At Easter, the station proclaims the death and resurrection of Christ. George, who died in 2015, was the brother of Blackie González (Blackie changed the spelling of his last name), the founder of KCHF TV, the Christian broadcasting station.

The Church of Antioch at Santa Fe began in 1988. It is an independent Catholic church and not part of the Roman Catholic Church. The Church of Antioch is an alternative Catholic church that ordains women as priests and allows priests to marry, with celibacy optional. Its parishioners are encouraged to make their own informed decisions about birth control and abortion. The church recognizes that all people are on a spiritual path, including atheists and agnostics, who reject the traditional view of the external God and prefer to place their trust in their own experience. The Church of Antioch celebrates the seven sacraments of baptism, confirmation, Eucharist, reconciliation, anointing of the sick, the holy orders of the sacramental ministry for priests and matrimony.

The Holy Trinity Orthodox Church began in 1995. Members of the church come from a variety of different faiths and backgrounds, all of them

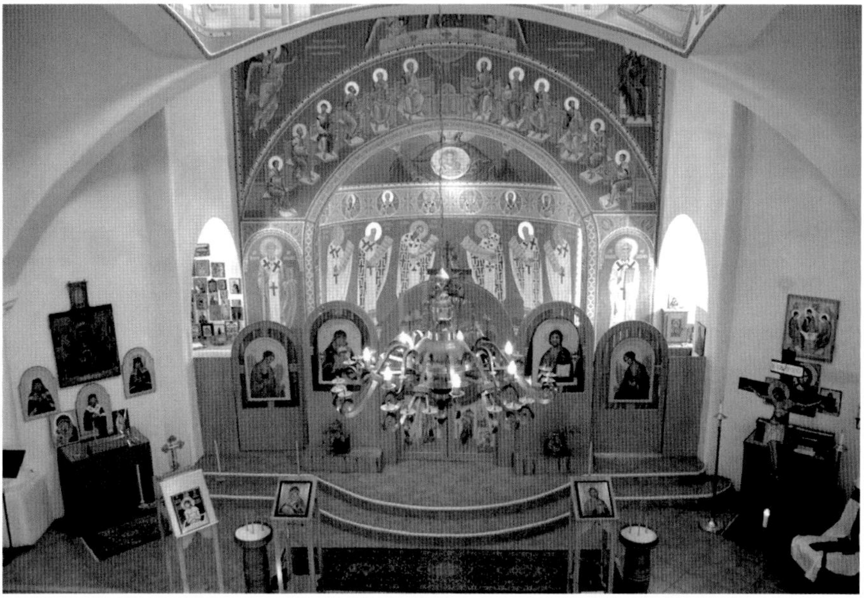

The altar at Holy Trinity church that began in Santa Fe in 1995. *Courtesy Holy Trinity Church.*

looking for a new spiritual path. Weary of both spiritual fads and secularism, they've chosen the ancient path of Orthodoxy. The parish is a part of the self-ruled Antiochian Orthodox Christian Archdiocese of North America in the Diocese of Wichita and Mid-America.

St. Elias the Prophet Greek Orthodox Church was established in Santa Fe in 1990 as a mission parish by Bishop Kalistos. The construction of the church began in 1992, and Father Demetri Colozzo (now Archimandrite Andonias) was the first *proistamenos* (parish priest). The Reverend Father Dimitrios Pappas (Papadimitropoulos) is the current priest. St. Elias is a parish of the Greek Orthodox Metropolis of Denver. St. Elias Greek Orthodox Church serves Santa Fe, northern New Mexico and southern Colorado. The church is located in the community of Eldorado, approximately ten miles southeast of the Santa Fe Plaza.

St. Juliana of Lazarevo Russian Orthodox Church began in Santa Fe in 1996. It is a parish of the Western Diocese of the Russian Church Outside Russia. The church is under the spiritual guidance of His Eminence Archbishop Kyrill of the San Francisco and Western American Diocese. The church is administered by priest David Starr. The church is named in honor of the sixteenth-century Russian Orthodox St. Juliana, who devoted her life to helping the poor.

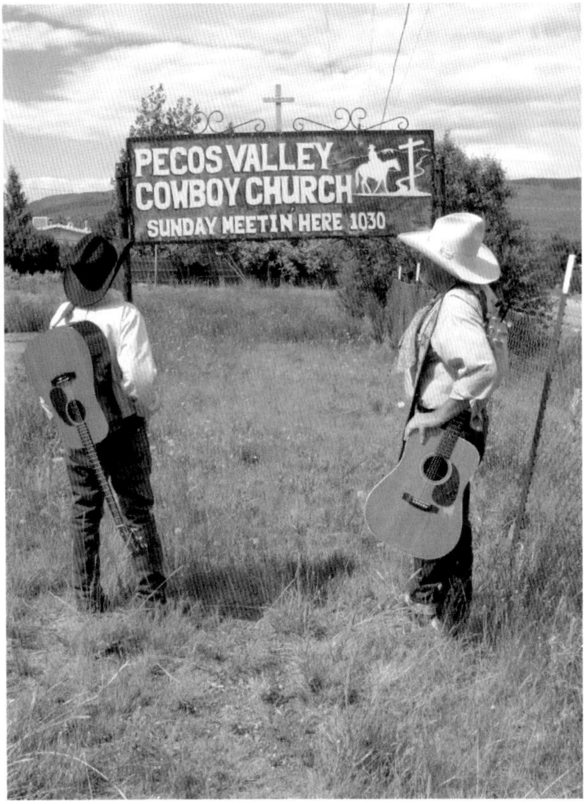

Left: Two member musicians of the Pecos Valley Cowboy Church. *Courtesy Glen Strock.*

Below: Julie Timmons and Sage at the Santa Fe Rodeo and members of the Sangre de Cristo Fellowship. *Courtesy Sangre de Cristo Fellowship.*

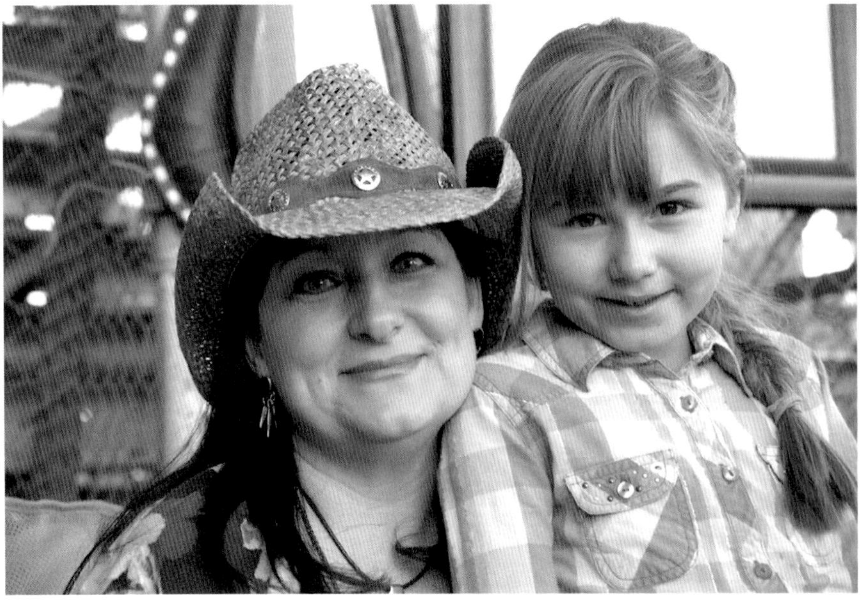

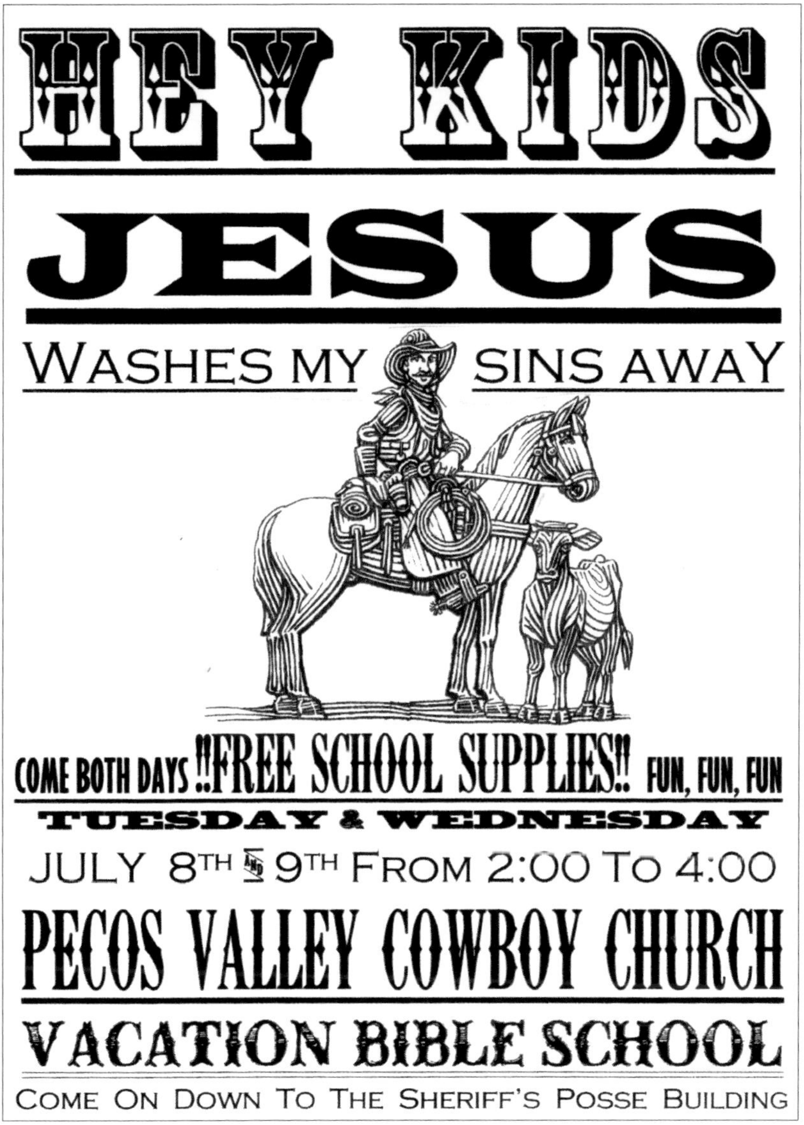

A poster for the Pecos Valley Cowboy Church Bible School. *Courtesy Glen Strock.*

One of the newest groups of Christian churches is the Cowboy Church of Santa Fe County, which is a member of the Christian organization Cowboy-Up International. The Cowboy Church began in 2011 and recently changed its name to Sangre de Cristo Fellowship. Under the guidance of Pastor Steve "Doc" Timmons, the church provides a comfortable setting for those raised in an agrarian lifestyle. One of the fastest-growing Christian churches in the West, the church is a place where cowboys feel right at home. Since the beginning, this congregation of true believers in the Holy Spirit has met weekly to share the word of Jesus in a western-style setting. Many non-cowboys have also become members, and all are welcome. There's also the Pecos Valley Cowboy Church under the direction of Pastor Glen Strock that began in 2006. Like all the groups that appear in this book, the Cowboy churches look to the future through their young people, making sure that they receive spiritual guidance.

Chapter 11

Messengers of the East

The first mention of the Baha'i faith in America occurred at the World Parliament of Religions held in Chicago in 1893. Baha'i, the youngest major world religion, began in Persia in 1844. It is an independent religion founded by Bahá'u'lláh, which means "the glory of God." Bahá'u'lláh is the most recent in a series of messengers from God who include Buddha, Moses and Jesus Christ. Today, there are twelve thousand Baha'i communities in 236 countries and territories with more than five million members throughout the world. They adhere to the belief that humanity is a single race. They work to investigate the truth and to unite religion, promoting the equality of men and women as well as the elimination of prejudice to provide the unification of all humanity into one global society.

Muriel Ives Barrow moved to Santa Fe in the 1940s with the purpose of sharing the Baha'i faith and building a community of believers. During the next few years, people of various backgrounds joined the group, along with members who moved to Santa Fe to be part of the community. They hosted private fireside gatherings in their homes and at public venues to garner interest from the public. By 1960, the group was large enough to form the Baha'i Spiritual Assembly. The Santa Fe Assembly helped support the National Spiritual Assembly by sending followers to promote the faith. Today, the Baha'i community of Santa Fe hosts study circles to examine the teachings of Bahá'u'lláh and enable the participants to apply the spiritual principles found in his teachings to their own lives and circumstances. Devotional gatherings are held in many homes throughout the city, where

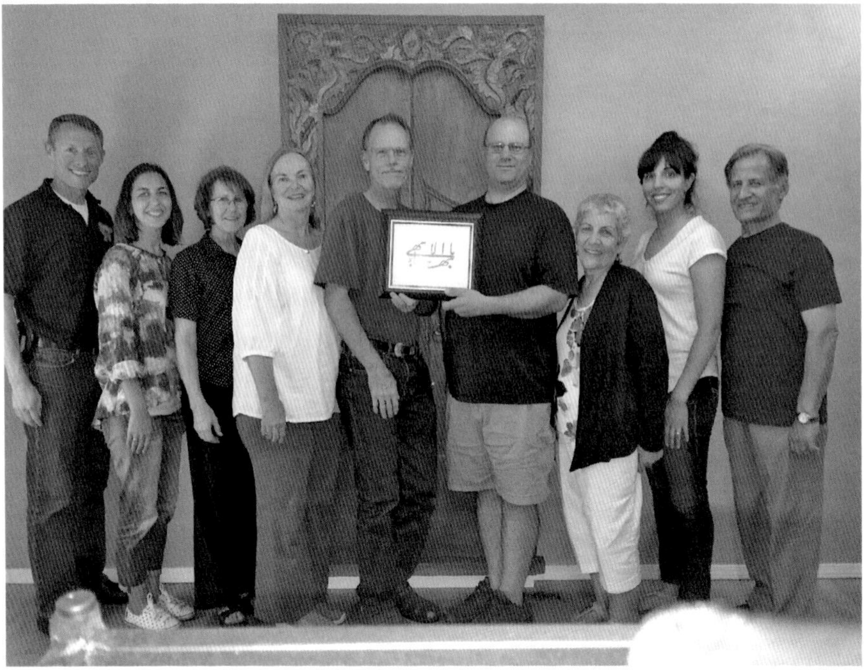

Members of Baha'i. *From left to right*: Stephen Fischer, Amelia Youssefi, Mary Mumford, Sue Khozein, Randy Freeman, Quill Head, Mahvash Yazdani, Neda Talebreza and Bijan Yazdani. *Courtesy Baha'i.*

groups of people from diverse backgrounds and faiths meet to share prayers, reflect on their spiritual natures and socialize. Children's classes are offered to encourage the acquisition of spiritual attributes so necessary to a healthy, productive life. Young people are encouraged in their transition into adulthood to reflect on their aspirations and build the skills necessary to communicate their vision of the future. The Santa Fe Baha'i community doesn't have a specific building where meetings are held. Instead, it devotes the resources that would be necessary to create such a space to building community activities.

At the beginning of the twentieth century, the Islamic faith was miniscule in North America. Today, it is one of the fastest-growing religions in the United States, with millions of followers. The teachings of Islam were brought to northern New Mexico in 1979, when Dar al Islam began near Abiquiu, New Mexico. The nonprofit educational center and mosque were established as an information center to share the culture and faith of Islam with the community. The mission of the center began at the Ka'aba in Mecca,

Saudi Arabia, at Islam's most sacred mosque. It was there that the vision to establish an American Muslim village to showcase Islam began. Northern New Mexico was selected for its serene and inspirational landscape. The mosque and school were designed by renowned Egyptian architect Hassan Fathy. Among the many programs offered are youth camps, teacher training and Muslim women's retreats. Dar al Islam's mission is to educate and share Islam's virtues of mercy and justice with the world.

The Islamic Center of New Mexico in Albuquerque began in 1986 to serve Muslim students at the University of New Mexico, who had been arriving since the 1970s. In 2006, a new and larger mosque was built to accommodate the growing community. The Islamic Center practices the religion of Islam based on the Holy Quran of the Prophet Muhammad. It also provides community services and events for the Muslim and non-Muslim community to introduce the general public to Islamic culture and religion.

The TaHa Mosque has been in Santa Fe for close to twenty years, and like many spiritual groups that began here, its members met privately in homes until the mosque opened on Barcelona Street in 2008. Because Santa Fe is a tourist destination, the mosque receives visitors from around

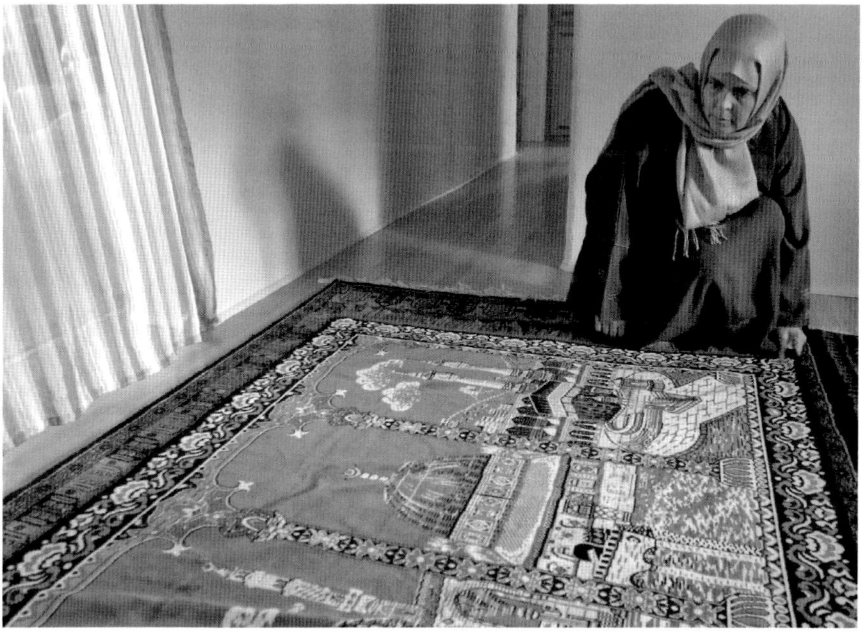

Preparing for Ramadan at Santa Fe's TaHa Mosque. *Photo by Sarah Wellver. Courtesy the* Santa Fe New Mexican.

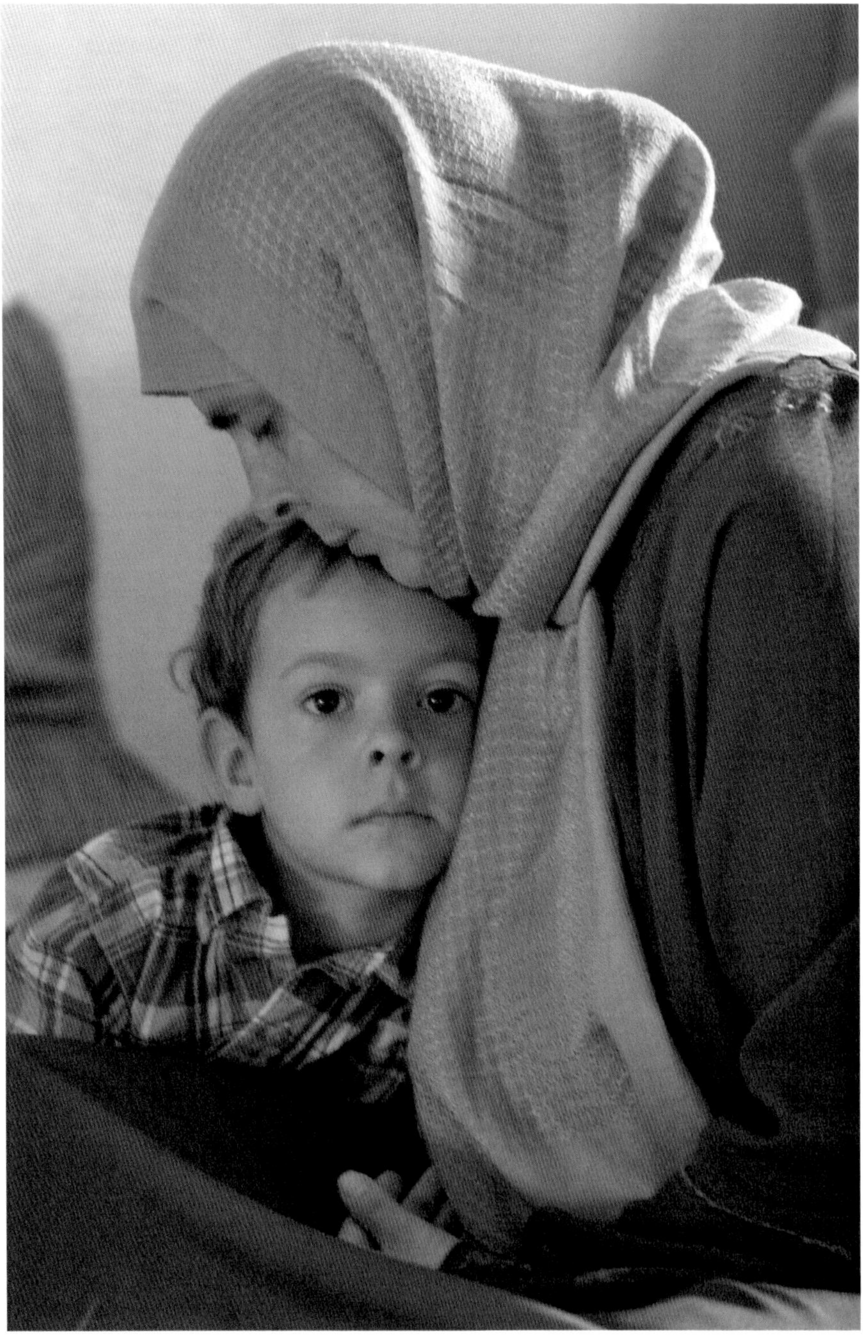

Sandra Tompkins prays with her son, Dakota, at the TaHa Mosque. *Photo by Sarah Wellver. Courtesy the* Santa Fe New Mexican.

the world, especially during the holy days of Ramadan. Santa Fe is so spiritually interconnected that people from Jewish temples and Christian churches also attend services at the mosque during Ramadan to get better acquainted with Islam.

Santa Fe has been home to an active community of Self-Realization Fellowship (SRF) members for almost three decades. In 1985, a small group of individuals following the Kriya yoga teachings of the society's founder, Paramahansa Yogananda, began meditating together. By 1990, they had formed an official group, which today continues to meet for meditation and inspirational services. Paramahansa Yogananda promoted the belief that truth must be experienced. He taught meditation techniques that enable the practitioner to experience a deepening inner peace and attunement with oneself and God.

Paramahansa Yogananda was born in Gorakhpur, India, in 1893 and received his spiritual training under the yoga master Sri Yukteswar, whose guru, Lahiri Mahasaya, revived the ancient science of Kriya yoga for the modern world. Yogananda came to the United States in 1920 as a delegate to the International Congress of Religious Liberals. That same year, he founded Self-Realization Fellowship. His teachings became so popular that in 1927, during a visit to the nation's capital, he was invited to the White House by President Calvin Coolidge. Paramahansa Yogananda's life story, *Autobiography of a Yogi*, is a bestselling spiritual classic today.

The Santa Fe Meditation Circle of Self-Realization Fellowship is a branch of Self-Realization Fellowship, an international nonprofit religious organization headquartered in Los Angeles. The teachings are based on original yoga as taught by Bhagavan Krishna and original Christianity taught by Jesus Christ. The activities of SFR are coordinated by members of its monastic order, under the guidance of its president, Sri Mrinalini Mata, one of Yogananda's closest disciples. Paramahansa Yogananda passed away in 1952 at the age of fifty-nine. It is said that several weeks after his death, his physical body showed no signs of decay.

Sri Mata Amritanandamayi Devi, or Amma (mother), as she is known throughout the world, first came to Santa Fe in 1987. After her first visit, Amma, like so many people, felt at home in Santa Fe. As Jonathan Crews, one of her local tour coordinators, said, "Amma loves Santa Fe because she knows that there are so many sincere spiritual seekers and that it's a mecca of spiritual transformation."

During that visit, Amma traveled to many sacred places in New Mexico, including the Lama Foundation, the Hanuman Temple, at the

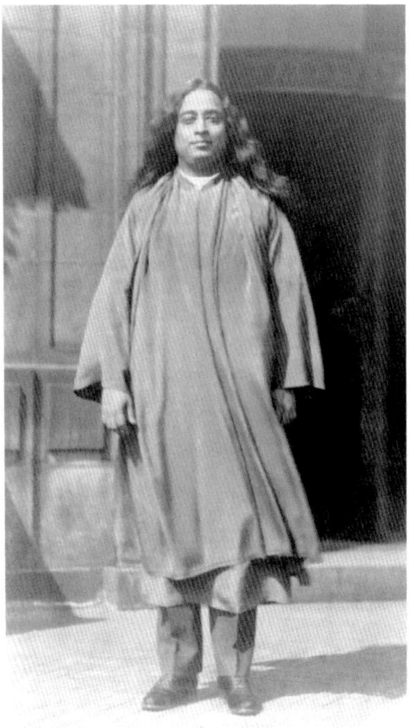

Left: A 1926 photo of Paramahansa Yogananda, founder of the Self-Realization Fellowship. *Courtesy Self-Realization Fellowship Los Angeles.*

Below: Amma in 2014 at the Amma Center on her way to the ashram, accompanied by Swami Ramakrishnananda, Swamini Krishnamrita and other devotees from India and Santa Fe. *Courtesy M.A. Center, San Ramon, CA.*

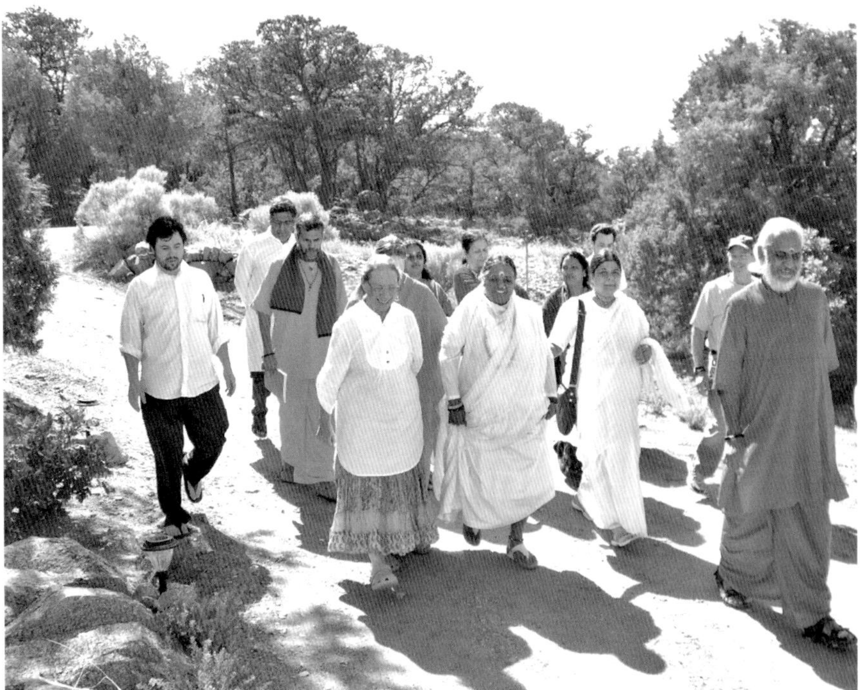

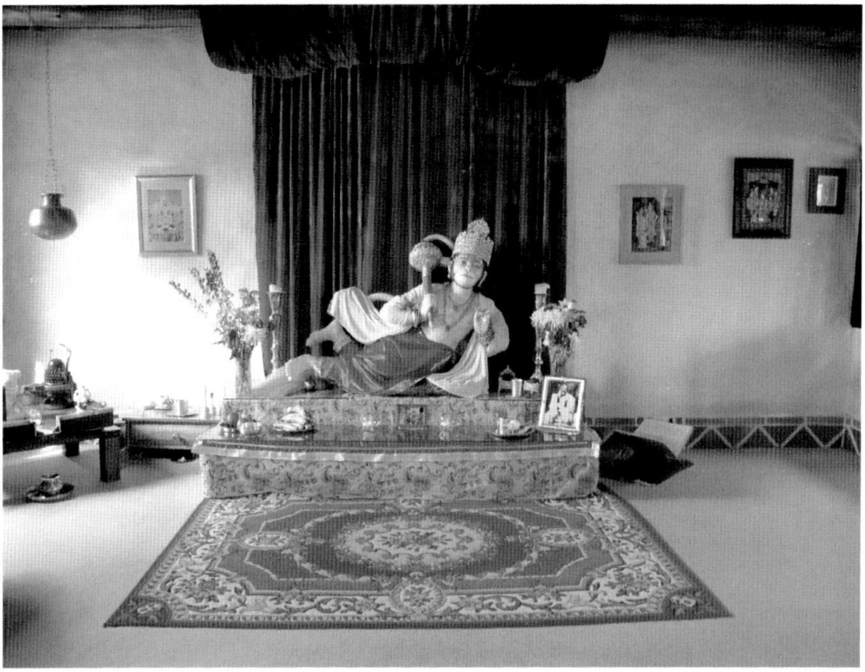

The Hanuman statue at the Neem Karoli Baba Ashram in Taos. *Photo by Lisa Law.*

confluence of the Rio Grande and Rio Pueblo, where she washed her feet. She conducted the traditional ceremony to consecrate the foundation stone for a future temple. It is the only place in America where Amma has performed this ceremony. Those same temple stones now reside at the site of the Amma Center and are lovingly cared for in a small shrine in the courtyard entrance to the Santa Fe ashram, awaiting their future.

In 1994, the Amma Center of New Mexico was built in Seton Village near Santa Fe. Regular gatherings are held at the temple and ashram, where various forms of *sadhana* (spiritual practices) are held to emphasize a connection with the Universal Consciousness. The center also provides charitable works that include collecting food and clothing for the homeless and conducting fundraisers to aid Amma's charitable organizations locally and worldwide.

Born in the remote coastal village of Kerala in southern India, Amma began her quest to rid the world of suffering while still a child. She would go from house to house delivering food to the poor and elderly, and she always had time to listen to their woes. During these formative years, Amma began to ask herself, "Why are there so many contradictions in this world? Why is there no real love? What is the real cause of suffering and what is the solution?"

Amma was born a Hindu and incorporates the universal aspects of Sanatana Dharma (Hinduism) into her life but has said that her religion is love. She experiences the Divine in everyone and sees that they are all connected by that fundamental unity of consciousness and love. After years of meditation, Amma began to experience her oneness with all creation and realized that her purpose in life was to uplift ailing humanity. Thus began her spiritual mission, which today includes nine months of traveling around the world with her message of love and hugs. In the past thirty years, Amma has physically hugged more than twenty-four million people from all parts of the world.

She has been hailed by world leaders as the greatest humanitarian of our time through the work of her organization, Embracing the World, one of the largest humanitarian operations in the world. Hundreds of volunteers in India and throughout the world provide global humanitarian work that includes providing disaster relief, housing, orphanages, food, medicine, pensions, legal aid and homecare for the elderly.

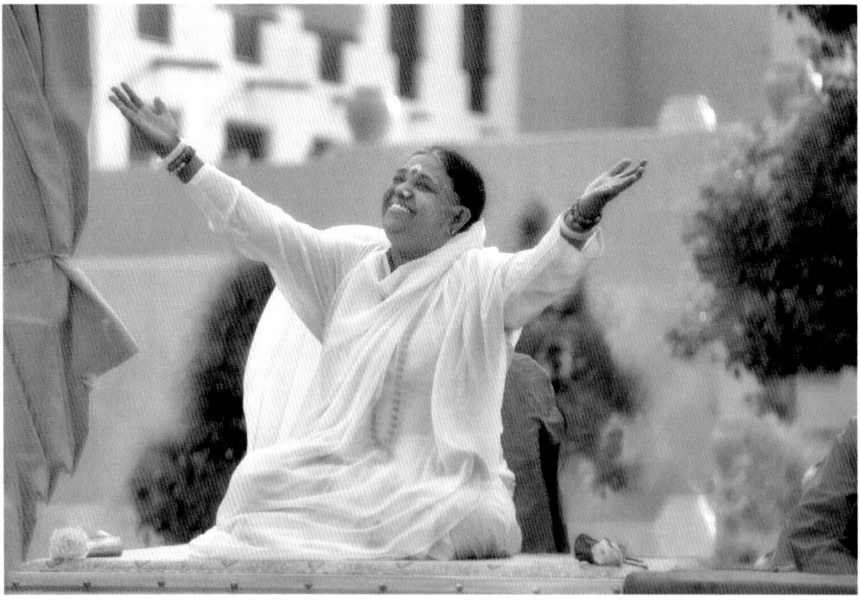

Amma in 2015 at an outdoor meditation gathering at the Buffalo Thunder Resort. *Courtesy M.A. Center, San Ramon, California.*

Amma visits Santa Fe every year during the third week of June. In 2015, thousands of her followers crowded into the Buffalo Thunder Resort and Hotel to share meditation, words of wisdom and, most importantly, a hug. At the gathering, Amma said, "Love is our true essence. Love has no limitations of caste, religion, race or nationality. We are all beads strung together on the same thread of love."

Chapter 12

A Different Take

A book on spirituality in Santa Fe wouldn't be complete without mentioning two belief systems born out of misery and mysticism. Phineas Quimby was the father of the New Thought movement, which began during the nineteenth century in America. Quimby was a mesmerist and healer who suffered from tuberculosis. Through his own experience with the disease, he came to believe that all disease was mental in origin and could be cured by right-minded thinking. This process of continued insight into infinite intelligence, or God, which exists in all individuals, differs through its different branches. New Thought doesn't have a set doctrine but, rather, the common belief that in the presence of goodness, impartiality and availability of God, people can avail themselves of God's gifts of health, wealth and happiness.

Mary Baker Eddy sought out Phineas Quimby in 1862 because she was in poor health, becoming one of his earliest students. She developed a movement out of his ideas that she integrated with her own Christian faith in 1879. Known as the Church of Christ, Scientist, this belief combines biblical teachings with the textbook she wrote in 1875, *Science and Health with a Key to the Scriptures*. More than ten million copies of the book have been sold, and it has been translated into sixteen languages. In 1919, four students of Christian Science began meeting in private homes in Santa Fe. By 1930, the group was established as the Christian Science Society of Santa Fe. The first Christian Science public lecture on the power to heal all illness, both physical and mental, was held at the Elks Club in 1932 before a capacity audience. During that year, a Christian Science Reading Room also opened, and it has been in continuous operation ever since. Today, the public can learn more about the Science of Mind tenets while they study and pray at the current location on the Plaza on San Francisco Street. The church was incorporated in 1948 in the state of New Mexico. In 1968, a church was built on Cordova Road, where followers continue to be inspired by the word of the Bible and learn about the ever-expansive power of the thought process.

The Science of Mind and Spirit found its way to Santa Fe in 1960 through the enthusiasm and dedication of businessman Richard J. Gregory Jr. In 1946, while living in Salt Lake City, he discovered the philosophy of Science of Mind. Impressed with its core concept—that Christ's universal presence lives within and that immortality continues on another plane once the body has outlived its usefulness—Gregory wanted to learn more. He traveled to Los Angeles to meet Ernest Holmes, a writer, teacher and proponent of New Thought who began the Science of Mind movement in 1927. After meeting Holmes—who stressed the system of thought that affirms the unity of God and man, the perfection of life and the immortality and infinite expansion of the individual soul—Gregory devoted his life to the movement. When he moved with his family to Santa Fe, he began distribution of the *Science of Mind* magazine. Within months, he was distributing over one hundred copies to interested people, who soon began a discussion group at the First National Bank on the Plaza. In 1965, he founded the Center for Spiritual Living on the corner of Grant Street and Paseo de Peralta. He brought in its first minister, Dr. Robert Stevens, who was ordained by Robert Holmes. The group attained church status in 1967 and became the Santa Fe Religious Science Church. Later, the church moved to Camino de los Marquez, where it resides today.

In 2010, a second location, the Everyday Center for Spiritual Living, opened on Fifth Street, run by the Reverend Gayle Dillon. Each Sunday, a group of seventy members gathers to listen to music and inspirational talks and learn the process of working on spirit. When Dillon moved to Santa Fe in 2007, she was immediately taken with the city's tranquil nature. As she says, "I was amazed by the spiritual consciousness of the people here. There's a strong human connection and a foundation that I believe stems from the long history in Santa Fe."

Together, the two centers provide the basic foundation of what the New Thought writer Elizabeth Towne described as "the fine art of recognizing, realizing, and manifesting the God in the individual."

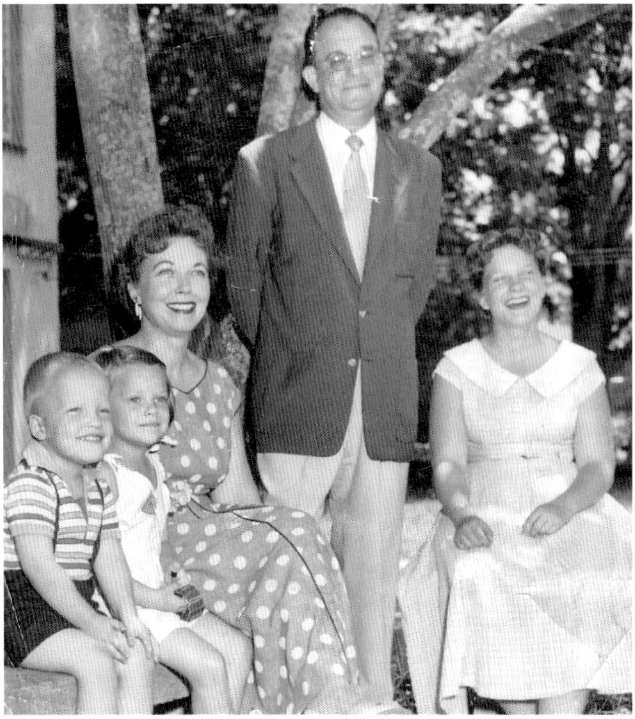

Left: Richard J. Gregory Jr., who brought the Center for Spiritual Living to Santa Fe, with his family in 1960. *From left to right*: Rick, Micki, Mary Jane, Richard and Patty. *Courtesy Patty Berry.*

Below: Reverend Gayle Dillon at the Everyday Living Center on Fifth Street. *Courtesy Everyday Living Center.*

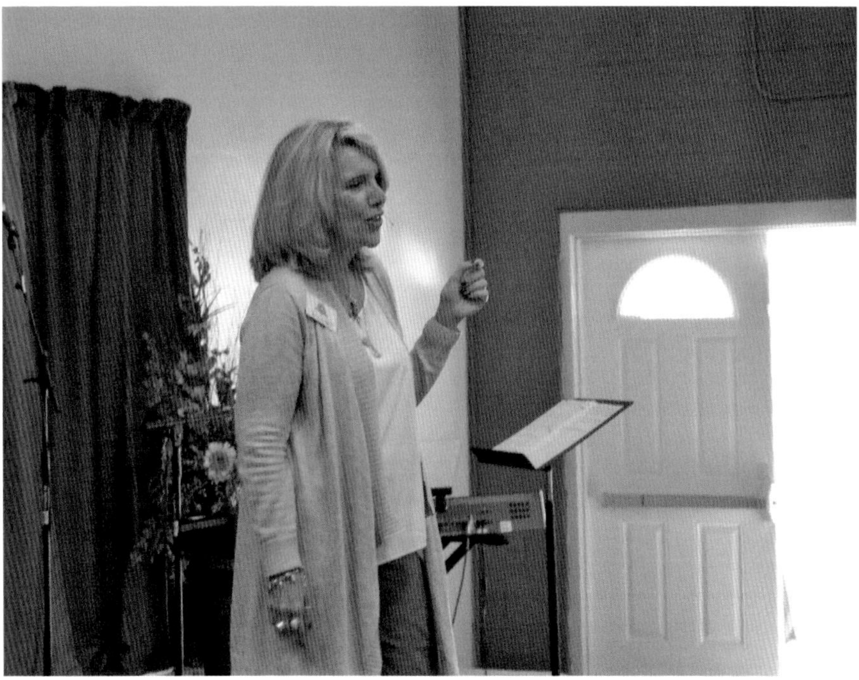

The bacterial infection that causes tuberculosis was also the impetus for the founding of the Unity movement. One of its founders, Myrtle Fillmore, was healed from the disease when her thinking changed. She had a deep-seated belief that her illness was inherited. After hearing a lecture on metaphysics, she suddenly grasped the idea that she was a child of God and did not inherit sickness. She prayerfully applied her new insight with great success, and her health instantly began to improve. Unity, which was founded by Myrtle and her husband, Charles Fillmore, in 1889, has no set dogma or creed. The spiritual movement offers a way of life that emphasizes humanity's Divine nature and the goal of expressing that nature in every area of life. One of Unity's fundamental working propositions is that the way we think and feel about ourselves, our fellow human beings, our world and God is a determining factor in the expression of that Divine nature.

Unity Santa Fe was founded as a study group in 1974 by Reverend Jean Beggs. The church was incorporated in 1977 and became a member of the Unity Worldwide Ministries in 1978. For the next twenty years, Unity Santa Fe met in different locations around town. In 1999, it moved into its own church off Highway 599 on a street now called Unity Way. The members all pitched in to build the church, which includes a bell tower, a bookstore, classrooms and administrative offices. Today, the organization continues to grow through the realization of the spirit of its followers.

The first *Big Book* of Alcoholics Anonymous was brought to Santa Fe during the time of the Manhattan Project. In 1942, a visiting doctor brought that blueprint for recovery from alcoholism to town, probably thinking that it could be of benefit during such a stress-ridden era. However, it wasn't until 1968 that a group of alcoholics began holding meetings in a private home in Tesuque. A decade later, as the need and interest grew, Santa Fe's Friendship Club began. Alcoholics Anonymous, which started in America in 1935, can be traced in part to the Oxford Group. This spiritual movement, which uses prayer and meditation, was popular in America and Europe in the early part of the twentieth century. Along with prayer, meditation and the belief in a higher power, the group advocated for self-improvement through performing self-inventory, admitting wrongs, making amends and carrying the message to others. This formula proved so successful that the noted psychoanalyst Dr. Carl Jung referred suffering alcoholics to the Oxford Group.

Today, close to sixty weekly AA meetings are held in Santa Fe, advocating unity, service and recovery. Over the past eighty years, AA has grown into a worldwide fellowship helping millions of people recover from alcoholism. Several other self-help groups for everything from

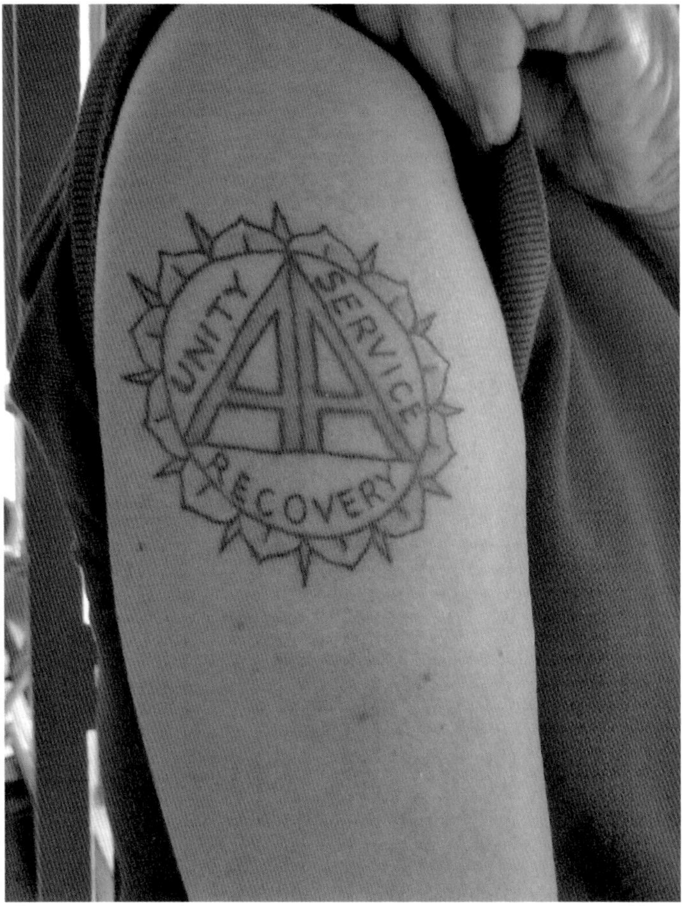

A tattoo of the Alcoholics Anonymous symbol for unity, service and recovery. *Photo by Ana Pacheco.*

gambling addiction to overeating have adopted the twelve-step format of Alcoholics Anonymous.

The Celebration is an independent spiritual community that was founded in 1989 as the Forum Celebration by Reverend Carol Bell Knight. In 1991, the nondenominational congregation became leaderless when Knight left, but for the past twenty-four years, it has continued to prosper. The group honors all spiritual paths through inspirational readings, meditation and music. Members welcome people from all walks of life who yearn to learn and be embraced by unconditional love. They believe that a higher power exists in each individual and all are a part of God. Therefore, they do not endorse a particular creed or dogma.

The international New Age movement of the 1970s and '80s is believed to have originated with theosophy, the occult movement of the nineteenth century with roots in ancient Gnosticism (knowledge through transcendence) and Neoplatonism (reuniting the soul through trance or ecstasy). New Age is not a religion but, rather, a vast syncretism of numerous religious and philosophical ideas. It is a free-flowing spiritual movement that has no text, central organization, dogma or creed. It adheres to astrology, channeling, Hinduism, Gnostic traditions, neo-paganism, spiritualism and Buddhism. Astrology is used as a method of foretelling the future. Crystals and volcanic rocks are thought to be sources of healing or energizing power, and tarot cards are believed to aid individuals with life decisions. New Agers have a nontraditional definition of the nature of God, believing that God is a state of higher consciousness that can be realized through personal human potential.

Since the hippie movement of the 1960s, Santa Fe has had a huge New Age presence. There are schools for healers and spiritual teachers, as well as various types of meditation and yoga. There are several vegan and vegetarian restaurants in town, along with many establishments that provide massage and other bodywork. Many people in the community make full-time livings as consultants, delving into the world of numerology, tarot cards, sidereal and other forms of astrology. The Ark Bookstore has been in business on Romero Street for thirty-five years, selling everything from oils to crystals to books on ancient eastern religions, as well as books on the metaphysical plane. Beth Wright is a spiritual healer and former owner of a shop of spirituality that hosts a show on all things interrelated to spirituality on Transitions Radio (KBAC-FM) that broadcasts on Sunday mornings. And the monthly magazine *Natural Awakenings* keeps everyone connected on the latest New Age spiritual news.

The Eckankar Religion of the Light and Sound of God began in Santa Fe in the early 1990s. People of all beliefs are welcome at the service held at the Santa Fe Women's Club on the third Sunday of the month. A community HU chant (song to God) is held on the first Sunday at Santa Fe Soul as a service to the community. People of any religious belief can sing HU to uplift their spirit and open their hearts to God's love. Eckankar, a teaching with ancient roots, was introduced as a modern-day religion in 1965 by Paul Twitchell. It teaches that there is one supreme God, the Creator, neither male nor female. God's spiritual essence is light and sound—the ECK, or Holy Spirit, which connects everyone with the heart of God. Personal experience with the light and sound of God is the cornerstone of Eckankar. Its current spiritual leader is Sri Harold Klemp, known as the Mahanta, the

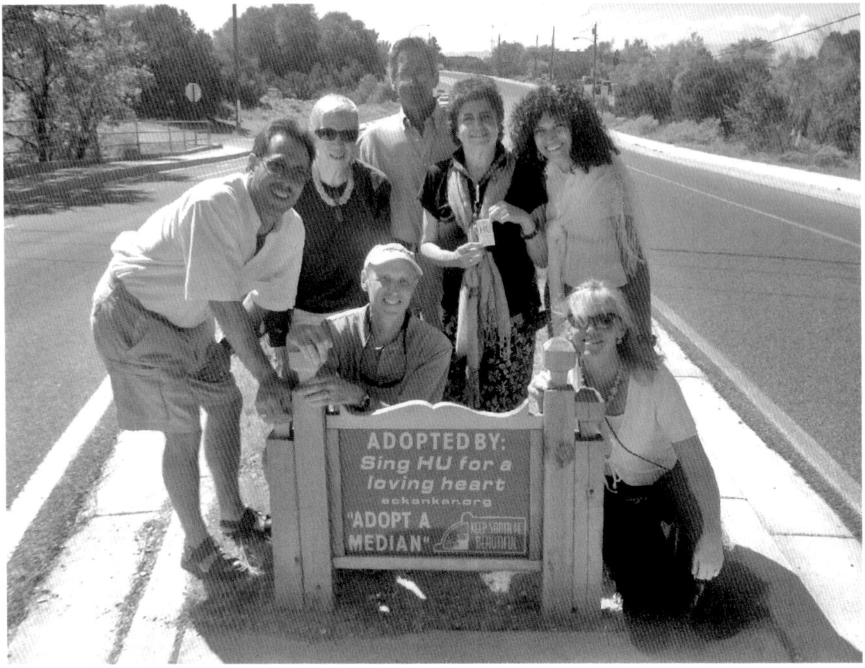

Members of Eckankar have been holding services in Santa Fe since the 1990s. *Courtesy C. John Graham.*

Living ECK Master. Eckankar's spiritual home, the Temple of ECK, and its international headquarters are located in Chanhassen, Minnesota.

Oneness, a belief that expands people's consciousness, began in Santa Fe in 2006. This phenomenon is also known as Deeksha, which is Sanskrit for "blessing." Oneness is the transfer of energy from one person to another. It is believed that through this practice a neurobiological shift occurs in the brain that activates the frontal lobes and deactivates the parietal lobes. This is said to result in a change of mind that is associated with prolonged meditation. Deeksha fosters consciousness while promoting inner peace. After a short period of time, people begin to live their lives from the higher platform of consciousness and experience what Oneness calls "awakening." The results are a quieter mind and a closer bond with the Divine of the individual's own choice, which result in a better phase of life regarding health, wealth and relationships.

Margo Baldwin was the first Santa Fean to be trained by Oneness University near Chennai, India, to give Deeksha. Over the past ten years, thousands of people in town have received the Oneness Blessing. Several

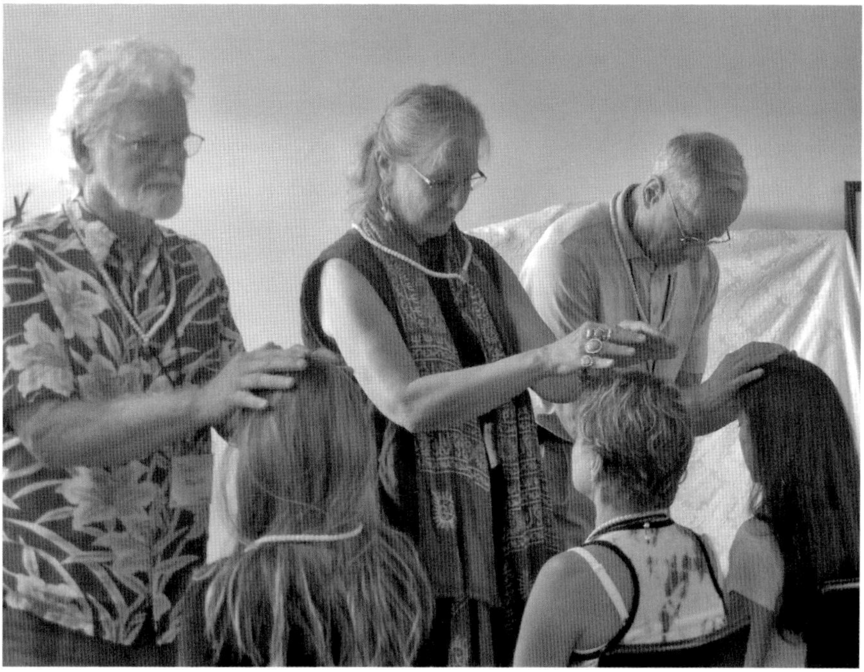

The members of Oneness attending a blessing ceremony. *Courtesy Peter DeBenedittis.*

people have been initiated as Oneness Blessing Givers. At these events, participants clear the emotional blockages that stunt spiritual growth. At the end of the ceremony, people kneel before a representation of the feet of their personal Divine, asking for Deeksha directly from God to heal them.

Kirtan is the Hindu-based practice of chanting names of deities to attain higher consciousness to connect with the Divine. It began in sixth-century India as part of the Bhakti yoga practices and was first introduced in the United States in the 1920s. The practice was made popular in the 1960s by the Hare Krishna, the followers of Krishna, the eighth avatar of the god Vishnu of Hinduism. Beatle George Harrison was a devotee of Kirtan and brought it to the forefront with his hit song "My Sweet Lord." The Beatles were also responsible for popularizing Transcendental Meditation, which was introduced by Maharishi Mahesh Yogi during that era.

Anne Goodwin is a leader of the Kirtan practice in Santa Fe. In addition to the songs sung in Sanskrit, she includes Jewish, Christian and Buddhist chants in the various events and festivals held throughout the year. The practice of Kirtan has grown exponentially in the United States in the past ten years. People claim that by being immersed in rhythmic repetition, they are able to connect to God.

Gong bath meditation is also popular in Santa Fe. Based on quantum physics, it uses the scientific principles of vibration and resonance to bring the body back to equilibrium in a natural state. No water is involved in the bath; the individual is bathed in the sounds and vibrations of gongs, Himalayan and crystal bowls, chimes, rattles, drones and the human voice. These sound waves alter the brain-wave patterns from the beta waking state of mind to the meditative state known as theta and delta. This practice is believed to aid the body by synchronizing the brain to restore balance and harmony in the human system. Followers of this ancient practice have found it to help with physical ailments as well as depression and anxiety. The use of sound baths is also used as a form of meditation.

DeeDee Downs, who runs the Gong Studio on Second Street in Santa Fe, is a sound healer, also known as a sounder. She has lived in Santa Fe since the 1960s and is well versed in many New Age and spiritual practices. Through her work, she has found that the gong vibrations relax brain-wave patterns during an hour-long session by putting the individual's body in harmony with the sound waves that enable meditation. The mainstream yoga community has helped spread awareness of sound baths. The gongs typically vibrate at around 439 hertz, creating an intense envelope of sound that leaves the "bather" fully relaxed and energized.

Nature-based religions also fall under the category of New Age spirituality. In many of these disciplines, the modern world is seen as being permeated by spirit. The União do Vegetal (UDV) Christian spiritist religion began in Santa Fe with a ceremony in July 1990. It was part of a movement of people from California, New Mexico and Colorado seeking to preserve and develop a deeper connection with God through communion with Divine Nature. Since its arrival in Santa Fe, the UDV has discreetly and slowly grown into a small congregation consisting of people of many different races, professions and economic classes. The UDV center in Santa Fe was the first to be authorized outside Brazil, where the religion was founded in 1961. In 1992, UDV members put up a yurt in the neighborhood of Arroyo Hondo to serve as a temple. On November 1, 2014, local UDV members began construction of a permanent temple on the same land.

UDV is now practiced by more than seventeen thousand people in six countries. The UDV headquarters are located in Brasilia, Brazil, from where it supervises the work of the UDV in the United States. Santa Fe was the first of nine centers in this country. The name "União do Vegetal" in Brazilian

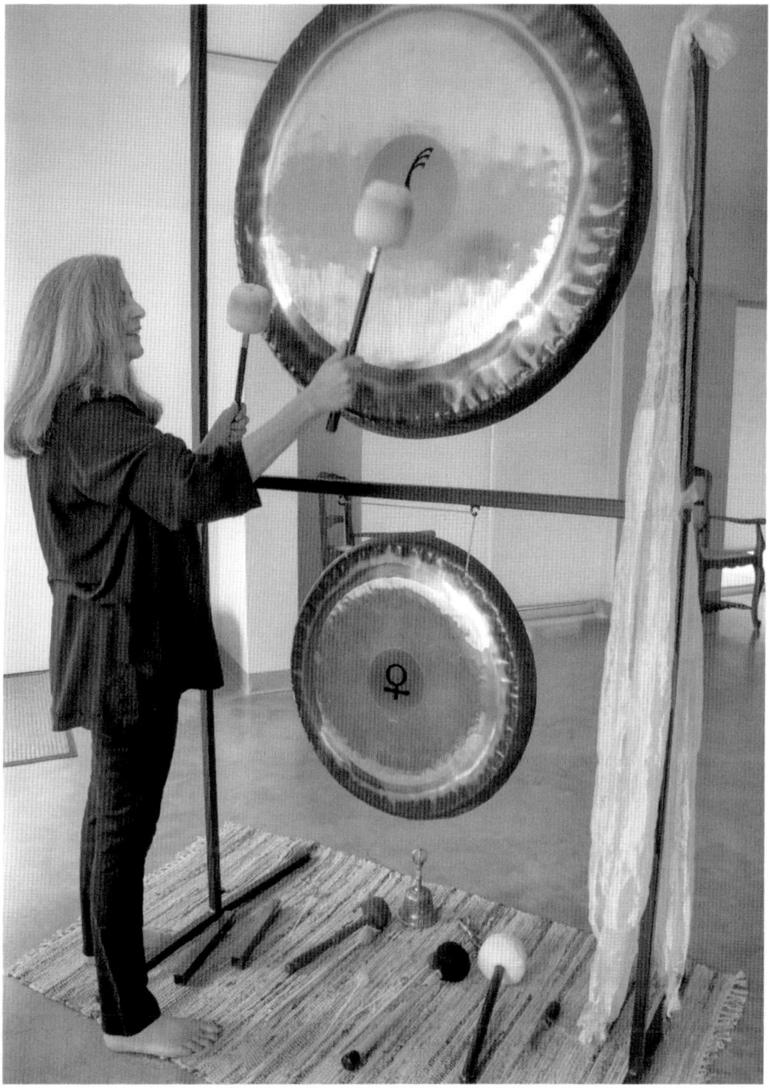

DeeDee Downs in 2014 at the Gong Studio on Second Street. *Photo by Lisa Law.*

Portuguese means the "union of the plants." The name refers to the union among the people who participate in the religious practice of drinking *hoasca* tea as well as the union of the two plants used to make the tea, *banisteriopsis caapi* and *psychotria viridis*, from the Brazilian Amazon. The tea is revered as a sacrament serving to heighten spiritual understanding and perception to bring the practitioners closer to God.

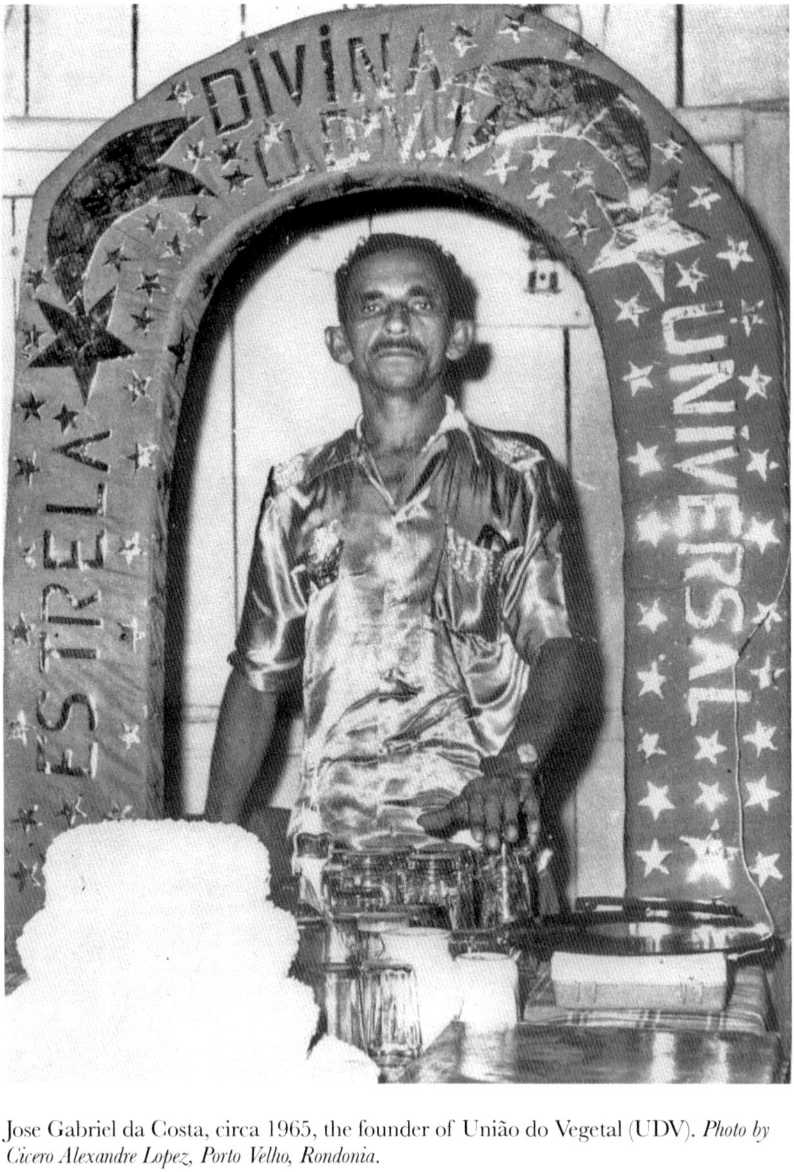

Jose Gabriel da Costa, circa 1965, the founder of União do Vegetal (UDV). *Photo by Cicero Alexandre Lopez, Porto Velho, Rondonia.*

The União do Vegetal was founded by Jose Gabriel da Costa, or Mestre Gabriel, as he is called by UDV members. Mestre Gabriel was born on February 10, 1922, the eighth in a family of fourteen children. In the 1940s, he worked as a rubber tapper in the Amazon. He drank *hoasca* for the first time on April 1, 1959, in the Amazon forest and began distributing the tea to associates and disciples shortly thereafter. In 1961, while still in the forest, Mestre Gabriel announced the creation of the União do Vegetal. Many of the men and women trained by Mestre Gabriel in Brazil in the '60s have visited Santa Fe to train the congregation and faithfully transmit the teachings of Mestre Gabriel. Since its founding in 1961, the União do Vegetal has worked for the improvement of the human being, developing moral, intellectual and spiritual virtues, and is considered by its members to be a place of peace, goodness and harmony. Mestre Gabriel founded the União do Vegetal to serve as an example of seriousness and transparency and to focus on respect for secular and spiritual laws in order to fulfill his goal of bringing peace to humanity.

Our Lady of the Woods is a Los Alamos–based group of devotees of Wicca, a neo-pagan belief system that incorporates multiple deities of all genders. They believe that these deities exist within us and can be transcended to others. Wiccans have a commitment to environmental awareness and are known for their spiritual and magical practices. The equinoxes and solstices are central to Wiccan practices, and adherents hold festivals and gatherings during the changing seasons. Many of these celebrations incorporate aspects of Greek mythology as well as Native American practices. They emphasize the importance of communal rituals rather than the individual pursuit of spiritual well-being. Wiccans and others associated with the New Age movement are generally social liberals who seek personal and religious freedom.

Timeline of Arrival in Santa Fe

AD 900	Native American
1610	Roman Catholicism Sephardic Judaism
1816	El Santuario de Chimayó (Chimayó, New Mexico)
1848	Ashkenazi Judaism
1849	Baptist
1866	Presbyterian
1863	Episcopal
1881	Methodist
1896	Mormonism
1909	Freemasonry
1914	Lutheran
1917	Baptist Church Resettlement
1919	Christian Science
1920	Quakers
1942	Buddhism I AM
1946	Baha'i
1948	Our Lady of Guadalupe Abbey
1952	Unitarian Universalism
1959	First Assembly of God (Pentecostal)
1960s	Evangelistic and Charismatic Church
1964	Monastery of Christ in the Desert (Abiquiu, New Mexico)
1965	Center for Spiritual Living

1968	Alcoholics Anonymous Gideon International
1969	Sikh Dharma
1970	Full Gospel Business Men Fellowship
1972	Shalom Prison Ministries
1973	Maha Bodhi Stupa
1974	Unity Santa Fe Capital Christian Church Salvation Army
1975	Kagyu Shenpen Kunchab Center
1980	United Church of Santa Fe Project Tibet
1984	Son Broadcasting, KCHF TV-11
1986	Bodhi Stupa Self-Realization Fellowship
1987	Hinduism/Amma
1988	Church of Antioch at Santa Fe
1990	Upaya Zen Center
1991	The Celebration KSWV AM 810 (Qué Suave Radio)
1992	Eckankar UDV Congregation St. Elias Greek Orthodox Church
1995	TaHa Mosque Holy Trinity Orthodox Church
1996	St. Juliana Russian Orthodox Church
1997	Tibetan Association
2002	Phende Rigzod Khan Center
2006	Oneness Light at Mission Viejo Pecos Valley Cowboy Church
2008	La Luz en Santa Fe Pema Khandro Ling Center
2010	Thubten Norbu Ling Tibetan Buddhist Center Everyday Center for Spiritual Living
2011	Sangre de Cristo Fellowship
2012	Kirtan
2013	Wicca (Los Alamos, New Mexico)
2014	Gong Meditation

Bibliography

Chapter 1

About. "Geography of the Rocky Mountains." www.geography.about.com/od/unitedstatesofamerica/a/rockymountains.htm.

National Park Service. www.nps.gov/petr/planyourvisit/volcanoes.

New Mexico Museum of Natural History and Science. "New Mexico: Land of Volcanoes." www.nmnaturalhistory.org/volcanoes-of-nm.

U.S. Department of the Interior. "Colorado Plateau Rapid Ecoregional Assessment (REA)." www.blm.gov/wo/st/en/prog/more/Landscape_Approach/reas/coloplateau.html.

Chapter 2

All Trips. "Monument Valley: History." www.allmoab.com/monument_valley/history.php.

The American Southwest. "Chaco Culture National Historical Park." www.americansouthwest.net/new_mexico/chaco_culture/national_historical_park.html.

Bernalillo County. www.bernalillo.nmgenweb.us.

Bureau of Land Management. "Who Were the Ancestral Pueblo People (Anasazi)?" www.blm.gov/co/st/en/fo/ahc/who_were_the_anasazi.html#who.

Exploratorium. "About Chaco Canyon." www.exploratorium.edu/chaco/HTML/canyon.

Indian Pueblo Cultural Center. "The 19 Pueblos of New Mexico." www.indianpueblo.org/19pueblos.

Maya, Inca, Aztec. "Compare and Contrast the Maya, Inca, and Aztec Cultures." www.mayaincaaztec.com/prinazci.

National Park Service. "Mesa Verde." www.nps.gov/meve/learn/education/upload/ancestral_puebloans.pdf.

Spiritual Travels. "Amid the Cliff Dwellings of Mesa Verde." July 24, 2014. www.spiritualtravels.info/2014/07/24/amid-the-cliff-dwellings-of-mesa-verde.

Chapter 3

Chavez, Angélico. *La Conquistadora: The Autobiography of an Ancient Statue*. Santa Fe, NM: Sunstone Press, 1975.

———. *My Penitente Land*. Albuquerque: University of New Mexico Press, 1974.

Dunnington, Jacqueline. *Santuario of Our Lady of Guadalupe*. Santa Fe, NM, 2014.

Kamen, Henry. *Empire: How Spain Became a World Power, 1492–1763*. New York: HarperCollins, 2003.

McCracken, Ellen. *The Life and Writing of Fray Angélico Chávez*. Albuquerque: University of New Mexico Press, n.d.

Silverberg, Robert. *The Pueblo Revolt*. Lincoln: University of Nebraska Press, 1994.

Slade, Carole. *St. Teresa of Avila*. Berkeley: University of California Press, 1995.

Torrez, Robert J. "Franciscan Friars and the Golden Age of Missions." New Mexico History. www.newmexicohistory.org/people/franciscan-friars-and-the-golden-age-of-missions.

Udall, Stewart L. *Coronado and Our Spanish Legacy: To the Inland Empire*. New York: Doubleday, 1987.

Weber, David J. *The Mexican Frontier, 1821–1846: The American Southwest Under Mexico*. Albuquerque: University of New Mexico Press, 1982.

Chapter 4

Bell, Lance. Author interview, July 16, 2015.

Drucker, Malka. Author interview, July 16, 2015.

Hordes, Stanley. Author interview, May 19, 2015.

———. *To the End of the Earth*. New York: Columbia University Press, 2005.
Jewish Virtual Library. www.jewishvirtuallibrary.org.
La Mont, Barb. Author interview, July 16, 2015.
Levertov, Rabbi Berel. Author interview, July 9, 2015.
Mahon, Kathy Kahn. Author interview, July 28, 2015.
New Mexico Jewish Historical Society. "Montefiore Cemetery." www.nmjhs.org/montefiore-cemetery.
The Santa Fe Life. "Peter Weiss' Annals of the Ancient City—The Secret History of Santa Fe—Part 2." April 11, 2011. www.thesantafelife.org/2011/04/peter-weiss-annals-of-ancient-city.html.
Silver, Marian. Author interview, August 12, 2015.

CHAPTER 5

Ball, Jean. Author interview, First Presbyterian Church, July 30, 2015.
Church News. "New Monument in New Mexico Memorializes Mormon Battalion—Marker Replaces One Built in 1940." October 5, 1996. www.ldschurchnewsarchive.com/articles/27418/New-monument-in-New-Mexico-memorializes-Mormon-Battalion-----marker-replaces-one-built-in-1940.html.
Gross, Denise. Author interview, St. John's Methodist Church, August 20, 2015.
History. "Manifest Destiny." www.history.com/topics/manifest-destiny.
Horowitz, Mitch. *Occult America*. New York: Bantam Books, 2009.
Irick, Dan. Author interview, Scottish Rite Temple, July 24, 2015.
Krause, Lynn. Author interview, First Baptist Church, July 15, 2015.
Lehmberg, Stanford. *Holy Faith Santa Fe*. Albuquerque, NM: LPD Press, 2004.
Porter, Anne. Author interview, Jesus Christ of Latter-Day Saints, July 18, 2015.
———. *A History of the Church of Jesus Christ of Latter-Day Saints in Santa Fe, N.M.* Santa Fe, NM: Church of Jesus Christ of Latter-Day Saints, 2014.
Reynolds, John Lawrence. *Secret Societies*. New York: Arcade, 2001.
Semon, Reverend Ken. Author interview, Church of the Holy Faith, June 9, 2015.
Szasz, Ferenc M. *The Protestant Clergy in the Great Plains and Mountain West, 1865–1915*, Albuquerque: University of New Mexico Press, n.d.
Szasz, Ferenc M., and Richard W. Etulain. *Religion in Modern New Mexico*. Albuquerque: University of New Mexico Press, n.d.
Watson, George. Author interview, Scottish Rite Temple, August 6, 2015.
Wroth, William H. "Stephen Watts Kearny." New Mexico History. www.newmexicohistory.org/people/stephen-watts-kearny.

CHAPTER 6

Escue, Reverend Douglas. Author interview, Immanuel Lutheran Church, August 28, 2015.

Lutheran Peace Fellowship. "Lutherans and Conscientious Objection to the Draft." members.tripod.com/~lutheran_peace/lutheran_co.htm.

Metro Lutheran. "Gustavus and Social Justice." July 23, 2012. www.metrolutheran.org/2012/07/gustavus-and-social-justice.

Rabinowitz, Harold, and Greg Tobin. *Religion in America*. New York: Sterling, 2011.

Raphael, Bettina. *Olive Rush: An Independent Spirit.* Santa Fe, NM, n.d.

Unitarian Universalist Santa Fe. www.uusantafe.org.

US History. www.ushistory.org.

Word & World. www.wordandworld.luthersem.edu.

CHAPTER 7

Downs, DeeDee. Author interview, Buddhism, June 3, 2015.

Kagyu Shedrup Chöling. "Current U.S. Stupas." www.kagyu-sfla.org/current-u-s-stupas.

Law, Lisa. Author interview, Buddhism in New Mexico, May 1, 2015.

Many Mountains. www.manymountains.org.

New Mexico PBS. "Moments in Time: Remembering the Santa Fe Japanese Internment Camp." www.youtube.com/watch?v=ewkDuQ7yZlI.

O'Brien, Barbara. "How Buddhism Came to Tibet." About.com. www.buddhism.about.com/od/vajrayanabuddhism/a/tiberthist1.htm.

———. "Zen 101: An Introduction to Zen Buddhism." About.com. www.buddhism.about.com/od/chanandzenbuddhism/a/zen101.htm.

Santa Fe Internment Camp. "Japanese-American Internment Camps in New Mexico." August 3, 2012. www.santafeinternmentcamp.blogspot.com/2012/08/japanese-american-internment-camps-in.html.

Sherab, Geshe Thubten. Author interview, Thubten Norbu Ling Buddhist Center, June 11, 2015.

Sherpa, Lama Venerable Mingma. Author interview, Kagyu Shenpen Kunchab Center, July 13, 2015.

Stamatov, Suzanne. "Japanese-American Internment Camps in New Mexico, 1942–1946." New Mexico History. www.newmexicohistory.org/people/japanese-american-internment-camps-in-new-mexico-1942-1946.

Stupas of North America. www.stupasofnorthamerica.com.

Upaya. www.upaya.org.

CHAPTER 8

Amarante, Betty. Author interview, I AM Sanctuary, June 30, 2015.

Ascension Research Center. "Guy and Edna Ballard Interviewed by *Chicago Herald and Examiner*, October 10, 1938." www.ascension-research.org/Guy_and_Edna_Ballard_interviewed_by_Chicago_Herald_and_Examiner.html.

Blavatsky, H.P. *Collected Writings*. Vol. I, *1874–1878*. Wheaton, IL: Theosophical Publishing House, 1977.

Horowitz, Mitch. *Occult America*. New York: Bantam Books, 2009.

St. Germain Foundation. www.saintgermainfoundation.org.

CHAPTER 9

Dunnington, Jacqueline. Sikh Dharma Mural of Our Lady of Guadalupe. Santa Fe, NM, 2014.

Hacienda de Guru Ram Das. www.espanolaashram.com/pages.

Kaur, Bibiji Inderjit. Author interview, Sikh Dharma International, September 15, 2016.

Khalsa, Gurumeher. Author interview, Sikh Dharma International, July 23, 2015.

Khalsa, Sada Kaur Bahar. Author interview, Sikh Dharma International, July 23, 2015.

Law, Lisa. Author interview, Sikh history in New Mexico, May 1, 2015.

McClure, Bruce, and Deborah Byrd. "When Does the Age of Aquarius Begin?" EarthSky. January 9, 2015. www.earthsky.org/human-world/when-will-the-age-of-aquarius-begin.

Miller, Susan. "Age of Aquarius." Astrology Zone. www.astrologyzone.com/forecasts/millennium.html.

Rabinowitz, Harold, and Greg Tobin. *Religion in America*. New York: Sterling, 2011.

The Sikh Encyclopedia. "Partition of the Punjab." www.thesikhencyclopedia.com/the-modern-history-of-sikhs-1947-present/partition-of-the-punjab.

Weaver, Sandra. "The Age of Aquarius Traits Are Building as the Next Great Age Begins." Spiritual Growth Prophecies. www.2012-spiritual-growth-prophecies.com/age-of-aquarius.html.

Chapter 10

Archiveque, Vickie. Author interview, Son Broadcasting, June 25, 2015.
Beaty, Mrs. David. Author interview, Gideon International, August 3, 2015.
Bethancourt, Reverend John. Author interview, Holy Trinity Orthodox Church, August 7, 2015.
Greene, Deborah. Author interview, Salvation Army, August 4, 2015.
Heavens Cross. "Gideon." www.heavenscross.com/Gideon.
Hodges, Olinda Hodges. Author interview, Light at Mission Viejo, August 18, 2015.
Monastery of Christ in the Desert. www.christdesert.org.
Our Lady of Guadalupe Monastery. www.pecosmonastery.org.
Pappas, Reverend Dimitrios. Author interview, St. Elias the Prophet Greek Orthodox Church, July 28, 2015.
Rabinowitz, Harold, and Greg Tobin. *Religion in America*. New York: Sterling, 2011.
Rodriguez, Rudy. Author interview, Full Gospel Business Men's Fellowship, July 8, 2015.
Starr, Reverend David. Author interview, St. Juliana of Lazarevo Russian Orthodox Church, July 28, 2015.
Strock, Glen. Author interview, Pecos Valley Cowboy Church, July 28, 2015.
Timmons, Steve "Doc." Author interview, Sangre de Cristo Fellowship, July 27, 2015.
Vasquez, José. Author interview, Barnabas Institute Center for Christian Community, July 28, 2015.
Walker, Reverend Doug. Author interview, Church of the Antioch, July 21, 2015.
Welcome to Holy Chimayo. www.elsantuariodechimayo.org.

Chapter 11

Amma Center of New Mexico. www.amma.org/groups/north-america/amma-center-new-mexico-0.
Aziz, Imam. Author interview, TaHa Mosque, July 15, 2015.
Crews, Jonathan. Author interview, Amma Center of New Mexico, June 11, 2015.
Khozein, Sue. Author interview, Baha'i, July 20, 2015.
Landress, Lauren. Author interview, Self-Realization, August 4, 2015.
Rabinowitz, Harold, and Greg Tobin. *Religion in America*. New York: Sterling, 2011.

Chapter 12

Alcoholics Anonymous. *Big Book*. New York: A.A. World Services, Inc., 1976.

———. www.aa.org.

Berry, Patty. Author interview, Santa Fe Center for Spiritual Living, July 15, 2015.

Bixby, Tai. Author interview, UDV congregation, July 25, 2015.

Bonewits, Isaac. "Defining Paganism." Neopagan. www.neopagan.net/PaganDefs.html.

Christian Science. "Mary Baker Eddy—Discoverer, Founder, Author, Teacher." christianscience.com/what-is-christian-science/mary-baker-eddy-discoverer-founder-author.

DeBenettis, Peter. Author interview, Oneness, July 21, 2015.

Delore, Dianne. Author interview, the Celebration of Santa Fe, June 30, 2015.

Dillon, Reverend Gayle. Author interview, Everyday Center for Spiritual Living, June 12, 2015.

Downs, DeeDee. Author interview, New Age, June 3, 2015.

Gong Bath Meditations. "What the Heck Is a Gong Bath?" June 1, 2015. gongbathmeditations.com/2015/06/what-the-heck-is-a-gong-bath.

Graham, John. Author interview, Eckankar, July 21, 2015.

Horowitz, Mitch. *Occult America*. New York: Bantam Books, 2009.

Our Lady of the Woods. www.ladywoods.org/index.php.

Rabinowitz, Harold, and Greg Tobin. *Religion in America*. New York: Sterling, 2011.

Index

About the Author

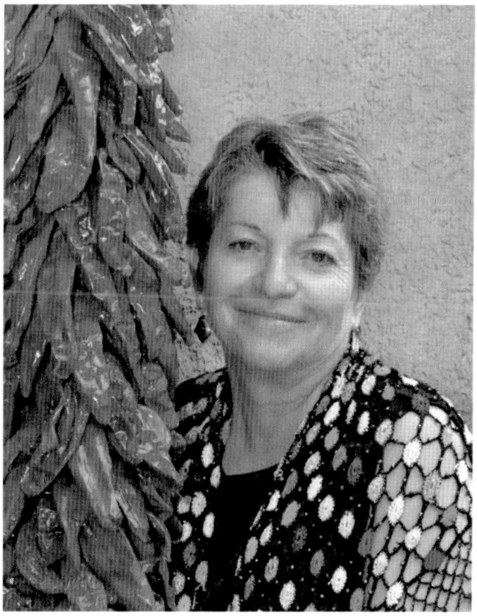

Photo by Linda Carfagno.

Ana Pacheco is the city historian of Santa Fe. This is her seventh book on New Mexico history as the author/editor. She was the founding publisher and editor of *La Herencia*, a quarterly magazine on New Mexico history that she published from 1994 through 2009. From 2007 through September 2013, Pacheco wrote the weekly column "A Wonderful Life" for the *Santa Fe New Mexican*, documenting the oral histories of the elder community. In 2010, she published the official magazine for Santa Fe's 400th anniversary.

Pacheco is the daughter of Jesús Pacheco and Natalie Ortiz. Her Ortiz ancestors settled in Santa Fe in 1694. Her mother was a descendant of Diego de Vargas, who led the resettlement of Santa Fe after the Pueblo Revolt in 1692. Don Gaspar Avenue is named after Natalie's great-great-grandfather Don Gaspar Ortiz. The Ortiz Room at the Santa Fe Hilton Hotel and Ortiz Street located in the plaza area are named in honor of

Nicolás Ortiz, her grandfather seven times removed. Her Pacheco ancestors arrived in Santa Cruz, New Mexico, in 1739 and moved to Santa Fe in the late 1800s. The busy thoroughfare Pacheco Street is named after Ana's great-grandfather José de la Cruz Pacheco.

In 1976, Pacheco moved to New York, where she began her publishing career. She was a freelance writer and also held various positions with entertainment, Hispanic and financial service publications as an advertising and international marketing executive. Pacheco returned to Santa Fe in 1992 and served on the board of directors for the National Hispanic Cultural Center for the state of New Mexico for seven years. She hosted a weekly Hispanic radio show for Citadel Communications for three years. Pacheco also served on the Wells Fargo Community Advisory Board and Santa Fe Fiesta Foundation board for several years.

Pacheco became a Paul Harris Fellow of the Rotary Foundation of Rotary International in 2010. The award was in appreciation of tangible and significant assistance given for the furtherance of better understanding and friendly relations among people of the world. In 2009, Pacheco received a Certificate of Appreciation from Santa Fe County for her work with the Hispanic and elderly communities. She received the 2008 Heritage Preservation Award by the City of Santa Fe for Excellence in Community Traditions for her work with *La Herencia*. Pacheco is a 2007 recipient of the New Mexico Community Foundation *Luminaria* award for her leadership and contributions to the state of New Mexico. In 2006, she was awarded two national awards by the National Association of Press Women. She is a 2004 recipient of the Governor's Award for outstanding women of New Mexico. In 2004, she also received an award from PEN New Mexico for her efforts to preserve Hispanic culture, history and language. PEN New Mexico is the state's affiliate of the largest international professional association of writers, editors and translators. For more information, visit www.anapachecosantafe.com.